CAN CULTURE SAVE THE WORLD?

The Nerve Of Peace

Driss Ferar

DEDICATION

I would like to dedicate this work, first and foremost, to His Majesty King Mohammed VI and to His Excellency Mr. Trump, President of the United states of America.

I also dedicate it to academic and governmental institutions, and to the leaders of public and private organizations.

Furthermore, this book is intended for anyone from any culture who cherishes peace and living together without exclusion or conflict.

ACKNOWLEDGMENTS

My apologies are first presented here for any fault, inattention or omission, to quote the name of an author, a theory, idea, phrase or paragraph that I am led to quote to argue the writing of this book.

My thanks go to all those close by who have helped and contributed, directly or indirectly, to the realization of this work.

My thanks go directly to Mr Jacques Igalens, spiritual father of the GRH, who kindly offered to preface this book. That the founder of the scientific community of HRM research, Jaques Igalens, finds here my gratitude.

My thanks go finally to the hierarchy, for its strategic view aimed at building the performance of the institution and safeguarding its fundamental values in its motto (God, Homeland, King).

PREFACE

Jacques IGALENS
Emeritus professor at the University of Toulouse
Honorary Director of (Toulouse Business School)
Founder of the AGRH (Association Francophone de GRH)
Past-president of the IAS (International Institute of Social Audit)

Corporate Social Responsibility (CSR) must evolve into a broader a cultural responsibility. This is true for all companies, but the Cultural and Creative Industries (CCI) bear an increasing responsibility. The CCI are made up of many micro-enterprises, but also by giants such as Apple, Amazon, Google, Meta, Tencent who address billions of «available brains». As Pascale Thumerelle emphasizes, "If global warming is a real danger to life, the spirits must also receive our full attention."[1] Prejudice, hate speech, and misinformation act as pollutants - detrimental to individual development and social cohesion. It is time to react, but this requires a solid knowledge of the nature of culture: what is culture, how to define it, how to appreciate the issues that underlie it, how to make it evolve and how to appreciate its relationship with the economy, management, ecology and sustainable development.

Driss Ferar's book, « **Culture to Save the World. The Nerve of Peace**» allows us to understand what is currently going on around culture and which could contribute to world peace if minds are willing to open up to new ideas.

The author has had several lives since he was a responsible executive (RE), in an important institution of his country, that he is doctor in management sciences since 2011, teacher-researcher in MRH and senior consultant in strategic management of companies.

---

[1] Pascale Thumerelle, « Warming of the minds, social responsibility of cultural industries », Ed, Actes Sud, 2024

This diversity in the course certainly explains the richness and originality of the subject, because it is necessary to "dare" to think and write that "culture can save the world" at a time when the world is experiencing new crises in Africa, armed conflicts in Europe and a climate situation of great concern around the globe.

In 1945, speaking to Churchill who spoke of the influence of the Pope, Stalin replied: "The Pope, how many divisions?". And yet material forces cannot do everything, the book of Driss Ferar amply demonstrates this. Drawing on scientific literature, Driss Ferar evokes all levels of culture, the highest level with Kant for whom culture covers the aspiration of man to transcendence, the level of nations with local or regional cultures and for example the works of Hofstede and his epigones who have managed to measure them and finally the level of enterprise with the works of Thévenet or Godelier. The state of the art provided by Driss Ferar is both complete and orderly, and I particularly appreciated his contextualization effort since it also reports on important works by Moroccan researchers such as Benabdeljalil, El Amrani, Chebihi, El Aoufi for the current authors as well as those of the previous century as Ali and Wahabi.[2]

But this book is not only a work of scholarship, it is also to defend a thesis, the one that exposes the title of the book: can culture save the world? This is the heart of the subject and to deal with it the author introduces essential concepts such as **cultural intelligence**. As the author writes: «cultural intelligence is not merely intercultural competence, because intercultural competence does not necessarily imply the ability to produce strategic information for the organization. » Cultural intelligence is at the intersection of economic intelligence, cultural expertise and intercultural skills.

[2] The references of these authors are given at the end of the book.

Cultural intelligence, aided by artificial intelligence, can play a crucial role in solving global problems. By facilitating cross-cultural understanding and cooperation, it enables the design of adapted and globally accepted solutions. As the world continues to face complex and interconnected challenges, cultural intelligence is emerging as an indispensable skill for building a more peaceful, equitable and sustainable future. This is crucial in a global world. But it is not enough to know "what" to do, it is also necessary to know "how" to do it and Driss Ferar addresses in the penultimate chapter of the book the broad topic of change management methods in organizations.

It is in the last chapter that lies the essential contribution of Driss Ferar both to the theory and to the practices of management improvement with the concept of «**cultural leadership**», a leadership at the same time humanist and transnational. The question of leadership style is indeed an important issue that management literature has already dealt with extensively and there are more than a dozen identified and documented styles. To my knowledge, only one article has so far been exclusively about cultural leadership; it is devoted to the way in which this type of leadership innovates by creating or modifying organizational cultures. Driss Ferar's proposal is more ambitious, because he envisions with the cultural leadership "a real dynamic synergy between demand and kindness, between commitment to vision and attention to people, between concern for others and energy of action."[3] Driss Ferar is also a teacher so he addresses one last issue related to higher education management.

---

[3] Trice, H. M., & Beyer, J. M. (1991). Cultural leadership in organizations. Organization science, 2 (2), 149-169.

Are management schools sufficiently preparing their students to become humanistic and transnational cultural leaders? The author's answer is negative and he is certainly right when comparing the current situation to what it could be in an ideal world... However, I find that progress has been made in management schools and a recent book bears witness to this. Under the term «Humanism and Management», a current of thought is currently developing in the French school of management and it is totally in phase. with Driss Ferar's analysis of the transformational role of culture.[4] The author's ambition remains: «the goal is to live together without rejection or discrimination, in this planet Earth governed by a law for all, and under the aegis of an independent supranational and planetary leadership»[5], it is noble and deserves us to act in that direction. Driss Ferar, in this book, opens avenues for practitioners as well as academics, hopefully they will be taken. So as Churchill said (again...) we will seize the **nerve of peace**.

---

[4] Bachelard, O., & Flamand, G. (2023). Humanization of management by management schools. Management Prospective Éditions.

[5] Igalens, J. (2015). Culture: Factor of Integration: Introduction to the 12th day symposium, Humanism and Management. Management & Social Sciences, (1), 4-7.

SUMMARY OF THE BOOK

The book proposes to ask the question of whether culture can rethink management and save a society in crisis, sick with management.

The key insight for the reader is that culture is not just part of the probable world but a solution to managing the planet. The book seeks to explore avenues for reflection and provide insights to contribute to the solution of the crisis in management and leadership. In the knowledge management approach (Brown, 1999) advocated by cultural leadership, the book is not about material and scientific knowledge, but rather about intelligence, the value of knowledge, which is a lasting and immutable value.

Addressing the cultural dimension is not limited to referring to one science, but to several, because culture is not unique, but diverse and diversified. People are born into culture and carry it throughout their lives. Culture is not part of the life of a company or an organization, but it is the very life of the organization.

Thanks to cultural intelligence as a cultural quotient, the book explains that cultural intelligence is now increasingly fed by artificial intelligence. The latter is distinguished by its merit to bring with economic intelligence, an added value in the direction of progress, change and evolution of culture. Cultural intelligence fosters the development of an intelligent cultural leadership capable of guiding cultural evolution toward adaptability and progress. The knowledge of researchers, their ideas, their vision of the world, and management of men, has produced in the past and can continue to produce added value to management sciences and humanity.

The new paradigm of supranational cultural leadership, proposed to the reader, could cure the sick society of management and save the world. It would be, in fact, an alternative supplanting the other types of historical and contemporary leaderships, which have not managed to think humanity, humanize management and allowed to live together in a village named planet Earth. To develop these ideas and answer the questions, the book is presented in three parts.

Part One highlights the importance of the mosaic of culture as part of human policy and the human species. In the second part, it proposes to deal with culture and sustainable development. In the third part on culture that can save the world, the book develops the peculiarity of the influence of culture and suggests a new type of supranational cultural leadership, able to cure the sick society of management and save the planet from endless conflict crises.

TABLE OF CONTENTS

GENERAL INTRODUCTION

What divides us is pale in comparison with what unites us.
- Edward Kennedy

This book aims to explore key aspects of culture by integrating insights from interdisciplinary literature, field observations, and management practice. As with all scientific endeavors, this work acknowledges its limitations and the inherent provisional nature of knowledge (MacMillan, 1982; Calmar, 1987), recognizing that scientific understanding is always subject to refinement. Human error, in the context of research, remains a learning task and an innovation lever that releases confidence, creativity and imagination (Sample, 2005; Cost, 2006).

This volume seeks to elucidate the broad characteristics of culture, examining its definitions across social sciences, anthropology, psychology, occupational health, and other social domains. Given the challenge for sustainable development, the cultural dimension appears crucial because of its influence on managerial and technological practices. However, the notion of culture can be confused with religion, tradition, custom or any other term referring to the daily habits and practices of society.

Motivation

The book is distinguished by its vision of renewing interest in the scope of culture and revaluing its purpose—as fostering acceptance and coexistence on Earth, free from cultural domination and exclusion. Cultural studies have experienced an alarming decline over the past decade (2014-2024). According to the thesis site These.Fr, there were 239 theses on the term ‘culture’ in 2014, dropping to only 14 in 2024. In ten years, research on culture decreased by 225 theses - a decline of over 94%. On the term influence of culture, the site shows 40 theses and only two theses in

2024. In ten years, the work on the influence of culture has decreased by 38 theses, a decline of over 95%. On the term leadership, the thesis site. Fr, lists 19 theses in 2014, and only one thesis in 2024. In ten years, the work on leadership decreased by 18 theses, a decline of over 94%. For 'culture and leadership', the site shows 6 theses in 2014 and none in 2024, a decline of over 99%.

The motivation to deal with culture and develop theses on the cultural dimension has decreased significantly each year by more than 90% during the last decade. Does this decline in interest indicate a saturation in the existing literature? Or does it reflect a shift of interest towards technical or technological subjects, such as digitalization and artificial intelligence? This decline in interest in studying cultural issues can only be explained by the importance given to other disciplines at the expense of culture, which is the very heart of the development of any discipline and science. The culture continues, however, to stimulate researchers towards more change, more performance and sustainable development of organizations. The terms chosen in the inventory of previous works (culture, influence of culture, leadership) are the key words and backbone of this work. This book contributes significantly to reviving the cultural dimension within management. It explains how and why culture remains a powerful driver of cross-reflection for change, performance and sustainable development for humanity.

Interest of the research

The interest of work, reflexively of the book, is to participate in the emancipation and progress of management. Another aim is to go beyond mere probabilities and offer solutions to management issues. The book seeks to explore ideas and insights to help solve the crisis of management and leadership. The approach, continued in the book, is based on a cross-reference literature, field observation, experiences and knowledge of men's management (Boyer, 2006). In this approach of knowledge management (Brown, 1999) advocated by cultural leadership, the works contained in the book do not aim at material scientific knowledge, but rather at intelligence, the value of knowledge, which is a lasting and unchanging universal value. If knowledge is power according to the expression of Bacon (1561–1626), the purpose of knowledge management is above all, to optimize decision support by promoting the availability of intelligence and facilitating strategic analyses. Knowledge management serves as a counterbalance to globalization, individualism, exclusion, and the obsession with profit.

From the point of view of knowledge management, it would be pretentious to really want to define a culture of management, because the notion of culture does not lend itself to one definition, but to several. Treating the concept of culture is not reduced to a single discipline, but several. Approaching the content of culture is not limited to referring to one science, but to several. Culture is not about one activity of an organization, but all activities of that organization. Culture is not unique, but diverse and diverse. People are born with a culture and die with their culture. Culture is not part of the life of a company or an organization, but it is the very life of the organization. In knowledge management, the book aims to explore different approaches to the concept of culture by trying to draw the contours of the various definitions that characterize it.

Justification

The reflexive work in this book aims to answer the central question of how culture can save the world. Thanks to cultural intelligence considered as a cultural quotient in the American and French approach, our work explains that cultural intelligence is today increasingly fed by artificial intelligence. It is notable for its contribution to advancing progress, change, and the evolution of culture.

The use of artificial intelligence in a globalized world, makes it possible to analyze the issues of artificial intelligence in relation to cultural intelligence. Artificial intelligence helps build a smart business by automating its operations, driving innovation and making the right decisions. A leader—an executive relying on artificial intelligence—would develop cultural intelligence that integrates AI and intelligent enterprise. In other words, artificial intelligence and intelligent enterprise are justified by the profile of an intelligent leader, which would promote the emergence of cultural intelligence. The term "intelligence" would be, from this point of view, the qualitative and common denominator to artificial intelligence, cultural intelligence and intelligent enterprise, that is, intelligent leadership. There is indeed a significant relationship between intelligent enterprise, that is, intelligent leadership, artificial intelligence and cultural intelligence.

The triangular relationship between company, chief leader and intelligence reflects this performance challenge sought by the three actors of power, to achieve sustainable development and save the world and present future generations. This interaction between artificial and cultural intelligence demonstrates that cultural intelligence is dynamic and adaptable, evolving with the world and drawing upon other scientific disciplines. Cultural intelligence powered by artificial intelligence allows the emergence of an intelligent cultural leadership capable of initiating the evolution and change of culture towards a dynamic of adaptability and progress.

Theoretical basis

The theoretical basis producing knowledge, knowledge that Girin (1989) calls «ordinary scientists», allows to be inserted into a dimension of practical research which requires to stick to facts and causality relations between facts. Second, knowledge gives science an opportunity, among others, to know the world and bring benefits to humanity through acquired knowledge. In the wake of this doctrine that favors priority, facts, our observations and our experiences remain at the heart of practical research which does not advocate a deductive mode (theory validated or refuted by facts), but inductive (theory based on observations). While the book does not claim to present a definitive theory, it offers hope that future researchers can develop one based on these observations.

The ambition that is outlined in the book is to shed light on a type of leadership suitable for saving the managerial world in time and space. Researchers' knowledge can contribute to the development of management sciences, society and people. Their contribution is not exclusively the fruit of conventional quantitative or qualitative surveys, but also emanates from reflections, thoughts and observations that are the result of several years of field experience and management of men.

The ideas of researchers, their vision of the world, and management of men, have produced in the past and can continue to produce added value to management sciences and humanity.

Science itself progresses through ideas, observations, and trial and error. « Scientific knowledge is not proven knowledge, but it represents knowledge that is probably true» (Chalmer 1987). Knowledge of management and leadership stems from experimentation, the right to error (MacMillan, 1982), reflection, and imagination (Sample, 2005; Cost, 2006). The new paradigm of supranational cultural leadership that the book defends to save the sick world of management would be the emergence of a new alternative paradigm. This would likely supplant the other types of historical and contemporary leadership that have failed to think about humanity, humanize management and allow people to live together in a village called planet Earth. This goal, based on knowledge, would be realistic and possible, far from being utopian based on selfish desires, because "there are no bad soldiers, there are only bad leaders," said Douglas Mac Gregor (1906-1964). Similarly, "there are no underdeveloped countries, but only under-management countries" (Drucker, 2005).

Architecture of the book

To develop the chosen concepts, the book is structured in three parts. The first part deals with the importance of culture. Part Two explains culture and sustainable development. Part Three shows how culture can save the world. In the first part, the book presents a first chapter relating to a mosaic of culture which is part of a human policy. The culture - adopts different definitions of culture, its characteristics and universal meaning. Culture pertains to humanity itself, intersecting with anthropological and sociological perspectives to guide change and evolution. This mosaic of cultures explains the issues of culture in relation to its usefulness for science and the world (chapter 2).

In the second part, the book deals with culture and sustainable development. In chapter three, he explains the theories of sustainable development and the debates they provoke on cultural management. The question is whether culture can contribute to sustainable development and, from this point of view, how it is perceived according to the United Nations and UNESCO. Another question is whether the cultural dimension can be a factor of sustainable development for Africa and other countries, or whether it would be an obstacle and a lure for development in Africa. Culture and cultural diversity are then dealt with in chapter four. It aims to highlight the concepts of national culture, corporate culture and cultural management crossed in the French, Moroccan and United Nations space.

In the third part, which deals with the culture that can save the world, the book develops in chapter five, the influence of culture in the world. This influence may be perceived as negative by some researchers (Defrenne and Delvaux, 1992), insofar as it constitutes a handicap to adaptability and an obstacle to sustainable development. Indeed, for Defrenne and Delvaux, culture kills adaptability because it subjects individuals to resignation, protection and defense, while adaptability means progress. Culture becomes for authors a synonym of alienation, and weakens the adaptability that comes with progress. For Defrenne and Delvaux (1992), progress means a better future, but probably uncertain unknown.

In contrast to the work of Defrenne and Delvaux, which consider culture as alienating from progress, other researchers (Thévenet and Vachette, 1992; Ulrich, 1989; Ketter and Hess, 1992; Tylor, 1996) support a dynamic and evolving culture. For example, in Thevenet and Vachette (1992), culture develops through a learning process and changes throughout history as it confronts problems encountered in companies. Tylor (1996) introduces the concept of movement in culture and shows that culture is not static and can add, modify elements that will be acquired by all members of a same culture. In the same vein, Demorgon (2000) supports a dynamic overall culture that combines the past, present and future. The founder of the European community, Jean Monnet, defends this idea of a dynamic and unfrozen dimension of culture when he says in substance: «If I had to face the challenge of European integration again, I would probably start with culture».

Monnet's advocacy of starting with culture raises the question: How and whether culture can save the world. Chapter six of the book deals with this question and provides some answers. The emerging idea is that the dynamic and evolutionary character of culture towards the idea of saving the world, is adopted by several ideologies that speak of abstract humanity and not of man located in his culture. Levi-Strauss (1967) considers that all these ideologies call for a false evolutionism of progress, because a cultural evolutionism must envisage for all societies the same development converging towards the same goal. Franz Boas (1858-1942), the founding father of American anthropology, approaches the study of cultural progress by distinguishing two criteria for progress that he considers antagonistic: Progress based on invention and knowledge and cultural progress based on the harmonious use of daily time and leisure. Levi-Strauss (1967) notes that this progress, mentioned by Franz Boas (1858-1942), whether quantitative or qualitative, has been the sole property of Western civilization for more than a century. This progress, a source of cultural diversity, can lead, according to Lévi-Strauss, to the homogenization of cultures that must be preserved in order to face the unification of a humanity characterized by monoculture.

This cultural progress, in the form of "coalition" or hominization of cultures, developed by Lévi-Strauss (1967), means for others (Benjamin Pelletier, 2012) a cultural intelligence. Indeed, for Benjamin Pelletier (2012), intercultural management trainer and head of the economic war school, author of several literary narratives, cultural intelligence is a new notion that is quite floating and blurred. Between cultural intelligence, as the intelligence of cultures in its broad concept and the intelligence of cultural industries in its very narrow concept, Benjamin Pelletier (2012) proposes a general definition of cultural intelligence, addressing it in its strategic dimension.

The author has defined it as both an exercise of intercultural competences and a production of cultural information useful to the activity of a public or private organization. He asserts that cultural intelligence underpins economic intelligence. For the author, the two notions: intercultural skills and cultural information are included in their strategic dimension as they contribute to the security of the organization. Cultural intelligence meets economic intelligence (security, surveillance, influence) in a relationship as essential as that of roots. For the author, cultural intelligence must be seen in close solidarity with economic intelligence, which is two sides of the same coin. Without economic intelligence, cultural intelligence loses its strategic dimension. Similarly, without cultural intelligence, economic intelligence is uprooted from its operational dimension. A cross-literature developed further justifies the currents of thought of each other.

Indeed, in a world that is changing "only change is permanent", said Heraclitus, cultural change fueled by cultural and artificial intelligence is needed today to change the management of the world towards a better, more just and humanistic world. Cultural change means a change of cultural leadership that is an independent supranational cultural leadership capable of saving the world from management disease (Gaulejac, 2005). The seventh and final chapter of the book proposes to defend this new paradigm of supra-national cultural leadership as a savior of the planet. It explains that the influence relationship between culture and leadership shows that supranational cultural leadership is underpinned by political, economic and ideological power Moreover, supranational cultural leadership is grounded in humanism, emphasizing humanity's role in transforming society and the world.

The work reported in the book shows that humanized leadership can be the responsibility of management schools as it can be the responsibility of decision-makers leaders themselves. It is indeed a management accident between the management schools which have not seen far enough in their pedagogical teaching to avoid the accident, and the decision-makers who have not applied the leadership teachings, so as not to commit an accident. This failure stems from leaders' reluctance to abandon negative notions of power rooted in force and symbolic violence. The other reason explained by Freud (1913) lies in the complex of power and domination of the human species.

The book is structured in three parts and seven chapters developed in the following paragraphs.

PART ONE
THE IMPORTANCE OF CULTURE

We (human beings),
An original mosaic
of mundane elements.
Jean Rostand (1894-1977)

2.2.2. Everything is cultural

Introduction of the first bet

This first part aims to expose the different fundamental approaches to the definitions and characteristics of culture in its broad sense in relation to its socio-economic environment. This first introductory part, structured into two chapters, presents a certain mosaic that is relevant to both human politics and the human species, which will be developed in the first chapter. The cultural issues arising from this are justified by the relationship between culture and science and the world, which is the subject of the second chapter.

CHAPTER 1
MOSAIC OF CULTURE

Me, complicated? No,
I am simply a mosaic
of several people in one
Francis Scott Fitzgerald (1896-1940)

Introduction

Culture is a multifaceted concept that encompasses scientific, political, social, and spiritual dimensions. Understanding culture requires recognizing its role as both a human policy and a defining trait of the human species. From this point of view, it becomes useful to ask whether culture is a matter of human policy or of the human species. The answer to this question requires first to treat culture as a human policy and then explain that culture would fall within the scope of the human species.

Section 1.1. — Culture is a human policy.

1.1.1. Definitions of culture

1.1.2. Cultural characteristics

1.1.3. Universal sense of culture

1.1.4. The universal, exercise of the mind

Section 1.2. — Culture is a matter for the human race.

1.2.1. The anthropological meaning of culture

1.2.2. The sociological sense of culture

1.2.3. The evolutionary meaning of culture

1.2.4. The meaning of cultural change

Section 1.1. — Culture is a human policy.

Human politics—our collective actions and choices—differ from the natural processes governed by the human species as a whole. This distinction frames culture as a transcendent, universal policy shaped by human agency. Culture has long been the work of the human, and remains a significant characteristic of humanity. It is therefore necessary to question the definitions, characteristics and universal meaning attributed to the concept of culture.

1.1.1. Definitions of culture

The word "culture" originates from Latin "cultura," meaning "to inhabit," "to cultivate," or "to honor." It signifies humanity's active engagement with its environment—both physical and spiritual. In the first sense, the word means to cultivate the earth. Figuratively, the word means to cultivate the spirit, the soul. Félix Gaffiot (1870-1930), in his dictionary Gaffiot believes that Cicero was the first to apply the word culture to humans: "A field as fertile cannot be productive without culture, and it is the same for humans without education."

Man lives in several dimensions of space-time. He evolves in space, where the natural environment exerts a permanent influence on him. It evolves in time, which gives it a historical past and a future. In this respect, man is not unique. All animals take space and time into account and form societies to adapt to other members of society. From this point of view, it appears that what distinguishes man (this social animal) from other species is culture. It seems to give man the means to adapt to the complexities of the world and gives him the paradoxical feeling of being his creator and at the same time his creature, "the basis of cultural anthropology" (Herskovits, 1950).

The word "culture" has several definitions. For anthropologists such as Alfred Krocher and Clyde Kluckhohn (1952), there are more than 164 definitions of the word culture included in their work: a critical review of concepts and definitions. For political and economic decision-makers, the definition is not the one found in the humanities or in "general culture". Entrepreneurs speak of the concept of "corporate culture", while engineers prefer to speak of "technical culture". Some definitions are reported in the literature.

The notion of culture is relatively new, dating back to the late 19th century. Anthropologist Edward B. Tylor was one of the first to develop a definition of this concept in 1871. The first definition of culture given by Tylor (1832–1917) in primitive Culture (1871) is found in all Anglo-Saxon or Francophone anthropologists: This complex set that includes knowledge, beliefs, arts, mores, laws, customs and all other abilities and habits acquired by man as a member of society. This complex set of thinking, feeling and acting reflects the cultural process of human social life and is for some authors a means of learning and transmitting a social heritage. Although this definition is the most widely used in anthropology, in France the notion of culture has succeeded the notion of civilization as employed by Mauss (1971) and the proponents of the French School of Sociology.

Thus, culture remains a complex whole that includes knowledge, faith, art, morality, law, customs and all the faculties and habits acquired by man as a member of a society (Tylor, 1924). Kroeber and Kluckhohn (1946) identified over 164 definitions of culture. Among these, the most representative for anthropology and sociology is:

1. It is transmitted and perpetuated not by the genetic mechanism of heredity, but by the interconditioning of zygotes.

2. Whatever its origins in or through individuals, culture is rapidly tending to become supra-personal and anonymous.

3. It fits into patterns, or regularities of form, style and meaning.

4. It embodies values that cannot be formulated (explicitly, as rules) or felt (implicitly, as popular traditions) by the society that carries this culture; It is part of the anthropologist's job to characterize and define them. »

It is clear from this definition that culture constitutes a determining concern in our existence, and yet seems to appear rarely in our conscious thinking (Herskovits, 1952).

The unconscious nature of culture

This unconscious structuring of culture manifests on two levels: first, in how cultural meanings escape individual subjective intentions; second, in the distinction between "real culture" and "ideal culture," as defined by Paul Mercier. The latter includes "models, and categories submitted by the individuals themselves". The Bescherelle National Dictionary of 1862 defines culture as a set of general knowledge of an individual, called "general knowledge". Le Petit Larousse (1980) gives culture an individual and collective conception, that is to say a set of social structures, religious, and intellectual, artistic manifestations which characterize a society. Thus, this second definition which goes in the direction of the anthropological definition is supplanting the old definition of individual culture. There are currently two different meanings for the word culture: the individual culture of each, giving the general culture; and the culture of a people.

Individual culture involves a dimension of elaboration, construction considered as evolutionary and individual. On the other hand, collective culture targeting values inserted in the community evolves only very slowly, because its value corresponds to stability fixed in the past, which appeals to history and not the present and even less the future. Collective culture thus contains a component of rigidity that can oppose the development of individual cultures, knowledge that can only be positive, because science is always evolving. In Canada, for example, the 2018-2023 Government

Action Plan on Culture is part of this cultural human policy to stimulate creativity, innovation and individual and collective development through culture (publication available on the Ministry of Culture and Communications website).

In the Census of 164 Definitions, American anthropologists Kroeber and Kluckhohn (1963) provide the best-known definition: «a culture is the configuration of learned behaviours and their outcomes, whose component elements are shared and passed on by members of a given society». If culture is one of the most complicated words in the English language. According to Raymond Henry Williams (1921, 1988) cited by Piller (2011), the American anthropologists Kroeber and Kluckhohn (1963) always cited by Piller (2011), have identified 156 definitions of the term culture which is essentially in the field of anthropology and constitutes an original and complex organization.

Kroeber and Kluckhohn (1952) first proposed a definition which was widely followed: «Culture is a set of patterns (some explicit, some implicit) that describes past behaviour or determines future behaviour; which the individual acquires and transmits through symbols; which constitutes the distinctive mark of a human group, Including the objects (or artifacts) by which this group expresses itself. The essential core of culture is made up of traditional ideas (that is, passed on historically and then selected) and particularly the values attached to them. Cultural systems can sometimes be considered as the conditioning elements of a future action ».

Ten years later, Kroeber and Kluckhohn (1963) formulated a simpler definition as follows: "A culture is the configuration of learned behaviours and their outcomes, the components of which are shared and passed on by members of a given society". Kroeber thus aligns himself with the founders of anthropology, such as Spencer and Tylor, on the nature of culture which they see as a system, with interdependent variables conditioned by their own past. For Piller

(2011), there is ultimately no single definition of "culture" and the term means many things to many people. For Barnouw (1963), culture is: "the way of life of a group of individuals, the combination of all the more or less stereotyped patterns of learned behaviour that each generation transmits to the next through language and imitation". Goodenaugh (1971, 24) defines culture as «a set of beliefs and norms, shared by a group of people, that help the individual decide what is, what can be, how it should be felt, what to do and how to proceed in order to achieve this ».

Hofstede (1983), prefers to define culture as a collective mental programming, that is, a conditioning shared by the members of a society. According to Hofstede (1987), culture could be defined by an interactive set of common characteristics that influence a group's response in the same way that personality determines the individual. Later, Hofstede (2001) defines culture as the collective mental programming of a group of individuals. Daniels and Radebaugh (2001) define culture as «Culture is the specific learned norms of a society, based on attitudes, values, and beliefs." Griffin and Pustay (2005) describe culture as "culture is the collection of values, beliefs, behaviors, customs, and attitudes that distinguish one society from another ».

From this point of view, culture can be defined by a set of knowledge of human beliefs and behaviour in relation to nature and the environment. It is an acquisition and not an instinctive, natural and innate inheritance. Since culture is acquired by learning, people are not born American, Chinese or peasants, soldiers or aristocrats, scholars, musicians or artists, saints: they learn to be." These remarks by Dobzhansky (1966) show the modern notion of an acquired culture, before becoming one through learning. A brief and useful definition of this concept could be as follows: "culture is what in the environment is man-made", says Herskovits (1950). It emphasizes the understanding of the nature of culture by resolving three paradoxes.

1. Culture is universal as human acquisition, but each of its local manifestations can be considered unique.

2. The culture is stable, but also dynamic and shows continuous and constant changes. The only completely static crops are those that have died. It is easy to see, according to Herskovits (1950), that changes occur before us, often so slowly that we perceive them only by confronting the present with the past. The author gives an example of a photograph taken a few years ago that reveals changes in fashion. These changes are indeed always noticeable if one observes a society for a certain time.

3. Culture determines the course of our lives, but rarely imposes itself on our conscious thinking. Seeking to solve a psychological and philosophical problem, Herskovits (1950) seeks on the psychological question to discover how human beings acquire their culture. On the other philosophical question, the author asks whether culture is a function of human mentality or if it exists in and by itself.

If the term culture is grouped into several definitions according to the context to which it refers, it should however avoid reducing culture to its scientific definition, but must refer to values allowing us to choose also our relationship to science (UNESCO). In other words, culture is a matter of human politics or of the human species?

1.1.2. — Cultural characteristics

Abdoulaye Sow (2009), Coordinator of the Interdisciplinary Center on Cultural Rights at the University of Nouakchott in Mauritania, questions how to define culture, cultural rights, cultural identity, a cultural community, cultural freedom and cultural diversity. Sow (2009) explores whether respect for cultural rights serves as an indicator of civil peace, democracy, and development, or whether failure to respect these rights could lead to conflict within societies.

Regarding the definition of culture, Sow (2009) gives a generalist definition of culture as follows: The term culture covers the values, beliefs, languages, knowledge and arts, traditions, institutions and ways of life by which a person or group expresses the meanings it gives to its existence and development.

On the identity approach, Sow (2009) considers cultural identity as "all the elements of culture that involve the universal and the individual integrating the freedoms and dignity of the person. For Sow (2009), it is a substance specific to the person whose violation would constitute an attack on the integrity of the human person. Sow (2009) wants to use the Fribourg Declaration, adopted on 7 May 2007 by an international group of experts, on "Cultural rights, an underdeveloped category of human rights" as a basis for his views on cultural rights., aimed at the protection of cultural rights within the human rights system. Sow (2009) therefore wants to define cultural rights more concretely as being "the rights of a person, alone or in common, to freely choose and express his or her cultural identity, to access the resources that are necessary for his or her identification process". Considering cultural rights as universal Sow (2009), stresses their indivisible and interdependent nature in relation to other human rights. The author realises that, in the end, this principle of indivisibility and universality often remains confined to the level of rhetoric rather than facts. From the analysis of the various cultural forms explained above, Rocher (1992) proposes four main characteristics:

The first characteristic of culture encompasses all forms of expression, feelings and rules governing society. This expression means that culture is an action experienced by people. Indeed, it is because it obeys a given culture that action can be considered as social action. The second characteristic of culture considers these forms of expression more or less formalized in a code of laws, ritual formulas, ceremonies, theology in some areas, rules that govern people who know each other for a long time. The third characteristic of a society's culture, not that of a group, includes a plurality of people, because the culture of a global society is necessarily shared by a large number of people to show that it is indeed rules of life having acquired a collective and therefore social character. Although individualized, culture in the anthropological and sociological sense of the term is not individual by nature; it is common to a plurality of people. As a result, the notion of culture, which at first could only apply to individuals, now takes on a collective meaning. The fourth characteristic concerns its mode of acquisition, which is not innate but biologically or genetically inherited and results from different learning mechanisms. Several authors have adopted this characteristic of culture as a <<social heritage>>. Other researchers talk about everything an individual must learn to live in a universal society.

1.1.3. Universal sense of culture

The universal sense of culture can be seen as a reflection of human agency—our collective efforts to shape and share values across societies—distinguishing human actions from natural processes.

The first, a sense of culture that is part of human politics in search of a dominant universalism, seems to arouse the interest of some researchers in anthropology or political science such as Ingrid Piller (2017). For him, the new sense of culture that is universal and dominant emerged in the nineteenth century. It was not only a part of colonialism, but made colonialism a universal moral obligation called the "burden of the white man". It is explained that the definitions of the notion of culture can contain two meanings: one relative to a universal acceptance and a relativistic meaning concerning the customs of peoples.

An example of this new sense of "culture" comes from the first professor of anthropology at Oxford University, Edward B. Tylor (1832-1917), who published a primitive book Culture in 1871. Tylor argues that «crops» could be measured scientifically by comparison with each other. Tylor's fanatical ideas of a global cultural hierarchy were not the ideas of one academic, but they were rooted in the socio-political context of the time as a particular way of life. For Tylor (1832-1917), this new vision of culture that emerged in the 19th century was not limited to academia and anthropology, but found its application in a multitude of popular discourses. Before Tylor, the plural use of the concept of culture was understood by the German polymath Johann Gottfried Herder1 (1744-1803). He was the first to advocate the use of cultures in the plural by referring to "specific social, economic and variable cultures in different nations and periods".

Emmanuel Kant (1724 - 1804), a German philosopher and founder of criticism and the so-called «transcendental idealism» doctrine considered in the same sense as Tylor that culture represents man's aspiration to transcendence. He observed the true progress of humanity in its desire to cultivate, civilize and moralize. Nature, according to Kant (1724 - 1804), seems to follow a plan that aims at «the perfecting of man through the progress of culture». From this point of view, Kant states the universal law that transcends particular cultures: "man is by reason destined to be in a form of society with other men and to cultivate himself, to civilize himself and to moralize himself in society through art and science."

A century later in the 19th century, Pierre Bourdieu (1930 - 2002), goes in the same direction as Tylor (1832-1917), to think of the existence of a dominant and legitimized culture, antagonistic to a dominated culture whose values are not recognized. The author considers that each individual, endowed with a social and cultural capital determined by his social field, is forced to adhere to the norms recognized by the dominant field in order to be able in turn to be recognized. For Mattei, Jean-François. (2011), «the encounter between European culture and the cultures it has discovered obeys what Hegel called the necessity of the concept». The author recalls that the universality of European culture, which tried to bring other cultures into abstraction, imposed itself on Europe in contrast to other societies which were closed and did not open up to other cultures. The author gives the example of Hegel who expresses the destiny of our history, «the reason seeks its other, knowing that in him it has nothing but itself, it seeks only its own infinity». Mattei (2011) thus considers that this ontological law, which forces the Other to bend to insertion in the same while revealing his identity as another, appears on the plane of civilizations, as an anthropological law.

When Freud in Unbehagen in der Kultur, imputes in 1929 to Europe the Malaise in civilization or culture, a few years later Edmund Husserl (1859-1938), mathematician by training, supports the equally pessimistic idea that «the malaise of intellectuals stems from a crisis in European sciences, that is to say, from the very idea of a rational knowledge which would now be sterile». This expression "crisis of European sciences" is the first part of the title of Husserl's last book, written between 1934 and 1937 and unpublished during his lifetime 4 entitled: « La crise des sciences européennes et la phénoménologie transcendentale », Paris, Gallimard, 1976.

1.1.4. The universal, as an exercise of the mind.

Husserl (1859-1938) viewed the universal as an intellectual exercise, lamenting the spiritual crisis of Europe and the decline of its cultural and scientific vitality. In the face of this renunciation of the spirit, men today no longer believe, according to Husserl, in the mission of Europe which wanted to be civilising towards all humanity. Today, with the creation of the new ministry, successively named Ministry of Culture and Environment, Communication, Major Works and Bicentenary, National Education and Francophonie Culture, and finally the Ministry of Culture in short, the generic and indefinable term "culture" was going to replace the term "art", or even "fine arts".

The ministerial policy was well founded on a desire for "democratization of culture". The decree of 24 July 1959 gave it the mission to make accessible the capital works of humanity, and first of all of France, to as many French people as possible. In his speech on the occasion of the inauguration of the House of Culture in Amiens, Malraux (1966) questioned on 19 March 1966 the technique that created "empty time which did not exist. Called leisure, this "empty time" is identified with the "modern world". He defined culture as "what responds to the face that a human being has in the ice when he looks at it and what will be his face of death" and therefore, "what responds to man when he wonders what he is doing on earth". This culture based on the primacy of psychological shock that one looks at his face in the mirror implied a metaphysical rupture destined to fill an universalist spiritual void, not a historical rupture. Often minimized, this psychological shock is a phenomenon that can in some cases lead to depression, anxiety and social exclusion from the culture of the host country.

At the international level, after the end of the cold war, we are witnessing a deliberate attempt at cultural domination, because the fall of the Berlin Wall in 1989 brought to light a predominantly liberal American model, but very heavily involved in the arms and computer industry. The American hold is thus manifested from the fundamental components of culture (values, education, language and cinema). For some observers, this Anglo-Saxon model tends to impose a form of cultural and linguistic imperialism that results in consumption and production patterns that are not compatible with today's societal constraints. Faced with this form of domination, some countries such as France promote cultural diversity through forms of action concentrated around the state (public aid and subsidies).

At the individual level, to limit somewhat the effect of this phenomenon of cultural domination, theorized by multiple psychologists, a solution advanced by some would be to prepare well for expatriation in advance, to learn about contemporary culture, take some language courses or talk to people who have lived in the country of arrival. Because the fact that you can't communicate, for example, either orally or in writing, increases your sense of anxiety. Often a simple time of adaptation in the host country leads to permanent hostility towards the host country, fear of going out, anxiety crisis, withdrawal into oneself and its culture. Staying at home is not the solution. It is necessary to create friendships, landmarks, integrate a social network, a professional or sports group. It's about finding the way to live your experience abroad. While some people find solace only with people of their nationality and do not change their way of life; others, on the contrary, seek to meet the other, get involved with the local population and soak up their rituals, until a real «acculturation» where the fact of returning to the country of origin becomes more difficult to stay in the host country.

In keeping with this perspective of the mind evoked by Malraux (1929) and Husserl (2011), the term culture means the sense that aims to exercise the mind on itself in order to make it better. This philosophical designation is in fact expressed by the Latin word culture which corresponds to the verb «cultivate» to mean the development of the qualities of the spirit that appeared in France in the eighteenth century. Indeed Vauvenargues (1715-1747), Officer of rare merit, philosopher, moralist, expresses his maxims as follows: "You must have a soul to have taste." Those who despise man are not great men. And above all his maxim, which he is the first to use in culture: «Whatever flatters the most, our vanity is based only on culture, that we despise».

It seems that society is increasingly distancing itself from the culture that created it. The fracture of society with culture or in other words the cultural crisis of society generates economic, financial and today health crises. In the same philosophical sense of culture. The lesson of culture teaches that a world is ordered and manifests the order of the universe. It is a blossoming of life in the world. Culture thus makes the world as long as it makes sense by involving the spirit in a limited fullness of life.

Section 1.2. Culture belongs to the human species.

Alongside culture as a matter of human politics, the culture of the human species encompasses its anthropological and sociological dimensions. This cultural heritage is living, evolving, and has changed over thousands of years. While the term "culture" has multiple definitions depending on context, it is important not to reduce it solely to its scientific meaning. Instead, culture should be understood as a set of values that influence how we relate to science, society, and ourselves (UNESCO). This section will explore the relativistic meanings of culture from an anthropological and sociological perspective. First, we will examine the anthropological definition, followed by the sociological and evolutionary interpretations. Finally, we will discuss cultural change and innovation.

1.2.1. The anthropological meaning of culture

Alongside the philosophical understanding of culture as a manifestation of the human mind, anthropology offers a distinct meaning. One of the earliest definitions was provided in 1871 by British anthropologist Edward Burnett Tylor in Primitive Culture. Influenced by Gustav Friedrich Klemm's ten-volume Histoire universelle de la culture de l'humanité (1843–1852), Tylor initially equated culture with civilization. Tylor defined culture as "that complex whole which includes knowledge, beliefs, art, law, religion, customs, and all other skills and habits acquired by man as a member of society." This anthropological conception of culture was adopted and developed by pioneers such as Edward Sapir, Franz Boas, Alfred Kroeber, Ruth Benedict, and others in the United States and Britain. In the United States, anthropology has even come to define itself as the science of culture, while in England we distinguish between physical anthropology (study of the development and growth of the human body) and social anthropology. The Americans contrast cultural anthropology with physical anthropology.

In France, Perrineau (1975) explores culture from an anthropological and scientific perspective, emphasizing cultural relativism—distinct from the human rights framework later discussed by Sow (2009). Perrineau (1975), believes that cultural relativism is the only one that allows a scientific approach to the cultural phenomenon. It is based on Herskovits (1950), when he considers in his work «the bases of cultural anthropology» that the principle of cultural relativism is linked to judgments. The latter are based on the experience and interpretation of this experience by each individual within the limits of his own acculturation. "Judgements are based on experience and each individual interprets the experience within the limits of their own enculturation."

Herskovits (1950) notes that all peoples naturally make value judgments about other societies, leading to classifications and moral evaluations of different cultural practices. Intangible facts like true and false, normal and abnormal, splendid and ordinary permeate the individual from childhood. From this point of view, Herskovits argued that even perceptions of physical phenomena—such as time, distance, weight, and height—are shaped by social conventions and cultural frameworks. Cultural relativism in the sense of Herskovits (1950), is a philosophy that, while recognizing the values erected by each society, calls for tolerance for different conventions from ours. Instead of emphasizing differences, the relativist view considers any system of norms and values it represents to be valid. Herskovits (1950) also makes a distinction between the "absolute" and the "universal" in cultural relativism. The absolutes, for Herskovits (1950), are fixed as long as they are conventions that cannot vary from culture to culture. On the other hand, universals are the common denominators that manifest themselves in all phenomena of the natural or cultural world. The author gives the example of law, and education, which are also universals of culture, stabilizing in each society patterns of behavior and supporting their values.

Herskovits emphasized that cultures contain both elements of stability and change, noting that every culture has its "rebels" who challenge or deviate from established norms. It is nevertheless necessary, according to the author, to distinguish cultural relativism from the relativity of individual behavior, which would deny any social authority on behavior. In a culture where absolute values have great force, it will indeed be difficult to understand the relativism of a world that contains several types of cultures. But Herskovits (1950), seems confident in the contribution of techniques and data, which will force individuals in a group of societies to adopt a position of humility and tolerance of cultural relativism.

According to Perrineau (1975), the term "culture" encompasses multiple meanings within anthropological literature. Over the twentieth century, anthropology developed a more scientific understanding of culture, gradually moving away from its classical, broad definitions. The goal of Perrineau's (1975) thought is to delimit the theoretical field of the notion of culture by the scientific practice of anthropologists of the late nineteenth and twentieth centuries. According to Pérrineau (1975), this field is constituted by the different definitions of the word culture (acculturation, cultural diversity, contacts between cultures, etc.) and the different concepts that revolve around the notion of culture (civilization, progress...), which arise in opposition (nature, personality...).

Thus the concept of culture, once accepted by men of science, will develop in many anthropological works and take several meanings. Thus, if the first philosophical sense of culture was originally a personal and rational one, then the second anthropological sense of culture was originally a collective and social one.

1.2.2. The sociological sense of culture

In sociology, culture is often defined as the set of material and spiritual characteristics that enable groups—whether public or private—to live and interact together. UNESCO's definition expands this to include beliefs, customs, moral values, and material aspects that facilitate social cohesion. According to the Quebec sociologist Guy Rocher (1969, 88), culture is, "a connected set of more or less formalized ways of thinking, feeling and acting which, being learned and shared by a plurality of people, serve in an objective and symbolic way to constitute these people into a particular and distinct community."

French-language sociology and anthropology, however, were slower to incorporate this neologism. It was only in the new generation of French sociologists that the term culture emerged after the last war and became popular in France under the influence of American sociology. Borrowed from French, retranslated from German to English, the term is each time added a new connotation, always by extension or analogy, without losing its original meaning, but taking on new meanings ever more distant from the first. The term culture was also quickly adopted by early American sociologists, especially Albion Small, because the great precursors of sociology such as Comte, Marx, Weber, Durkheim did not use it. But it is now part of the vocabulary of sociology as well as anthropology.

Sociology therefore proposes to analyze cultural phenomenology in the plural. It aims to explain that there are cultural practices according to place and time, the social position occupied by individuals, and gender, the work they do. Each cultural practice is closely linked to representations, which the French sociologist Pierre Bourdieu (1930 - 2002) calls «habitus» way of being. Thus, each individual, living among other men, accustomed to social practices that he considers «normal», makes his own social representations of what is legitimate and not legitimate, good or bad.

If culture is a daily affair, Norbert Elias (1897-1990), German writer and sociologist, in his major historical sociological work, "On the Process of Civilization", believes that the «Culture is a dynamic of successive transformations linked to social changes and technical developments». For the author, culture reveals forces that coexist, repel and merge with each other.

Sociologically, Rocher (1993) explains that the main function of culture is to bring together a plurality of people in one society. However, other factors may also contribute to the same result of bringing together a plurality of individuals in a specific community. For example, according to Rocher (1993), blood ties become kinship ties that define the rules of marriage and the norms governing kinship relationships. The author gives other examples of geographical proximity, work and cohabitation in the same territory, which are themselves factors for gathering food together in the same society. Thus, from the bonds of blood and cohabitation, the culture adopted contributes to building ideas of nation, homeland, property, social hierarchy and social class.

From a psychological point of view, Rocher (1993) considers that culture imposes itself on the personality, allowing flexible adaptation and individual assimilation to common values. It is then possible to argue that culture forges the personality, in the sense that it attributes to it a form of life allowing it to emancipate itself in a given society. This view is a kind of socialization of culture (Rocher, 1993). In the sense of the consolidation of the individual's personality by culture, the notion of culture can take the form of a general culture which could indeed correspond to the body of knowledge that the individual possesses in the world and in his education. The general culture would be defined according to Édouard Herriot (1878-1957), central figure of the French state of the Third Republic, as "a culture that remains when one has forgotten everything". Today, general culture can include knowledge that encompasses history, music, art, science, literature, astronomy, geography, cinema, sport and philosophy, all of which contribute significantly to the individual's emancipation. Although this view may appear to be somewhat elitist, it is nevertheless a necessary reference that an individual must possess in order to integrate into today's society. Beyond this psychological meaning given to culture, it remains fundamentally sociological and can be perceived by certain representations (1221), and social forms (1222) explained below.

1.2.2.1. Social representations of culture

A representation of culture can be made up of four elements passed down from generation to generation: values, norms, institutions, and artifacts. Julien Sorel Huxley (1887-1975), a British biologist, eugenicist theorist and UNESCO's first director, advocates another form of division into ideological, sociological, and technological subsystems. Socialization, from Huxley's point of view, depends on the belief subsystem. Thus the sociological subsystem aims at the interaction between people while the material objects and their use form the technological subsystem. From this point of view, archaeologists are interested in material culture, while anthropologists favor symbolic culture and assign it a meaning in relation to social practices. The four components of social representation are explained by values, norms, institutions and artifacts.

Values relating to a society contain ideas and beliefs that make up the culture of that society. If, for example, the values of village societies are concerned with the balance between man and nature, the values of nomadic societies are more concerned with solving the problems of nomadic groups established on the same territory. Anglo-Saxon societies are more interested in the law (culture of Common Law, and Rule of Law). In France, the French Revolution introduced a civil status for all society regardless of beliefs, but did not long reject the transcendent power of Catholic tradition. Everywhere else in Europe, the two religions and cultures of the «Book» are composed: the Jewish tradition, and the Muslim tradition that develop values both common and specific to each culture.

Standards are the ways in which people should behave in various social situations. Norms as a law are imposed on the members of society. Institutions are the founding pillars of society through which members of a society develop the values and norms they have assumed. In the United States, cultural industries have developed to implement the foundation of a cultural management based on a business model. Since the 1950s, the American film industry based in Hollywood has dominated not only economically but also culturally through large-scale distribution of films and the display of big stars.

Unlike the United States, the cultural institutions of France, among the first modern democracies to have a ministry of culture in 1959, are based on public management or associations (academies, museums, libraries). France was then followed by many other countries in Europe, but according to formulas adapted to their respective contexts. The Netherlands, Finland, Austria or Portugal have a larger ministry (education for example) in their respective government organizations, to which is attached a State Secretariat for Culture. Countries with a federal structure have equivalents in their regions (federated states) that exercise cultural competence. In Germany, for example, the government of each Land has a department for culture and arts, most often attached to education, research and vocational training (this is explained in particular by the importance of art education institutions). Spain had a Ministry of Culture in 1978, as soon as the page of Franquism was turned.

Whether in France or in Europe, local authorities (municipalities, departments and regions) have for some 30 years now adopted their own cultural policy by regulating local cultural life, often in partnership with government services. Moreover, since the Maastricht Treaty, certain aspects of culture are now part of the responsibilities of the European Union, particularly in terms of subsidiarity principles. These two different viewpoints show two distinct cultural models: the American model focused on the private sector in cultural matters and the European cultural model mainly public.

1.2.2.2. The social forms of culture

The collective culture explained above as a human species in the relativistic sense of the term, both anthropological and sociological, can take several forms. Culture manifests across various domains: artistic, technical, linguistic, environmental, and heritage-related, often influenced by processes like globalization.

In its artistic dimension, culture is closely linked to heritage—both material and intangible—reflecting traditional values and collective identities rooted in community memory. Traditional values relating to culture are much more characteristic of countries such as Europe, Asia, Africa than the United States for obvious historical reasons. The United States thus recognizes European cultural heritage in so far as it constitutes its cultural roots and shows its attraction for the acquisition of works of art in their artistic venues; patronage, and other places of musical exchange. The artistic heritage in question concerns built heritage, that is to say architecture, sculpture, painting, music, literature, folklore and language. In parallel to this cultural and material heritage, UNESCO's 2003 Convention established a program to safeguard intangible cultural heritage, focusing on: 1) identifying heritage in urgent need of protection; 2) maintaining the Representative List of the Intangible Cultural Heritage of Humanity; and 3) promoting best practices for safeguarding. Also, in Asia and Africa for example, it is possible to note the existence of an extraordinarily rich heritage, confined to civilizations: Chinese, Indian, Arab, Berber and African.

Secondly, in the linguistic cultural dimension, language would probably be the best means of conveying an oral or written culture. French culture developed in the Europe of the Enlightenment thanks to the pre-eminence and influence of the French language under the aegis of the French sovereigns in the 17th and 18th centuries. The English language today conveys a large amount of information in fields of science, finance and especially computer science. The accounting standards emanating from computing tend to impose a certain cultural model. After the Second World War, the French showed their willingness to react against this form of linguistic imperialism by re-establishing cultural links with the countries of the Francophonie, such as Spain with South America for example and the Britain with the Commonwealth. The Arabic language brings together and establishes cultural links with the Muslim world which conveyed a brilliant civilization between the WIII and WV — th century. Multilingualism is now referred to in European language policy as bearing a value of cultural diversity.

Third, the cultural and technical dimension is linked to science, especially the exact sciences because it stems from the applications of science in the community. The cultural dimension related to science would fall within the realm of misunderstanding and conflict. Some thinkers have appropriated this conflictual tendency between culture and technique, such as the French sociologist and theologian Jacques Ellul (1912 – 1994), who argues that technology imposes its values by denying man and his culture. Claude Allègre

(2003) does not share this view and advocates a complementary juxtaposition between culture and technique rather than a conflictual opposition. The author notes that in the name of a specialization always demanding, scientists have isolated themselves from general culture, and insists in his work a little science for everyone, "there is no future for any human knowledge outside of culture, and there can be no culture in today's world that keeps science at a distance".

The German philosopher Hans Jonas (1903 – 1993) goes in the same direction as Allègre and indeed shows, in Principe de responsabilité (1979), a best-selling philosophical book in Germany whose French version was published twelve years later, that man tends to adopt, towards science and especially technology, a forward-looking attitude. The author advocates the precautionary principle endorsed at the 1992 Rio Summit, which aims to adopt proactive risk management measures with regard to potential damage to the environment and health. From this point of view, Hans Jonas (1903 – 1993), who seems to be at the origin of the philosophical principles of sustainable development, is the first philosopher to have introduced the concept of responsibility of present generations towards future generations, adopted by the United Nations in the 1987 Brundtland report. The three dimensions of sustainable development (economic, social and environmental), which will be explained below, have been adopted by the United Nations for the benefit of present and future generations.

In 2004, the astrophysicist Jean Audouze was awarded the UNESCO Kaling Prize for his work on the dissemination of scientific knowledge. He notes that the important contribution of Islamic civilization in astronomy in philosophy, as well as in many other sciences (algebra, geometry, trigonometry, music, chemistry, mechanics, medicine, etc.), allowed fruitful exchanges and the development of the West in these areas during the Middle Ages. At the Arab World Institute, the astrophysicist Jean Audouze believes in 2006 that today's civilization owes much to Islamic civilization, which contributed to the cultural foundations of Europe, and its development during the Renaissance. Former director of the Institut d'astrophysique de Paris, he made the same observation as Claude Allègre in advocating a reconciliation between science and culture.

Fourthly, in the cultural dimension as intangible heritage, a society allows us to see the emergence of a dominant culture in the sense of universalism developed by Tylor (1832-1917), Kant (1724 - 1804) and Bourdieu (1930 - 2002). The formation of cultural groups in this same society should also be noted. These cultural groups are distinguished from the dominant culture in the sense of anthropological and sociological relativism defended by Edmund Husserl (1859-1938) when he speaks of a crisis of universality, or by Malraux (1929) and Husserl (2011), when they refer to a cultural crisis in society, or by Norbert Elias (1897-1990), when he considers that culture is a dynamic of successive transformations. The diversity of these cultural groups can take the form of popular culture, which UNESCO defines as an intangible and living cultural heritage according to the convention adopted on 17 October 2003 in the following terms:

This intangible cultural heritage, passed on from generation to generation, is constantly recreated by communities and groups according to their environment, interaction with nature and history, and provides them with a sense of identity and continuity, Thus contributing to the promotion of respect for cultural diversity and human creativity." To speak of intangible cultural heritage requires to evoke its corollary on cultural and material heritage. This concept of material heritage has evolved over the past 15 years or so. Indeed, already in 1972, UNESCO had formulated a list of world heritage sites in hundreds of places around the world. Indeed, the 43rd session of the World Heritage Committee had identified 1,121 listed properties, distributed in 167 states as follows: 869 are cultural, 213 natural and 39 mixed (cultural and natural). These properties are also listed according to five regions according to a UNESCO definition and not on geographical criteria. (See summary table).

Synoptic table of the world heritage

	Culturel	Naturel	Mixte	Total
Afrique	53	38	5	96 8,56 %
États arabes	78	5	3	86 7,67 %
Asie et Pacifique	189	67	12	268 23 ;91 %
Europe et Amérique du Nord	453	65	11	529 47,19 %
Amérique latine et Caraïbes	96	38	8	142 12,67 %
Total	869	213	39	1121 100 %

Source : UNESCO 1972

Then in 1992, another Memory of the World list identified documentary collections of universal interest (Declaration of Human and Citizen's Rights, Suez Canal Memorial, etc.). Finally, in 1997, when UNESCO defined the notion of the intangible oral heritage of humanity, it adopted a progressive orientation towards a conception of both tangible and intangible heritage.

Fifth in the cultural dimension in relation to nature

For many researchers, culture is synonymous with civilization—an advanced, evolved state of humanity that contrasts with the "wild" state of nature. However, works from the 17th to early 19th centuries, during the rise of the Industrial Revolution, often reflected ideas aligned with the natural, or state of nature, Many of the works carried out in the 17th century and early 19th century, marking the rise of the industrial revolution, are consistent with the state of nature. John Locke (1632–1704) was influenced by natural law theories in developing his political philosophy rooted in nature. Similarly, Robert Boyle (1627–1691), a physicist and chemist, combined Christian beliefs with experimental science in his writings on the scientific method and the philosophy of nature. However, in recent decades, many philosophers have questioned the scope of our relationship with nature. René Dubos (1901-1982), an American agronomist, biologist and ecologist of French origin, is also interested in ecology. Hans Jonas (1903 – 1993) advocates the responsibility of present generations towards future generations.

A recurring question for anthropologists is: where does culture begin and nature end? The notion of culture first defined by Tylor (1871) distinguishes between man and animal, thus giving rise to the opposition between nature and culture. Lévi-Strauss (1967), in The Elementary Structures of Kinship, argues that while humans are social animals, they are uniquely characterized by their use of speech and tools in their interactions with the environment. For him, the distinction between nature and culture is not primarily historical but methodological.

In modern philosophy, Claude Lévi-Strauss having exerted a major influence on an international scale in the humanities and social sciences, goes further in thinking of our relationship with nature by considering that culture is natural to man, because all men have a culture and that any attempt to reduce man to a state of pre-cultural nature would be utopian. Indeed, recent discoveries (Stoller, 1924 - 1991) tend to show that nature, the biological, influences culture. Robert Stoller (1924 - 1991), American psychiatrist and psychoanalyst, showed that forces of nature act "on a child's attitudes and behaviour through play, clothing, choice of playmates, etc. In other words, the innate can influence the acquired."

1.2.3.— The evolutionary meaning of culture

In the anthropological and sociological sense, human cultures are closely linked to the living world. They have evolved and often changed over thousands of years. Two contrasting perspectives emerge: one affirms that humanity belongs to nature, moving away from religious explanations (which locate human origins in divine will) and recognizing humans as animal species. The other, rooted in human and social sciences, rejects reductive naturalism, emphasizing the unique aspects of human behavior that distinguish us from other animals.

The contrasting approaches to cultural evolution—one accepting human closeness to nature, the other emphasizing human uniqueness—can be reflected in the distinction between "culture" and "civilization." In Germany, two classifications were proposed: first, viewing culture as encompassing collective means like science and technology used to control the natural environment; second, considering culture as embodying the spiritual, idealistic aspects of society rooted in values. In North America, however, American sociologists favour the second distinction above all because of the significant contributions made by the works of Ferdinand Tönnies 1855-1936) and Alfred Weber (1868-1958). However, many sociologists and anthropologists prefer not to fall into either the first or the second distinction in order to argue that the two terms culture and civilization are interchangeable.

Civilization thus remains, marked in history by both conflicting events and fruitful events from the point of view of cultural exchanges. Examples include maritime exchanges in ancient Greece, in ancient Rome, contact areas in Spain between Muslims, Syria after the Crusades conflicts, the Silk Road, the Kingdom of Roger II of Sicily (who brought cartographic knowledge to the West from Arab-Muslim knowledge). It should also be noted that this type of exchange has led to the drafting of several scientific, philosophical, economic and commercial treaties in the West. The term civilization may refer to an advanced stage of scientific and technological development and tend towards the adoption of an evolutionary concept. However, it remains clear that some contemporary sociologists and anthropologists adopt a distinction according to which the culture is linked to a society while the term civilization refers to a set of societies sharing affinities and values common. For example, Western civilization includes diverse national cultures such as French, English, German, Italian, and American.

Authors such as Mercier (19 661 967) follow this distinction between civilization linked to a set of societies and culture linked to a society, by specifying that culture is a coherent set of traits in a given society. For Mercier (19,661,967), functionalists such as Malinowski and Radcliffe-Brown believe that each cultural trait has a function in a global system, whereas structuralists, particularly Claude Lévi-Strauss (1958) Define any culture as a collection of symbolic systems. From this point of view, culture would be for

Mercier (19 661 967), both material and spiritual. In other words, culture would be both explicit (material phenomena) and implicit (knowledge, attitudes, shared values). On the other hand, Mercier (19,661,967) prefers to speak of civilization when it comes to cultural diversity, that is to say the international and general aspect of the various particular cultures that Mauss (1971) defines as follows:

A civilization is a kind of moral environment in which a number of nations are immersed and each national culture is only a particular form... The phenomena of civilization are essentially international, extranational. We can therefore define them in opposition to the specific social phenomena of this or that society: those of the social phenomena which are common to several more or less close societies...»

Having noted that cultural diversity is not indeed dependent on racial diversity and that there are more cultures than races, Levi-Strauss (1958) wonders whether this cultural diversity constitutes an advantage or a disadvantage for humanity. The author goes further in asking how then to explain the advance of white civilization if it is not due to race. For him, cultural diversity has two causes.

First, the isolation of each culture which is shaped by a geographical, social and historical context. Secondly, the closeness of cultures that leads to a «desire to oppose, to distinguish oneself, to be oneself». Lévi-Strauss (1958) shows that the field of nature is above all that of the absence of rules and that everything universal in man comes under the order of nature and is characterized by spontaneity. On the other hand, everything that is bound to a norm belongs to culture and has the characteristics of the relative and the particular.

From this point of view, it is necessary to ask whether the author does not seek in nature a foundation for culture. It seeks to arrive at an explanation according to which the universal unconscious is not a matter of scientific observation, but of philosophical induction.

According to Lipiansky; M. M. (1973) in his work the structuralism of Levi-Strauss, this one seems to lead progressively the reader from the particular to the general, from the diversity to the unity, from the conscious to the unconscious, from the Culture to the Nature.

Regarding the evolution of culture, many ideologies emphasize a notion of abstract humanity rather than focusing on humans within their specific cultural contexts. Lévi-Strauss (1967) criticizes these ideas as a form of false evolutionism, which assumes that all societies follow the same developmental trajectory toward a common goal. The main mistake of these ideologies is their confusion between the continuous development of techniques and the discontinuous nature of civilizations. Today, it is more or less consciously recognized that modern civilization will not suffer the same fate as past civilizations. The traditional view holds that all cultures follow a linear path—from savagery to barbarism, and ultimately to civilization.

In contrast to proponents of this evolutionary view, diffusionists focus on the spatial spread of cultural elements, studying how ideas and practices move across different societies rather than following a linear, historical progression.

1.2.4. The diffusionist sense of culture.

Diffusionists consider that the essential thing is the diffusion of cultural elements interconnected from one culture to another. According to Lévi-Strauss (1967), the reality of progress cannot be easily denied, but the conception of this progress is more debatable. The author argues that progress is neither necessary nor continuous, but proceeds by leaps and bounds. The author then considers that all these "cultural bonds" do not go in the same direction. Thus history for Levi-Strauss is cumulative only from time to time and cannot be the privilege of a civilization or an era. The author gives an example of the cumulative period of history that Latin America has known until the end of the Inca Empire.

Franz Boas (1858-1942), the founding father of American anthropology who rejected evolutionism to represent the school of diffusionism by introducing concepts of cultural relativism, the study of cultural progress by distinguishing two criteria for progress which he considers to be antagonistic: progress based on invention and knowledge, and cultural progress based on a harmonious use of daily time and leisure. Boas thus defines the problem of progress in Western societies as follows: «The impoverishment of the masses caused by our unfortunate distribution of leisure is certainly not a cultural progress».

Boas's view of cultural progress aligns with Lévi-Strauss's perspective, though they differ from Mauss (1971). Mauss primarily associates progress with technological discoveries and inventions, viewing culture as a collection of innovations. Lévi-Strauss observes that this form of progress—quantitative and qualitative—has been dominated by Western civilization for over a century, a process he terms the "universalization of Western civilization." He suggests that Western influence will continue to adapt to diverse cultural contexts, but warns that this process may lead to "culinary excess," or "bulimia," risking cultural homogenization. Despite these trends, Lévi-Strauss argues that global civilization should not be viewed as a universal standard but rather as a coalition of cultures that each retain their distinctiveness.

This conception of civilization resembles Mauss's (1971), which emphasizes a shared core—the common substance or collective achievements of societies. In our view, civilization represents a limit to cultural fusion rather than a principle of unified civilizations. Mauss describes civilization as a moral environment in which nations are immersed, each representing a particular expression of culture. While this progress fosters cultural diversity, Lévi-Strauss warns that it can also lead to the homogenization of cultures, which must be preserved to counteract the trend toward a monoculture in an increasingly unified humanity.

To develop a comprehensive science of culture, it is essential to consider all cultural forms, processes of integration, and the psychological dimensions of culture. Without appreciating the dynamic nature of culture, these approaches provide only a limited understanding (Herskovits, 1950). Given the diversity of perspectives on cultural dynamics—ranging from evolutionist stages of development to diffusionist reconstructions of migration—it is unnecessary to favor one over the other. Herskovits (1950) emphasizes that evolutionists viewed human progress as a series of socio-cultural stages, while diffusionists focused on tracing the migration of cultural elements across regions. More recently, functionalist schools have expanded this focus to include cultural integration and change, emphasizing ongoing processes over static reconstructions. This broader perspective allows for a deeper analysis of the historical forces shaping cultural evolution and renewal.

The dynamic historical analysis of the literature indicates that the main positive and negative considerations, which guided the thinking of the great scholars, contributed to the emergence of the notion of evolution in Euramerican thought. To understand cultural evolutionism, it is necessary to understand it outside the biological theory of evolution. Teggart (1916), for whom historical criticism must free itself from literary concerns to submit to the philosophical and scientific discipline, showed that Darwin's work on the origin of species appeared in 1859, "was just too late to act on the evolution of ethnology". Furthermore, Teggart (1916) demonstrated that cultural and biological evolutionism differs in theoretical aspects, and explained that Tylor in 1873 and MeLennan (1876), denied their dependence on Darwin and remained faithful to an earlier tradition. The first authors, like their successors, understood, however, that there was a fundamental difference between learned traits of behaviour and innate physical characteristics.

Like any important theory, the one of cultural evolution was the work of several enlightened minds. Some, the best known, sought to describe and explain the development of human civilization in its entirety. Others focus on particular aspects of culture, studying the evolution of art, state or religion. Among the evolutionary anthropologists, Herskovits (1950) cites famous names such as: Pitt-Rivers, Lubbock and McLennan in England, Bachhofeu in Switzerland, Bastian and Wundt in

Germany, Count in France. In the wake of these remarks, Herskovits (1950) wants to distinguish three main elements appearing in the thinking of the proponents of cultural evolutionism:

1. The history of humanity represents a unilinear series of institutions which denote the principle of the psychic unity of man.

2. The comparative method makes it possible to establish the evolution of human institutions by comparing their manifestations among existing peoples.

3. The survival of customs among peoples proves that these societies have passed through earlier stages whose characteristics are visible in their current ways of life.

Morgan (1877) distinguishes in his Ancient Society three main periods in the socio-cultural development of man: Savagery, Barbarism and Civilization. The first two are divided into ancient, middle and recent periods, marked by social conditions called old, medium and recent state of Savagery or Barbarism. More than five decades later, Tylor (1924) moves away from Morgan's definition of cultural development, preferring to talk about the historical development capable of giving meaning to culture, and the large group he calls "survivances" able to trace the course of world civilization. This conception of survival was a feature of evolutionism in Europe more than in America.

The concept of survivals moves from the camp of evolutionists to that of anti-evolutionists. In his remarkable but controversial work, The History of Melanesian Society, Rivers (1914), he considered "survival" as a means to reconstruct the history of primitive peoples. The author goes further to consider survival as "the persistence of the useless". In the same sense, Father W. Schmidt, a German diffusionist who also attacked cultural evolutionism, evokes the term survival to search for the «origins» of religion in primitive societies. It demonstrates the existence of an original monotheism by the «supreme gods» that is observed in many tribes. The author indicates that these tribes regard the survival of a belief as one deity. But the question is whether, from this point of view, it is possible to reject the usefulness of cultural survival. Beyond the thought of a "survival" stripped of its cultural significance, Herskovits (1950) argues that there can be no culture emptied of meaning because culture is a component of ever-changing history. The author believes that no living culture is static in the life of a people, because even in a society marked by strong conservatism, it has indeed been observed that changes have occurred after a certain time. The rejection of evolutionism, by a large number of anthropologists, is in fact part of a methodology and thoughts of the time. Herskovits (1950) who admitted the real utility of cultural survival points out that the thinkers of their time doubted the conception of progress which prevailed at the time of evolutionism under the influence of a philosophy of cultural relativism which was based on values peculiar to The lives of "wild". Herskovits (1950) bases his arguments on Franz Boas (1858-1942), a German anthropologist of the diffusionist school and founding father of American anthropology. Having established scientific anthropology in North America, he also reacted against evolutionism by establishing cultural relativism in the following terms:

While the general pattern of evolution is no longer defensible, the problem of progress remains. Observation shows that man's discoveries and knowledge have spread with ever increasing speed, and we can speak of progress in technology, in the successful exploitation of natural resources and in knowledge, because each new advance adds to existing knowledge. Cases of loss of pre-existing knowledge are relatively rare and, for the whole of humanity, temporary. It is much more difficult to talk about progress in any other cultural activity, except that the aspects of cultural life that stop the progression of knowledge gradually disappear. The lack of change in basic ethical attitudes was noted. Progress in social organization generally refers to better adaptation to economic conditions and ethical requirements, conceived as if conforming to the general state of knowledge."

Franz Boas (1858-1942), then proposes to the anthropologists to be more interested in the particularities of each society rather than comparing cultures and making conjectural generalizations. Boas reaffirms his opposition to the conception of a direct relationship between culture and race, and rejects the idea of the existence of inferior and superior races, as proposed by some ultranationalists. Boas refuses to oppose also the «primitive» to the «civilized». The term "primitive" seems to indicate, by its etymology and history, the idea of an outdated evolutionism although it is defined by Lévi-Strauss (1958), as serving the political point of view: "A primitive people is not a backward or retarded people". If the primitive term has been rejected by the ethnological community, because it can serve a political point of view, it remains that its definition appears scientifically unfounded and is not based on any sociological or historical reality. Today it is appropriate to speak more often of indigenous or indigenous populations. This is how the doctrine of evolution entered the political realm as any other scientific hypothesis to become popular, concludes Herskovits (1950). The author indicates that this episode in the history of cultural and social evolutionism does not seem to have had much influence on anthropologists who persisted in analyzing existing hypotheses using technical data used in the field.

In addition, a century before Herskovits (1950), Herbert Spencer supported in 1857 in «Progress, Its Law and Causes», the idea of an evolutionary philosophy of transformation from simple to complex and considered that progress is not only technical to say a progress, but the general progress in all fields, that is to say all progress, a law of all progress. Regarding this progress that the individual organisms show in their evolution, the law of organic progress appears to be the law of all progress. Whether in the development of the Earth, Life, society, governments, businesses, trade, language, literature, science, or art. This same evolution from the simple to the complex, through a process of continuous differentiation, begins with changes until the last results of civilization. Thus, the transformation from homogeneous to heterogeneous is truly progress. Four decades later, Spencer (principle of evolution, as a response to Lord Salisbury, 1895), rejected in 1895 the idea of confusing Darwin's theory of natural selection with specific organic evolution or with evolution in general which he defends as the law of all progress. Known as one of the leading defenders of the theory of evolution in the 19th century, Hebert Spencer competed with Charles Darwin by introducing the expression "selection of the fittest" instead of Darwin's natural selection. His theory of evolution later became the «social Darwinism», considering society as a living organism, or a super organization.

CONCLUSION

This chapter has explored the concept of culture as part of human politics within a broader, universalist perspective. It presents a view of culture as both diverse and interconnected, aiming for universality and dominance. This mosaic of cultures reflects the collective actions and policies of the human species. The goal is to demonstrate that culture, as a characteristic of the human species, encompasses multiple dimensions: anthropological, sociological, evolutionary, and dynamic.

The anthropological perspective views culture as a scientific construct rooted in cultural relativism, emphasizing the diversity and adaptability of human societies. The sociological perspective relates culture to social representations, customs, values, and norms that shape daily life. The evolutionary approach compares culture to civilization, highlighting processes of development and change over time. We also discussed the challenges in identifying and fostering innovations, considering the resistance to cultural change due to its complex nature.

CHAPTER 2
CULTURAL ISSUES

Culture is an antidote to violence,
because it invites us to understand others,
and fertile tolerance, inciting us to
to meet other imaginaries and other cultures
- Renaud Donnedieu de Vabre

Introduction

Building on the mosaic of culture and its complex relationship with human politics and the human species, this second chapter explores another key challenge: understanding the stakes of culture in a global context. It first examines the enigmatic and often conflictual relationship between culture and science (Section 2.1), then analyzes the connection between culture and the world (Section 2.2). Finally, it reveals that, ultimately, everything is cultural (Section 2.3).

Section 2.1. — Culture and Science

Section 2.2. — Culture and the World

Section 2.3. — Everything is cultural

Section 2.1. Culture and Science

The relationship between culture and science can be understood through the transition from the philosophy of the human sciences to that of the exact sciences. Is the philosophy of social sciences not also a philosophy of culture? Or even a «science of culture» in the broadest sense, encompassing human cultural productions? From this perspective, researchers like Fournier (2009) see science as a form of cultural production—alongside art or literature—though not occupying the highest hierarchy of knowledge. The longstanding divide between the natural sciences and the spiritual sciences of culture persists. Building bridges between the philosophy of the exact sciences and that of the humanities and social sciences is essential for critical understanding.

According to Fournier (2009), there are two main groups: critical researchers who seek to challenge and critique the concept of culture, and practitioners who view ethnology as a resource for reflection and cultural action. Researchers focused on culture are often suspected by anti-culturalists of promoting the very notion they critique. At university, the culturalist positon is sometimes linked to a conservative ethnology, sometimes to «cultural studies», but still considered by anti-culturalists as an external label. The problem with the anticulturalist posture is that it itself creates an artificial divide between "culturalists" (considered outdated and backward) and those who have been able to overcome culturalism, and the divide between "bad" and "good" anthropologists. Thus, the anticulturalist posture conveys an ideological and hierarchical vision of anthropology, which strengthens the legitimacy of anticulturalists, because designating an enemy, in the sense of Fournier (2009), always allows to strengthen oneself.

To get out of this oppositional logic, Fournier (2009) recommends observing the different forms of culturalism and examining several ways of instrumentalizing culture. This seems to be the only way for anticulturalist anthropology not to fall back into the essentialist posture it denounces. Would it not be better to denounce the instrumentalization of the notion of culture, work on the scale of microhistory? the author wonders. More and more anthropologists today display an anti-culturalist posture, believing that the notion of culture is in itself dangerous because it contributes to chosify the facts it refers to. If the criticisms of the notion of culture were first carried by sociology or political science (Bayart, 1996), anthropologists themselves have not hesitated to defend this posture of interculturalism (Bensa, 2006).

The anti — culturalists show that they most often prefer to argue their criticism by theoretical reflection rather than by concrete examples on the harmfulness of the notion of culture. According to Fournier (2009), the main cause of this critical trend lies in the desire of postcolonial anthropologists to distinguish themselves from a certain naive ethnography, marked by the fol klore (in its popular acceptance, negative), and the positivism of critical intellectuals, who denounce the aberrations of the notion of culture.

On the other hand, ethnology represents a reservoir of reflection for researchers who are constantly suspected by the "anti-culturalist" to play into the notion of culture. Fournier (2009) points out that the analysis of culturalist and anticulturalist postures only deals with the situation in the three geopolitically «dominant» geographical areas (Germany, the USA, France), and shows that anthropology is also a «cultural» discipline. For the author, the usefulness of culture lies in connecting anthropology and the society to which it belongs.

Moving beyond these dominant regions, it is essential to consider the global dimension of culture, as discussed by authors such as Lipovetsky and Serrou (2008), who explore the concept of culture in the context of the entire world.

Section 2.2. — Culture and the World

Gilles Lipovetsky, an associate professor of philosophy joined by jean Serroy, a literature specialist (2008), believes that it is first necessary to remove a number of ambiguities about the nature of culture-world. For them, world culture is not synonymous with the Americanization of the world, but it is that of the triumph of planetary products. The culture-world is not synonymous with an erasure of convictions, because the revival of the religious contributes to this persistence of beliefs and divergences. It is not the advent of the «Return of the religious», but the individualization, denationalization of beliefs and practices, point out the authors.

Lipovetsky and Serroy (2008) describe the culture of the hyper-modern era as distinct from traditional social norms. It has transformed into a thriving economic sector often referred to as «cultural capitalism». This culture-world is driven by market forces, influenced by global stars and events, and characterized by the proliferation of museums, festivals, and cultural marketing aimed at attracting and retaining tourists.

The logic of this new situation, which researchers Lipovetsky and Serroy (2008) do not consider as bad in itself, implies new political ambitions capable of providing answers to the needs of a population conditioned by the planetary effects of culture-world. Fashion, advertising, tourism, art-business, star-system, urbanism, today nothing escapes the order of culture. It has become a culture-world, a culture of widespread technocapitalism, cultural industries, media and digital networks that transcend all borders.

In the age of cultural hypercapitalism, Gilles Lipovetsky and Jean Serroy (2008), while analyzing this cultural upheaval, propose possible courses of action aimed at reversing the growth of consumerism and the widespread disorientation of the time. The authors ultimately question whether the years to come would, paradoxically, be those of a «revenge of culture». Is it a culture in the world, inclusive, alienating or a culture of the world crushed or dominated? For Jean Paul Warnier, a field ethnologist (2004), the alternative in this sense seems clear: either a world culture under the sign of alienation or illusion, or a cultural crushing that is hardly better. Despite the barriers to migration flows, European, Arab, African, Asian countries have millions of their children in other countries and educational migrations, work, tourism and religion contribute to the globalization of cultural practices. As a result, states are deprived of control over these cultural flows on a global scale and continue to think about illusory fences in order not to be overrun. Warnier (2004), a field ethnologist, finds that factions, clans, camps, parties, social classes and regions are opposed, allied and divided according to their lifestyles, passions and interests. For a "world culture" to exist, there would have to be, according to Jean Paul Warnier (2004), a "world society", or a government of the world.

Hence the question that arises is whether a world culture can be shaped by an action of world cultures. The expression "culture monde" has the merit of highlighting the implementation of local cultures through the action of the globalization of flows, without being able to imply a "globalization of culture" which everyone thinks is not for tomorrow. Similarly, a single mass culture on the scale of the world would also be unlikely in the thought of Jean Paul Warnier (2004). However, in the English-speaking world, essays on "globalization" or "globalisation" have been a genre in their own right since the 1990s, to the extent that titles dealing with these issues are more the result of academic modes. and media curiosity.

It is worth noting that this approach to world governance serves as a foundation for the final chapter, which proposes a new paradigm of transnational cultural leadership capable of addressing the disorientation and mismanagement of the global order. Ultimately, for Warnier (2004), the question is whether it is possible to make a sociological and ethnographic analysis of cultural practices on the ground and on the whole planet. And at what possible price for the investigator? The author believes that it is possible to see a world culture emerge through the intersection of globalization of flows and local reinterpretations. Building on this idea of a global field survey, CNRS researcher Dominique Wolton (2004) advocates for cultural coexistence in a interconnected world, emphasizing that cultural identities should be open and relational. In world history, geopolitics according to Wolton (2004), often takes precedence over the cultural, because it refers more to the French Revolution than to the Enlightenment. From this point of view, almost all political actors agree that culture is fundamental to democracy and that it remains to be defined in what and how to implement it.

From "democratization" to "democracy", from "the exception" to "diversity", the cultural dimension has been strongly modified by the French writer and politician, André Malraux (1901-1976), and in particular by Serge Regourd (2004) Emeritus professor of universities and author of SOS Culture, indigenous editions, Bouzigues, 2021. André Malraux (1901-1976) and Serge Regourd (2004) advocate the rejection of any hierarchy in the cultural dimension: The originality of the policy we have wanted to conduct (...) is to reject, in a total, radical and absolute way, the opposition between what would be, on the one hand, great art, great ambition, great creation, and on the other hand, everyday culture. Indeed, for the authors, failing to work so that the cultural becomes popular, now we act in such a way that the popular becomes cultural. In May 1968, everything was political. For the authors, everything is now cultural.

Section 2.3. Now everything is cultural.

If for politicians, everything is now cultural, the themes related justify this analysis of Malraux and Regourd explained in a few recurring sentences:

The pandemic has caused a serious crisis in the cultural sector

Cultural policies

The cultural issue in election campaigns,

Artistic and cultural issues in recruitment

Ministers of Culture

Mass culture

The example of the Culture Pass, aimed at 18-year-olds

In the cultural categories

Ministry of Cultural Affairs

Cultural democratization

A certain cultural capital,

Cultural democracy

The scope of cultural activities

Everyday culture

The cultural becomes popular

Culture is everywhere and in all trades. The book illustrates this ubiquity of culture with examples from cinema—filmmakers, directors, actors, assistants, scriptwriters, producers, set designers, cinematographers, sound engineers, editors, video artists, makeup artists, presenters, journalists, and columnists—and from the visual arts—painters, sculptors, engravers, photographers, gallerists, illustrators, watercolorists, and art historians.

If everything is now cultural, can we talk about the revenge of culture (Laurent Nunez, 2015) in a world that has become soulless and moral? Would a world without culture be a world without soul? To explain the world that has become soulless, researcher Allan Bloom (2018) notes that when culture flourished, students who had a unified vision of the world were cultured, and had a kind of soul, and an identity. Unfortunately, those who are now in the big schools have no chance of grasping life as a whole as before, because according to Bloom, the purpose of the education they received is to make them open young people. Indeed, long before Bloom, Guuthier (1989) explained that in the great idea of relativism at the time, the school had developed more an attitude of tolerance towards ideas than a desire to seek or transmit truth. The young people whose soul is disarmed today are unable to judge, because they no longer have criteria for judging and deciding and pour in indifference. Thus, it seems that this contemporary doctrine of open-mindedness constitutes the great weakness of the West and remains at the heart of the problem (Gauthier, 1989).

The author considers that modern man, having lost his identity (unity, truth, finality), cannot say «no» because he considers that everything is part of culture and everything becomes culture. For Gauthier (1989), the crisis of general culture only reflects a crisis of education, an incoherence in the world, in short a crisis of our civilization. Consequently, the danger arising from this weakness is that the US will lose its political and intellectual supremacy in the world. Just as the responsibility for the fate of freedom in the world lies with politicians, so the fate of philosophy in the world lies with universities, because what characterizes the West is science, that is to say, the quest for knowledge of nature, culture, in other words the culture of the West is perceived as a culture in which people are imprisoned in the image of the cave that Plato assimilates to a culture. But Plato did not suggest as a solution to go to other cultures, but to discover nature, in which the cultures are only imitations aimed in the Nietzschean approach, to stimulate and increase the ability to create values.

Gauthier (1989) notes that the university has become disconnected from the universal, as the universal has abandoned academia. Today, issues like racial and sexual claims, and the generation of social demands, often dominate academic discourse, encroaching on reason. Bloom (2018) views this shift as part of a broader philosophical revolution—relativism—that challenges the Enlightenment's rationalism. Bloom argues that Enlightenment rationalism aimed to transcend faith while maintaining universal principles. In contrast, relativism constitutes a fundamental change in how knowledge is understood, rendering rationalism—once a pursuit of universal truth—unable to access an ultimate reality.

French anthropologist Yves Goudineau (2018) shares the views of Gauthier (1989) and Bloom (2018) on rationalism, adding two others relating to domination and values that he believes characterize the western world of enlightenment. The researcher asks the question of rationalism and its universality. He explains, as his predecessors did, that the notion of scientific universality has primacy over cultural differences and aims to reduce them. On the second question of domination, the author explains that Western science, and hence its values, would rely less on the superiority of rationalism than on domination by the conquests of colonialism. The «modern» science is part of the colonial heritage and has only imposed itself at the price of a radical negation of other scientific traditions which it has abruptly interrupted. On the third question of values, the anthropologist Yves Goudineau (2018) explains that the so-called «modern» science would be of western essence, intimately linked to the values of the Judeo-Christian or capitalist West, depending on the case, and thus, would attack the cultural foundations of other societies.

Given that modern science and Western culture have often been imposed through domination (Goudineau, 2018; Gauthier, 1989; Bloom, 2018), an additional question arises: can culture fundamentally distort or denature human nature?

The question of whether culture distorts human nature hinges on the classical opposition between nature and culture. Nature refers to our animal instincts, while culture differentiates us from animals through education and civilization. From this perspective, culture distances man from his innate nature, suppressing instincts and imposing rules. Rousseau (discourse on inequality) argued that humans are naturally good, and that culture—through social development—has become the root of evil, turning man into jealous, envious, and greedy beings. Similarly, Diderot described the peaceful life of the "wild man," living close to nature and free from possessiveness. Nietzsche took this further, suggesting that culture is humanity's greatest misfortune, inhibiting the full expression of our true, natural nature.

The concept that man has no nature deserves to be questioned. Indeed, the view that culture distorts the nature of man is not followed by Sartre's philosophical thought that considers that man defines himself as nothing and has no nature since his existence precedes its essence. For Sartre what makes a man a man is his fundamental freedom and his choices, not what comes from his nature. By pushing the reasoning of Sartre further, if man has no nature, culture does not distort him, but it constitutes him. Man is only culture in the end, falling back into the conception that everything is cultural as defended above by André Malraux (1901-1976) and Serge Regourd (2004).

In reality the nature of man is his culture, because the idea of a denaturation of man would be absurd: man opposes to the animal by its culture considered as part of the essence of man. Is it not legitimate to think that man is naturally cultural and therefore conforms to his nature? Moreover, it should not be forgotten that the animal in us is also part of human nature, and that it is demonstrated that only man can be inhuman.

CONCLUSION

The book suggests that the issues of culture in its relationship with its political and social environment, science and world appear complex and disparate. In relation to the sciences, it proposes to underline the old gap between the sciences of nature of life, and the sciences of mind of culture, still remains. From the philosophy of the exact sciences to the philosophy of the humanities and social sciences, a bridge can be established to constitute critical passages.

In relation to the world, culture cannot be seen as synonymous with the americanization of the world, but as the triumph of inclusive cultural hypercapitalism aimed at a world culture through the globalization of local reinterpretations. From now on, man is only culture and in the end everything is cultural.

CONCLUSION OF PART ONE

The first part underscores the importance of culture, beginning with a mosaic that portrays culture as both a human policy and an aspect of the human species. The second chapter explores cultural issues related to science and the world, ultimately affirming that man is defined by culture. Overall, the book clarifies how human politics shape this universalist conception of culture—one that seeks to be both universal and dominant. It shows that culture, as part of the human species, encompasses multiple meanings: anthropological, sociological, evolutionary, and dynamic.

The anthropological meaning which means a scientific anthropology based on a cultural relativism. The sociological meaning of peoples' customs is linked to social representations based on values and norms. The evolutionary sense of culture which translates into a comparison between the notion of culture and that of civilization. In the sense of cultural change, the book shows the difficulties of identifying innovations that reduce resistance to change due to the complexity of the phenomenon of cultural change.

In the second chapter, the book aims to explain that the issues of culture in its relationship with science and the world appear complex and disparate. In relation to the sciences, he describes the ancient gap that still exists between the natural sciences of life and the spiritual sciences of culture. From the philosophy of the exact sciences to the philosophy of the humanities and social sciences, a bridge can be established to constitute critical passages. In relation to the world, culture cannot be seen as synonymous with the americanization of the world, but as the triumph of inclusive cultural hypercapitalism aimed at a world culture through the globalization of local reinterpretations. From now on, man is only culture and in the end everything is cultural.

PART TWO
CULTURE AND SUSTAINABLE DEVELOPMENT

... in short, beauty is everywhere.
It is not she who is missing in our eyes,
it is our eyes that are missing to see...
- Boris Vian

Introduction

After having explained in the first part, the importance of culture which is distinguished by a mosaic of characteristics that confront themselves in their contribution to science and the world, the book proposes to study in this second part structured in two chapters (three and four), culture and its relationship to sustainable development.

The book deals in chapter three with culture and sustainability by explaining the notion of sustainable development in which cultural management cultivates a sustainable interaction. It raises the question of whether culture can contribute to sustainable development or vice versa, if it is perceived by some countries, in Africa, as a decoy.

In chapter four, the book deals with cultural diversity and the differences that exist between the concepts of national culture and corporate culture. It ends with a confrontation of culture and cultural management around the world.

CHAPTER 3
CULTURE AND SUSTAINABLE DEVELOPMENT

When poverty comes through the door, love goes out the window.
- French proverb

Introduction

Building on the discussion of sustainable development introduced in Part Two, this third chapter is structured into four sections. It begins by examining key concepts and theories of sustainable development (Section 3.1), then explores the relationship between cultural management and sustainable development (Section 3.2). The subsequent sections analyze whether culture can contribute to sustainability (Section 3.3) and scrutinize the perception of culture and sustainable development as a potential decoy (Section 3.4).

Section 3.1 Concepts of sustainable development,

3.1.1. Theories of sustainable development

3.1.2. Sustainable development debates

Section 3.2 Cultural management and sustainable development

3.2.1. Concept of sustainable management and development

3.2.2. The contribution of management to sustainable development

Section 3.3. Culture can--it contributes to sustainable development.

3.3.1. Culture contributes to sustainable development according to UNESCO.

3.3.2. The cultural dimension as perceived by the UN

Section 3.1. Sustainable development concepts

Sustainable development is addressed here through the search for a better quality of life and working conditions in the present and in the future. The book analyses these areas in a synthetic way, due to their wide scope and the complexity of their interdependence. It first presents the concept of sustainable development, decrypted by different theories. It then examines sustainable development through the lens of management sciences, including management and its contribution to the sustainability of organizations and businesses, particularly socially responsible enterprises (CSR). The book finally presents theories and cross-debates in the specific field of sustainable development.

3.1.1. Theories of sustainable development

Does sustainable development imply continuous growth in production and consumption to achieve greater well-being and happiness? In other words, does it promote the accumulation of material wealth? As early as 1848, John Stuart Mill—cited by Flipo (2011)—argued that material well-being required little growth, and that constant work could make life unpleasant. This perspective suggests that halting growth might be a route to happiness and well-being. Today, however, the potential halt of growth raises debates among three major schools of thought:

The first trend in favour of growth was initiated by Robert Solow in 1974, who believed that growth should not be limited and must continue so as to enable future generations to become richer and better equipped to combat poverty. multi-problem. According to this current of thought, growth does indeed deteriorate the environment, but this deterioration is the price to pay for industrialization and subsequently an improvement in living conditions and well-being (Flipo, 2011). Other analyses emanating from a tradition of economists such as François Perroux (1903-1987), French economist and Joseph Schumpeter (1883-1950), Austrian economist, known for his theories on creative destruction and innovation, prefer to distinguish between growth and development.

The second trend in favor of economic decline is defended by Nicholas Georgescu — Roegen (1906-1994), an American mathematician and economist quoted by Flipo (2011) to protect ecological wealth, because the current wealth is not acquired by technical progress, but by the indebtedness of the Third World, and the squandering of its essential riches. The proponents of decline believe that peak oil will lead the world into decline and it would be irresponsible for policymakers not to anticipate this situation.

A third trend is more concerned with the spatial distribution of wealth rather than growth or the cumulative level of wealth. Alf Hornborg (1993) shows, for example, that international trade is all positioned in a perspective of changing the distribution of «goods» and ecological «evils» rather than thinking about the increase of «goods» in industrialized countries that are the product of increased "ills" in other parts of the world (Flipo, 2011). This thesis embodies «the environmentalism of the poor» (Juan Martinez-Alier, 1992, 1994), often claimed by third world countries. It joins some analyses of Marx, of theorists of the dependence or theorists of the unequal exchange.

It should be stressed that while economics still dominates sustainable development analyses, other scientific analyses propose legal and ethical approaches which focus on the hierarchy of standards, because the world disorder can only be dealt with by a legal approach derived from the Declaration of Human Rights. It is ultimately a matter of understanding that the rule of law must apply to the entire planet.

If, however, trees cannot bring a complaint; since they do not have an entity that can represent their interests, the same question arises as to who can then represent the interests of future generations? Self-centered theories (protection of the environment) are opposed to biocentric theories (protection of living beings) and anthropocentric theories (protection of nature according to the interest of the human species). From this point of view, if the law accepts the three theories since always: the protection of domestic animals, environments and «remarkable sites», Jared Diamond, considers that human societies still do not know how to deal with their environment and may eventually disappear.

On one side, political scientists argue that sustainable development requires an evolution of institutions; on the other, sociologists advocate for social mobilization models to address conflicts related to production. In the 1970s, French sociologist Alain Touraine suggested that the core issue has shifted from controlling production to fostering a new conception of emancipation. Leslie Sklair, cited by Flipo (2011), contends that the environmental crisis results from a confrontation between an economic class and an ecological "class," both divided over wealth distribution. Surveys of managers reveal that business leaders concerned about environmental issues tend to blame the population, whereas the public believes that environmental degradation is primarily caused by companies and their managers due to their behaviors and marketing strategies.

The environment in turn will influence the content of developed countries' development. As a result, sustainable development becomes a diplomatic concept that contains major geopolitical issues whose solution is collective. Sustainable development is therefore not "the" solution, but a space for reflection and solutions. But the real question remains that of the priorities to be adopted by decision-makers to ensure sustainable development and safeguard the planet. Flipo's (2011) in-depth examination of sustainable development shows that it is not a concept, because it is not defined precisely, but rather a set of ideas and debates which do not all agree on one single truth, on what would be sustainable development.

3.1.2. Cross-cutting discussions on sustainable development

In the wake of these debates, we should ask ourselves, with Flipo (2011), whether sustainable development means limiting population or consumption to safeguard the planet's wealth and protect present and future generations. In other words, should we protect humans or nature? Should we give priority to diversity or universalism, wealth or standard of living in order to achieve the desired sustainable development? This question deserves to be discussed in the following paragraphs.

Limit population or consumption?

In his Essai sur le principe de population (1798), Thomas Malthus quoted by Flipo (2011) had estimated that the population increases exponentially or geometrically (1, 2, 4...), while resources grow arithmetically (1,2, 3...). It concluded an inevitable demographic catastrophe, if one could not prevent the population from increasing. Two centuries later, in 1972, the western countries began to point fingers, the demographics of the southern countries characterized by a high birth rate. Faced with this position of the Western countries, many third world countries have raised their voices to announce that the problem is not in the number of people but in the western way of life which damages the environment and squanders the planet's resources. (Flipo, 2011).

Today, the UN predicts that the global population will reach approximately 9 billion by 2050, accompanied by an estimated 21 billion domestic animals (e.g., 29 million in France and 300 million in China). If current trends continue, Flipo (2011) estimates that around 99% of the human population will reside in developing countries. This raises a critical question: how can we ensure a high standard of living for all? Flipo also questions whether reconciling economic growth with ecological sustainability is truly feasible or if it remains an unrealistic ideal. Wouldn't the only possible way be to change our conception of wealth?

Protecting people or nature?

In France, for example, several laws are being enacted to protect nature and the environment. The first was the Nature Act (1976), followed by the Laws on mountain environments (1985), forests (1985), coasts (1986), water (1992) and air (1996). There are currently, according to Flipo (2011), 13 global multilateral agreements and more than 500 international environmental agreements. Despite this legal approach to nature protection, the man/nature opposition still persists because once nature was immense and powerful and now it is becoming narrow and fragile. Must we now protect it, renounce its domination and thereby renounce progress? asks Flipo (2011). Some currents believe that it is up to the human being to continue his mastery of nature (conquest of space, genetic manipulations), while others note that success in these fields are becoming increasingly rare.

Diversity or universalism?

While sustainable development is universal, all diversity seemed to be disappearing in a planet characterized by a single model. Development was based on economic development, which had to be accompanied by progress in political freedoms and human rights. Beyond human rights, the question of living together is acute. Living together means living in a cultural diversity, because each culture is a particular way to practice the world. Development, to be sustainable, cannot, according to Flipo (2011), ignore the meeting of cultures for a better world. Thus culture and universal are not necessarily contradictory, for 3 reasons. First of all, culture is a constructed order giving it an appearance of immutability, because everything that is built, perhaps, according to Flipo (2011), deconstructed and translated by acculturation.

Then, if cultures are different practices of the world, the latter is not entirely left to their arbitrariness, because reality resists the diversity of cultures. Finally, Flipo (2011), believes that human beings can refer to an ethical and moral sense of which part is a universal aspiration. Flipo (2011) argues that part of the solution in this debate about cultural diversity and universalism is in general culture, which refers to a person's ability to understand different cultures.

Wealth or standard of living?

What most often characterizes the cross-debates on sustainable development would be to refer to the indicator GDP as old as its invention by Simon Kuznets (1901-1985) the third Nobel prize in economics Western countries have adopted the Simon Kuznets principle as a benchmark for their empirical interpretation of economic growth. Yet other indicators propose assessments of wealth that take two broad directions: social and environmental. Today, in the face of ever-increasing inequalities, scientists are proposing various social health indicators. This is the Human Development Index (HDI), which places Norway in first place, the United States in fourth, and France in fourteenth, behind South Korea (2010).

This new HDI indicator would also be applied at the enterprise level to assess economic, social and environmental wealth concepts.

Although these indicators are imperfect, just like GDP, Flipo (2011) nevertheless considers the example of Bouthan to be interesting insofar as the King of Bouthan Jigme Singye Wangchuck, to replace the GDP, had invented in 1972 an index of Gross National Happiness (BNB), now perceived as a new indicator built after a broad debate with society.

In short, the differences on ways of thinking and acting seem to be linked not only to political and geopolitical issues, but also to important differences between the supporters of sustainable development on what needs to be done to improve the current and future situation. Examination of the debates shows that these differences are not simply political, but a cultural state produced by industrialization which has entered into current customs. Ultimately, the greatest challenge of sustainable development may be its cultural dimension—shaping values, perceptions, and behaviors across societies. (Flipo, 2011). Sustainable development, as defined in the UN Burtland report (1987), aims at economic and social development, but also environmental development, that is to say, to preserve and promote ecological and environmental safety. This is specifically to protect the planet from certain disasters that the book cites as examples:

Environmental safety

The following disasters have revealed weaknesses in crisis management and especially in preventing crises and disasters that have led to significant changes in human life and activities: mercury pollution of Minamata Bay by the Chisso plant in Japan from 1932 to 1968 (nearly 900 deaths), sinking of the oil tanker Tomy Canyon on the coasts of Brittany in 1967, explosion of the Flixborough plant 260 km from London in 1974 (28 deaths, factory razed), chemical plant explosion at Seveso in Italy in 1976 (37,000 displaced persons), nuclear accident at Three Mile Iceland in the USA in 1979 (reactor fusion), chemical plant explosion at Union Carbide in

Bhopal (1984), fusion of the Chernobyl reactor in Ukraine in 1986 (x 5 000 km2 irradiated), sinking of the oil tanker Exxon Valdez in Alaska in 1989, explosion of the AZF plant in Toulouse in 2001 (30 deaths), gigantic oil leak on a BP offshore platformUnited States in 2010, etc. The costs of these disasters appear to be enormous. For Chernobyl, the figures range from 80 billion to several hundred billion euros plus the release of huge quantities of radionuclides.

Ecological Economic Security

The problem is that the security of one is linked to the security of another. Economic security is also reflected in the various solidarity systems such as unemployment insurance or social security, which make it possible to deal with unforeseeable accidents. Ecological safety depends on the stability of ecosystems, because according to Flipo (2011), the greater the diversity, the more stable the ecosystem. Today, the mechanization that requires to expand the areas cultivated for the same variety has resulted in a reduction of the space occupied by other varieties. As a result, in Europe half of domestic varieties have disappeared within a century, and 41% of the remaining 1,500 breeds are at risk of disappearing in the next 20 years. In the Philippines, 54 varieties of rice remain out of the 4,000 that were once grown. In the US, 86% of the 7,098 apple varieties grown between 1804 and 1904 are no longer stored in a gene bank. Approximately 75% of the genetic diversity of agricultural plants would have disappeared from the fields during the 20th century.

What are the levers of sustainable development?

Sustainable development imposes traditional issues of democracy, common good and new issues related to international space, ecology and the long term. Flipo (2011), believes that democracy can only exist if there is debate, if the issues are known and solutions are not taken in advance by the monopolies in place. Some ecological thinkers, such as Hans Jonas (1903-1993), have postulated an enlightened dictatorship to avoid the destruction of the conditions for a truly human life on Earth. The environmentalists want to impose a kind of "benevolent and enlightened tyranny", according to the expression of Hans Jonas and written by Michel Santo on August 2, 2019. Given the evidence of a "dictatorial" type proposal, the researcher, Ms. Szuda noted in the interview with the newspaper libération on July 30, 2019, that coercion does not necessarily mean dictatorship and provides proof of compulsory education up to the age of 16. This constraint is accepted by the population without difficulty, because Szuda considers it legitimate for the good of humanity. Indeed, it is not impossible to imagine that tomorrow a sovereign people sufficiently enlightened will consent to a drastic restriction of its freedoms and entrust the management to an «altruistic» and «benevolent» elite composed of scientists, intellectuals and philosophers.

The researcher Mathilde Szuda puts forward two arguments for a «muscled» intervention of politics: rationing during the Second World War and that practiced in Cuba. She points out that with these two examples the only modes of muscular intervention by politicians in the economy can be authoritarian in nature. In the wake of the contours of this «tyranny» or dictatorships to save the world, intellectuals have long ago identified the weak points of the representative democracy of this world: temporality and geography. In terms of temporality, elected representatives are considered as assigned to the short term because of electoral mandates that induce individuals to entrust their political freedom to representatives, while the environmental issue and living together on the planet, require thinking about long time. In terms of geography, this global issue takes shape in the nation-state, while it is a matter for all nation-states, that is to say, the global planet. But also, and above all, its founding principle: and thus enjoy another form of freedom, individual.

In modern democracy, which is part of an ever-expanding worldview, how can we make sure that citizens give up some of their individual freedom for a global purpose? For some, it is necessary to go through coercion, an idea born in the 70s, defended by the American political scientist William Ophuls who advocates a seizure of power by «king ecologists». A few decades later, in Green Dictatorship (Presses du Midi, 2010), the ecologist Michel Tarrier (2010), imagines an «ethnocracy», instead of democracy not arbitrary but coercive, led by intellectuals and scientists. This enlightened elite led to lead a global ethnocracy is itself stuck in the system, says Agnès Sinaï, co-founder of the Momentum Institute who does not doubt the laudable intentions of the elite, but wonders if this elite would be incorruptible? In the same sense of doubt addressed to this enlightened elite, the historian of science and environment Valérie Chansigaud, interviewed by Libération, believes that "it is an idea that is disconnected from the teaching of history": "Attacking freedoms in the name of a higher interest is the model for all authoritarian regimes, which always end up favouring one class". From this point of view, the «green dictatorship» must go through a referendum and that citizens are first informed and aware.

Ultimately, the researcher Luc Semal believes that the environmental danger is so imminent that the idea of the end of civilization would be staggering. He explained that "people would be able to give up certain things if they were trained, and if they had a sense of justice". Valérie Chansigaud points out that: "It is not individual freedom that leads to the degradation of the environment, it is the freedom of certain individuals. Is a totally unequal democracy really one?"

In the same line, Jonas Hans, interviewed by Der Spiegel magazine, asks the same question of modern democracy in the following terms: Could modernity have been a mistake that must be rectified? Is the path we have embarked on through this alliance of scientific and technological progress and increased individual freedom the right one?" For the environmental activist Michel Sourrouille, it is permissible to doubt the current democratic situation when he expresses in the following terms: "In the present situation, one can still think, but if one fails, in five or ten years, one risks a brutal rupture. When a country is in trouble, there is a tendency to entrust its destiny to a strong man or woman." Some already imagine that the green dictatorship would appear as a lesser evil.

Hans Jonas in his book the principle of responsibility, bestseller of philosophy in Germany did not say anything else in 1979. Thirteen years after the Principle of Responsibility, when asked by Der Spiegel about the possibility of a «kind of economic dictatorship», he replied: «A project of dictatorship can be sketched in the abstract with a view to saving humanity. But how to imagine that an effectively altruistic elite will arrive in power, that it will remain altruistic and that its selflessness will also be recognized? This is a kind of utopia that cannot be translated into reality." Hans Jonas considered the renunciation of individual freedom inevitable. As a result, Hans Jona was the first philosopher to introduce the concept of responsibility of present generations towards future generations. This principle was first adopted by the United Nations for sustainable development in the Brundtland Report of the World Commission on Environment and Development in 1987. The report is entitled "Our future for all": "A development that meets the needs of present generations without compromising the ability of future generations to meet their own.

While the prospects for sustainable development are linked to major political and geopolitical issues, Flipo (2011) considers that there remain important divergences which are not merely of a political nature, fuelled by industrialization. The issue of sustainable development for Flipo (2011), is also, and above all, a cultural one, following the idea of Hans Jonas (1903-1993), on the assumption of an enlightened dictator to achieve the sustainable development of the planet and avoid the destruction of the conditions for human life on Earth.

Building on Flipo's (2011) assertion that sustainable development is primarily a cultural challenge, and inspired by Hans Jonas' philosophy on the responsibility of current generations towards future ones, this book advocates for a new supranational cultural leadership. Such leadership would be capable of guiding global efforts to address environmental and social crises. Further development of this conceptual approach will be presented in the final chapter.

Section 3.2. Cultural management and sustainable development

If for Flipo, the challenge of sustainable development was above all cultural, it is therefore necessary to explain the concept of sustainable management in the cultural sense of the term defended by Flipo, and then examine the contribution of management to sustainable development.

3.2.1. Sustainable management and development

Based on the theories and cross-debates on sustainable development discussed above, it is now necessary to consider the content and scope of sustainable management. In the words of the book, it is a question of sustainable management of human resources, which is considered to be strategic management (Beaumont, 1993), and which aims as prospective management of the present and the future. Strategic management and foresight allow companies and organizations to think about the future without ignoring the present. If foresight and strategic management allow organizations to project themselves into the future with the actors of the present, it should be considered that their purpose is to seek to grasp the future without compromising the present. Strategic human resources management and foresight aim both at the continuity of the present and the achievement of the future and do not aim at the future to the detriment of the present.

In other words, the management of human resources that is concerned with the development of present and future practices is thus part of sustainable development. The HRM revisited by the prospective aimed at the sustainability of the company and the well-being of employees both in the present and in the future, can be described as a sustainable HRM. The concept of sustainable human resources management, the "HRDM" is a new and still delicate concept, even for human resource professionals who do not find a clear definition to this new expression. Nevertheless, the renewal of HRM approaches is currently moving towards integrating the concept of sustainable development into business practices and contributing to the development of CSR. The expression "sustainable human resources management" or "sustainable human resources management", as used by Poissonnier and Drillon (2008), has recently been introduced into mainstream language and managerial discourses.

An attempt to define sustainable human resource management as "HRDM" can be borrowed from the definition of sustainable development as set out in the Brundtland Report of the World Commission on Environment and Development in 1987, entitled "Our future for all": "A development that meets the needs of present generations without compromising the ability of future generations to meet their own. Two concepts are inherent in this concept: the concept of "needs", and more particularly the basic needs of the most deprived, to which it is necessary to give the highest priority, and the idea of the limitations that the state of our techniques and social organization imposes on the ability of the environment to meet current and future needs. Sustainable development, which makes it possible to reconcile economic and social progress and achieve the ecological balance of the planet, is at the confluence of three concerns: economic, social and ecological (see Figure 1).

Figure 1 : The three concerns of sustainable development

(Report of the World Commission 1987)

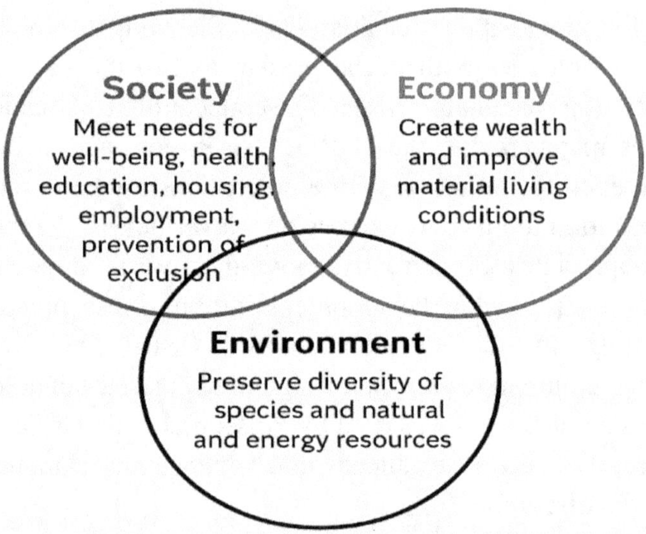

This notion of sustainable development is for Bourg (2006) a response to two major global imbalances: a very unequal distribution of wealth (20% of the population, or the 30 richest countries, still used 80% of non-renewable energy); a dangerous degradation of the biosphere which compromises the development and existence of future generations. Yet the current north-south disparity in the sense of Bourg (2006) is probably not foreign to the hatred, violence and terrorism that are developing within globalized modernity, which constitute a powerful obstacle to efforts towards more sustainable lifestyles. Beyond the political, environmental and economic implications of sustainable development, the issue for Bourg (2006) is that of a new civilization.

Why talk about sustainable development in management?

According to the 1987 Brundtland Report, sustainable development concerns all sectors—agriculture, industry, and services—and emphasizes the rational management of natural and human resources. This implies a form of human resource management (HRM) that is relevant not only for the present but also for future generations. Today, HR management is evolving to include perspectives such as responsible management, ethical management, and sustainable development management—concepts increasingly emphasized by decision-makers, especially in the aftermath of the financial crisis. In an article rich with futuristic perspectives, published in the journal of Haward Business, Hamel (2009) thinks that experts must first admit that they have reached the limits of management, and that they must create far-off futuristic plans called lunar plans.

Each lunar plane illuminates a path in the journey to management 2.0. According to Hamel (2009), the Lunar Management plan fuelled by foresight must focus tomorrow's practical management on the social dimension and noble objectives in the interdependent world of tomorrow. Future human resource management, guided by foresight, must move away from current practices rooted in win/lose relationships. According to Beaupré et al. (2008), a major challenge for HR professionals will be reconciling economic efficiency with social and environmental principles of sustainable development.

The major challenges of Human Resources Management in this perspective of sustainable development lie in managing succession (Beaupré, Cloutier, Gendron, Jiménez and Morin, 2008). That is, ensuring sustainability and continuity in the management of the organization and human resources. The HRM is now challenged to be a responsible and sustainable HRM. In other words, the current and future challenge for HRM is to become both an HRM responsible for balancing economic concerns, social and environmental aspects of the organization and sustainable HRM that can meet the managerial needs of present and future generations. The HRM, thus renewed by the concept of responsibility and sustainability, makes it possible to contribute to sustainable development and corporate social responsibility. It thus becomes a sustainable Human Resources Management (HRM).

To lay a strong foundation for genuine sustainable human resource management, organizations must be viewed as living systems rather than purely economic entities (Calisti & Karolewicz, 2005). Unfortunately, those involved in sustainable development and HR often overlook the link between living systems, sustainability, and a sense of belonging. Calisti and Karolewicz (2005) argue that living systems evolve through continuous learning—without which sustainability cannot be achieved. Therefore, developing HR is not merely a humane act but a responsible one that addresses current and future development needs.

In the same vein, Bourg (2006) points out that human relationships with living beings are at the heart of sustainable development, more than the depletion of natural resources. In the future, management systems would take into account community and citizenship, recognizing the interdependence of all groups involved. Tomorrow, to be able to adapt, organizations based on the precepts of foresight will be innovative and socially responsible, seeking new principles in fields as varied as anthropology, biology, design, political science, Urban planning and theology. However, It is important to distinguish between sustainable management, sustainable development management, and reactive emergency management. Bon (2009) warns against confusing sustainable management with the management of sustainable development—often referred to as the difference between sustainable business practices and planetary sustainability. Sustainable management focuses on microeconomic issues within a company, whereas sustainable development management addresses broader macroeconomic sustainability goals. Additionally, reactive emergency management—focused on responding to crises—is incompatible with sustainable management, as it fails to consider a balanced view of all sustainability dimensions. At the microeconomic level, sustainable development according to Bon (2009) is not decreed but built. Building a sustainable HRM is not an easy task. Gond (2006) indeed shows the societal problems that pose challenges to a sustainable HRM, which must now take up the challenge of integrating employees and society.

While sustainable management seeks to anticipate the future from present actions, sustainable human resource management aims to counteract fatalism by actively shaping a possible future through foresight. To do so, companies adopt strategic sustainable management—a concept whose significance is primarily cultural (Flipo, 2011). This vision does not focus on a distant, utopian future but on creating a desirable one (Lukacs, 2008)—a future grounded in cultural values and aspirations that support sustainable development. The HR management of tomorrow must indeed mark a break with current management characterized by winning/losing relationships. In current and future sustainable development for present and future generations, management systems would take into account community spirit, culture, thus recognizing the cultural interdependence of all groups involved.

3.2.2. Management for sustainable development

Sustainable development is a modern management vision that challenges the company's past practices (Porcedda and Lapierre, 2008). This questioning can only succeed, according to the authors, if it is followed by a real cultural, structural and relational change. Porcedda and Lapierre (2008) wonder if sustainable development finally allowed to think about management, or would it itself become another theory of management? But development will only be sustainable if the blurring of boundaries between public and private becomes more effective today as a mode of management constituting what Fray (2011), calls the «managérialism», from the Anglo-Saxon New Public Management. According to Asselineau and Piré-Lechalard (2009), sustainable development in the workplace involves "a reflection on temporality, space, collective need, well-being and growth".

At the micro-economic level, the authors suggest three dimensions: "economic efficiency, social equity and environmental integrity plus governance" (Elkington, 1998). Today, sustainable development is on the way to supplanting the term social responsibility under pressure from public opinion, the media and non-governmental organizations. Based on a moral and ethical concept, sustainable development would be for Bon (2009) a managerial phenomenon in many academic research. Bon (2009) argues that corporate social responsibility (CSR) and sustainability are linked, and that the use of the CSR concept allows for the integration of sustainability. The usual definition of sustainability leads companies to assess their social impact in the very long term.

Researchers closer to us (Massa, Tucciand Afuah, 2017) support in an article of the Academy of Management Annals, the same idea of sustainability that does not necessarily refer to a sustainable competitive advantage or similar concepts in the strategy lexicon. On the contrary, sustainability for these Anglo-Saxon authors refers largely to the integration of social and environmental concerns into corporate strategy and business models, creating environmental value for sustainable development. This explanation of the contribution of sustainable development to CSR allows the transition to the renewal of CSR called RDE, Sustainable Corporate Responsibility. On this assumption, the new RDE paradigm will find application in business practices. The second assumption is that the new RDE paradigm will remain more theoretical than practical, because the realization of the new paradigm of sustainable enterprise development is hampered by the age-old gap between theorists and practitioners on the quality of life in the world sought by sustainable development. For example, a 2020 quality of life table, based on the NUMBEO index, is the world's largest database of cities and countries.

Quality of life index by country year 2020

(according to 2020 NUMBEO)

Rank Country		Quality of life	Health care	Cost of living
1	**Danemark**	192,53	80,17	85,02
9	Germany	177,25	73,35	66,34
15	USA	169,78	69,20	72,47
16	Spain	167,05	78,69	55,27
17	Japan	163,23	80,23	86,22
18	Portugal	162,46	71,88	49,52
19	UK	161,20	74,88	65,67
21	Canada	158,88	71,77	66,18
22	**Qatar**	156,90	73,03	67,54
24	UAE	155,41	67,92	62,98
26	**French**	150,68	80,68	76,34

30	Saudi	148,94	60,42	49,15
36	Italy	138,97	66,95	68,95
39	South Africa	132,39	64,16	37,52
54	Kuwait	115,14	58,14	49,86
59	India	105,86	66,21	24,12
63	China	104,96	66,62	39,51
64	**Morocco**	104,94	46,32	34,44
70	**Russia**	101,57	58,01	33,66
74	**Egypt**	86,78	46,29	29,55
79	**Iran**	70,32	52,23	38,47

Sustainable development is treated so far from the perspective of a sustainable management that remains above all cultural in the sense of Flipo (2011), it is now necessary to consider whether the cultural dimension can provide a service to sustainable development as described in the following paragraphs.

Section 3.3. Can culture contribute to sustainable development?

The book analyses in this section whether the cultural dimension can serve and make a significant contribution to sustainable development, according to UNESCO, in the United Nations, Africa and other countries, or if, on the contrary, the contribution of culture to sustainable development would be a decoy.

3.3.1. Culture contributes to sustainable development according to UNESCO.

Sustainable development, which remains above all cultural (Flipo, 2011), today challenges UNESCO, which has endeavoured to launch an initiative on culture for sustainable urban development in its 2030 agenda. The UN organization estimates that by 2030, 70% of humanity will live in urban areas due to population growth and exponential urbanization. The idea of dealing here with sustainable development stimulated by the contribution of culture should be clarified. However, sustainable development in its three components (economic, social and environmental), as defined in the 1987 United Nations Brundtland Report; will be discussed later, when it comes to examining the cultural dimension and its influence on the management of organisations and the performance of enterprises.

While all countries and the United Nations seek to promote economic and social development through the cultural dimension, Irina Bokova, a Bulgarian politician and UNESCO's Director-General from 2009 to 2017, strongly advocates for culture as a key driver of sustainable growth for both developed and developing nations. The UNESCO 2030 Agenda for Sustainable Development initiative includes two types of reports: a global report and an international conference. The Global Report on Culture and Sustainable Urban Development presents the broad outlines and recommendations, based on the collection of information provided by partner institutions around the world. An international conference on "Culture for Sustainable Cities" (Hangzhou, China, 10-12 December 2015), and (Quito, Ecuador, October 2016) which focused on all important issues related to the culture of sustainable cities.

UNESCO's 2030 Agenda for Sustainable Development aims to foster prosperity for all people and the planet by promoting freedom and universal peace. It includes 17 Sustainable Development Goals (SDGs), designed to build upon and extend the Millennium Development Goals. These goals aim to eradicate poverty and hunger, protect the environment, promote prosperity, and foster peaceful societies through global cooperation. The 17 Sustainable Development Goals with 169 associated targets, formulated by the 2030 Agenda, are indivisible and reflect the commitment of world leaders through a common action and universal policy agenda. The book has the merit of telling the reader the titles of the following 17 objectives:

1. Ending poverty around the world
2. Eliminate hunger and promote sustainable agriculture
3. Ensuring a healthy life and promoting well-being for all
4. Ensuring equitable education throughout life
5. Achieving gender equality for all women and girls
6. Ensuring sustainable water availability for all
7. Ensuring access to affordable, sustainable energy for all
8. Promoting a sustainable economy, and employment for all
9. Building infrastructure, and sustainable industrialization
10. Reducing inequalities within and between countries
11. Making cities safe, humane and sustainable
12. Ensuring sustainable consumption and production patterns
13. Addressing climate change and its impacts
14. Conserving marine resources for sustainable development
15. Protecting ecosystems, desertification and biodiversity
16. Promote peace and justice for all at all levels.
17. Revitalizing the global partnership for sustainable development

Among the key contributors on this subject is Mehenou Amouzou (2015), who argues that culture is multilayered, an intrinsic value, and a crucial driver of economic and social development grounded in knowledge, tolerance, and creativity.

He likens culture to the light illuminating society, the roots of a tree grounding it, and a pilot guiding it. Amouzou advocates for reconciling tradition and modernity—between cultural heritage and knowledge—arguing that society cannot develop without balancing these elements.

3.3.2. The cultural dimension as perceived by the United Nations

Invited to the Chaillot forum on April 4 and 5, 2014 and answering questions from Valérie Abrial Director of publishing and image — La Tribune, Ms. Bokova defends with conviction the cultural dimension as a potentially significant strategy for economic and social development, capable of providing answers to the crisis problems faced by societies. For her, culture that withstands crises can be seen as a creative economy, which creates millions of local, green jobs in cultural industries around the world (UNESCO Global Report 2013).

The UN estimates that culture accounts for almost 4% of Argentina's GDP and 20,000 companies in the fashion sector in Bangkok. The world trade in cultural goods and services, which is growing by 12% per year over 10 years, represents an opportunity for the United Nations for all advanced or developing countries. In 10 years, the value of culture in national development policies has increased in countries that have invested in creative industries such as China, India, Indonesia and Brazil. So, Iceland, one of the first European countries hit by the crisis decided to build a concert hall to boost employment and confidence in the future. The same applies to the Louvre-Lens project in France. In the past, the cultural dimension that was at the centre of development strategies has now become a major challenge for building rapid and sustainable development (resolutions pushed forward and adopted by UNESCO in 2011, 2010 and 2013).

In the wake of this creative economy that unifies skills and potential for sustainable development, is not the cultural dimension becoming a new economy of culture? Indeed, it is to be noted increasingly an extension of the traditional vision of the economy of culture as entertainment towards a broader more creative vision of added value in the economic system of a country. The UNESCO Convention of 2005, ratified by 134 countries, promotes cultural diversity and recognizes culture as a driver of trade and development. However, culture should not be seen merely as a commodity; rather, it is a policy tool supporting diversity and fostering global creativity. In this context, the "economy of culture" aligns with a knowledge-based economy driven by creativity and innovation.

3.3.3. Culture as a factor of development in Africa

Mehenou Amouzou (2015) considers today that the advanced countries have become aware that social capital contributes significantly to economic development and helps to remedy the phenomenon of exclusion from prejudice and discrimination. Hence the importance of investing in culture. Is culture, therefore, a source of economic development? To this question, Mehenou Amouzou (2015) believes that the West has based itself on cultural values and knowledge to develop its economy. He gives the example of Adam Smith, whom he describes as the initiator of contemporary economy "Wealth of nations" (1776). Mehenou Amouzou (2015) wants to show that Mr Smith has demonstrated that «the pursuit of personal interest» is more important than the creation of money. Through his work, «Theory of moral feelings», by Adam Smith deals with what Mehenou Amouzou (2015), today called cultural values.

Mehenou Amouzou (2015), gives a second example of John Stuart Mill, 70 years after Adam Smith, "who came to the same conclusion when he wrote that cultural restrictions on individuals could have a more detrimental effect than the pursuit of personal financial gain." The third example that inspires Mehenou Amouzou (2015) concerns Max Weber when he describes how culture or even religious values could have a significant impact on economic production. According to Max Weber, social values can determine the success or failure of an economy. As a result, investment in cultural events has increased and helped to increase employment and gross domestic product (GDP) of countries.

To substantiate his remarks, Mehenou Amouzou (2015), is based on some work by Anglo-Saxon researchers. He cites Landes, David S (1998), in "The Wealth and Poverty of Nations: Why Are Some So Rich and Others So Poor", who believes that the success of national economies is driven primarily by cultural factors. He also mentions Amy Chua (2007), a Yale law professor from the Chinese minority in the Philippines. The author Amy Chua, in fact, goes in the same direction when she reveals in her book at the crossroads of economic and cultural politics, "Le monde en feu. Social violence and globalization", "World on fire", a hidden and dark face of globalization.

3.3.4. The cultural dimension in other countries

In France, for example, the Ministry of Culture points out that culture contributes seven times more to GDP than the automobile industry at 3.2% of GDP. In a joint report to the Ministry of Culture, the government notes according to Romain Renier (2014) journalist at Alternatives économiques and Alter éco and president of the company, but Sushi, that the impact of the cultural industry has reached 104 billion euros, almost 6% of the value added generated in France. According to the explanation given in the office of Culture Minister Aurélie Filippetti, from 2012 to 2014, the best way to get the economic weight of culture recognized is to undertake an unprecedented study to calculate a kind of "cultural GDP", relying on the methodologies of the European Union and UNESCO. The study concerns the added values of performing arts, cinema, visual arts, audiovisual, heritage, books as well as access to knowledge and culture.

The report's key achievement is establishing a "positive correlation" between cultural implantation and socio-economic development. Laure Kaltenbach, general director and founding member of the Forum d'Avignon, an expert in the links between culture, creative industries, innovation, and the economy, along with Olivier Le Guay, director of Singulars.fr and DG of the association Culture Papié, argue that, as early as 2013, the new economy can be viewed as a tool for exiting the crisis. The example is set by the US president. Roosevelt, who had included in his New Deal during the crisis of the 1930s, a great program of economic recovery through culture. Mitterrand also in 1980 had marked France by a significant support to cultural actors, under the leadership of Jack Lang. Finally, the example of Lille becoming the European Capital of Culture in 2004 demonstrates the relevance of choosing cultural investment. Metz, Lens and Marseille have chosen to follow the example of Lille to mean that culture is no longer the poor relative of the economy; but it has now become everywhere an essential factor for development.

In Ecuador, cultural activities contributed 4.76% of GDP in 2010 and 4% of household spending was spent on cultural goods. (UNESCO). In Spain at the end of the 1990s, the example of the Basque city of Bilbao is relevant. Hit by the end of the iron and steel industry, Bilbao is reborn in a spectacular way thanks to the establishment of a new museum of contemporary art, which has drained ten years after its opening, one million visitors per year and 4,500 jobs. Therefore, it is noticeable that cities and countries around the world want to follow these examples.

China has also distinguished itself with new cultural development policies through its ambitious project of 5000 new museums in

2014. For its part, Brazil, closely followed by Mexico, wants to build 300 art centres, as do India and Indonesia. Arab countries are embarking on the preparation of the post-oil era by investing huge sums in cultural infrastructures.

The "Louvre des sables" in Abu Dhabi is a typical example of this new economy. Indeed, this new economy that the English sociologists Scott Lash and John Urry (1993) presented as a concept of "culturation" of the economy was translated by Ms. Irina Bokova, Director-General of UNESCO (2009 to 2017) in the following terms:

This new approach positions culture within a knowledge-based economy, where innovation and creativity drive growth. Increasingly, national development policies prioritize cultural factors. For example, the US Bureau of Economic Analysis is preparing to revise how it calculates GDP by incorporating creativity into its economic accounts—marking a significant shift in how cultural contributions are valued. Thus, from 2013 onwards, the era of technological and scientific skills is no longer sufficient to make a product or service successful, but cultural, aesthetic and emotional dimensions have become essential. The Apple group of its founder Jobs Steve «the visionary artist» has indeed been leading to use aesthetic creativity to conquer new markets. And it is not without reason that today we see entrepreneurs becoming artists and artists becoming entrepreneurs.

Closer to us, authors such as Gilles Lipovetsy and Jean Serroy (2013) go so far as to consider this cultural and artistic dimension as an artist capitalism in the following terms: "The hypermodern era has developed this artistic dimension to the point of making it a major element in the development of businesses, an economic value sector, an increasingly important source of growth and jobs." The authors believe that today's reality is built as an image combining an emotional aesthetic dimension of stylization of «look» and affect in search of competitiveness by brands. In the wake of this artistic dimension of the economy defended by Lipovetsy and Serroy (2013), the example of the Louis Vuitton brand is significant when the management of the Louis Vuitton group distinguished itself by adopting in 2006 a strategy to display the Danish artist Olafur Eliasson in his windows, without displaying any of his products of the brand.

Similarly, the Galeries Lafayette Group cannot ignore the fact that art is inextricably linked to the history of the brand. Guillaume Houez, a leader at Galeries Lafayette and an advocate for contemporary art and sustainable development, emphasizes that "the connection to visual arts is part of the brand's genetic code." Since establishing the group's patronage branch in 2010, he has highlighted how cultural investments are embedded in the company's identity and strategy. In 2016, the Galeries Lafayette Foundation was born: Beyond our commitment to creation and its democratization, I am convinced that cultural investment responds to the major structural changes in the world. It was possible to enter easily into the era of the immaterial; to live a pivotal moment when the Internet has upset our habits. The relationship to possession is changed. The act of purchase will be done more and more on the Web; our stores will offer fewer products for more services. And to respond to this dematerialization of things, what could be more natural than offering moments of experiences and emotions."

Can we argue here that art has come to fill the void and effect a societal change? Culture has succeeded in reconciling political powers with an economic public policy that offers the hope of the birth of a new cultural economy. As part of the evaluation of this new cultural economy, a French qualitative study (2016) the General Secretariat for the Modernisation of Public Action on Cultural Public Policy involving eight ministries and local authorities that finance 70% of the country's cultural facilities, shows that the notion of culture refers to a sense that everything can be culture and that any activity can be cultural with a notion of civilization. Culture is thus seen in the Ministry's study as a source of enrichment, personal development and enjoyment that allows one to escape, entertain oneself, nurture one's imagination and creativity.

Culture appears as a polysemic term in the sense that to cultivate means to enrich oneself personally, to equip oneself with the means to understand the world and better evolve socially. In fact, however, the inhabitants of the territories interviewed say that they engage in relatively few cultural activities for economic and financial reasons and explain that there are several obstacles to cultural practice such as lack of time, Lack of money, loneliness, lack of identification of events, aging programming. But the question is how to measure the impact of culture on economic and social development. Faced with this difficulty in measuring the immeasurable impact of culture on economic development, UNESCO has adopted a Set of indicators which includes indicators relating to the economic weight of culture, social cohesion, participation in culture and individual freedoms. Thus, UNESCO, which welcomes this global recognition of the link between culture and development, now believes that culture has ceased to be perceived as the poor relation of the economy and reduced to its monetary dimension only. Cultural goods carry values, which are factors of inclusion and fulfilment. They directly address societies in crisis, because the problems they face are not only economic but also social and solidarity problems. The social values of inclusion and fulfilment make it possible to stimulate the search for scapegoats between countries and to protect minorities, immigrants and disadvantaged people from attacks that often have cultural connotations.

Valuing culture from this point of view requires a cultural strategy based on the adoption of measures to protect cultural heritage through international conventions, statistical tools and studies of the impact of culture on economic growth. A culture that is enriched by diversity can foster innovation, accelerate the renewal of ideas and strengthen international cooperation. Outside the European and North American countries discussed above, where culture appears as a factor of economic and social development, Mehenou Amouzou (2015) wonders why African countries are unable to develop despite their natural resources and the cultural education of their populations. The book aims to analyse whether in Africa culture is significantly correlated with sustainable development and whether it constitutes a decoy for some.

Section 3.4. Culture, promoting development, would be a decoy.

Sustainable development, which faces certain obstacles, is not spared some criticism from theorists and researchers. We first address the obstacles to development in Africa, then we analyze the critical approach of researchers on the contribution of the cultural dimension to sustainable development.

3.4.1. Obstacles to Africa's development

Mehenou Amouzou (2015), amputates the obstacles to development of Africa to two exogenous phenomena that are slavery and colonization and endogenous that are the vision and communitarian spirit.

Slavery

The slavery that destroyed African culture for centuries takes, according to the author, two forms: the form called "House Negros" and "Field Negros!" Indeed, House Negros is the type of domesticated black people who think, according to the author, that their colonial masters are gods and try to resemble them and collaborate with the colonists at the expense of the development of their well-being and country. The Field Negro wants to be free and gives priority to the well-being of his own community and demands dignity and respect. Slavery, humiliation and denial of human rights, inspired Mehenou Amouzou (2015), to think that the African has fallen into a loss of identity marker and begins to no longer believe in its cultural value that is at risk of disappearing.

Colonization

After slavery, colonization is perceived by the author as a continuation of slavery under the name of neoliberalism (80% of the independent resources held by former settlers), which has aggravated the phenomenon of corruption in the developing world. If the culture of African countries has thus become an obstacle to development, the leaders of these countries are very embarrassed by their customs, to speak their own languages. From this point of view the question is whether Africa does not value its own culture, who will.

No vision for 2030

The idea put forward by some countries claiming to be preparing to emerge in 2030 would be a decoy, a utopia due to the lack of vision and long-term agenda of African leaders. The United Nations has been warning African countries since 1998 about the shortage of water, the 70% increase in the cost of living, the lack of computer rooms, laboratories, infrastructure and equipment on the continent and universities.

Spirit of cohabitation and communitarianism

Democracy does not provide the solution for Africans, says Mehenou Amouzou (2015), because for him democracy is not exported from one country to another, much less from one continent to another. It is made up of culture and regulation put in place for many years." To want to impose on the African peoples a vision, a culture, a democracy is still a reminder of slavery, colonialism and imperialism. For the author, there is no country in the world that is the most civilized or the most democratic. There is no model to follow. Africa lived and coexisted with its different peoples, its different religions because religion was part of culture. On the other hand, the religion of extremism would be a manipulation initiated by certain third countries that tend to destabilize other sovereign countries.

After outlining some obstacles to the economic and social development of Africa, Ali Mazrui (1933 - 2014), researcher, professor, and Pan-Africanist, believes that to transcend the state of underdevelopment of Africa, it is necessary to adopt a policy of indigenization, That is, demonstrate greater use of Aboriginal techniques. It will be for Ali Marzui who deals mainly with African issues, Islamic studies andthe South, to return to the community spirit that enabled African ancestors to live together as one people, thus promoting unity and preventing crime. The idea that "cultural industry" has been involved in economic development for some years is not shared by researchers who tend to reduce this assertion.

3.4.2. Critique of culture for sustainable development

Isabelle Porter (2008), a journalist at the Le Devoir and correspondent in Québec City who is interested in politics of cities and regions, said in Culture Québec in May 2008 that culture would have only a limited impact on the economic development of cities. Other experts in the field of the city, participating in the congresses of the Acfas, go in the same direction of Porter. Professor Xavier Greffe (2004) estimates that the impact of culture is low in communities with fewer than 500,000 inhabitants. Others, such as Richard Florida (2012), a professor at the University of Toronto, in his book "The Rise of the Creative Class," argue that there is a correlation between economic development and large cities with more than one million inhabitants. The author explains this attractiveness for large cities by the desire of investors to have a cultural and educational environment that allows them to benefit from a more comfortable life. It states that culture is increasingly "metropolitan" in the sense that, for example, London and Paris account for more than 50% of cultural activity, while in major American cities this rate rises to 80%.

This economic, geographical and cultural correlation allows Florida (2012) to avoid the idea of separating economy and culture that academic researchers who are too locked in their disciplines adopt. Florida's idea of the essential importance of culture in the economic development of large cities is not shared by other researchers who tend to nuance and limit the importance of culture by bringing it back to its place and recognizing it for this that she is. Thomas Werquin (2008) of the Université de Montréal, President of the Association Axe Culture, considers that studies on the impact of culture are often "too positive" and "too partial".

He defended his position during his interventions at the ACFA symposium in Quebec City in May 2008 "the impact of cultural facilities and events on local economic development: between fantasy and reality", or in Boston in June 2008 "Impact of major cultural events and equipments on urban development, a critical analysis from case studies". Andrée Fortin (2000, 2015), sociologist and writer, emeritus professor at Laval University, warned about the economic weight of culture because for her "There is an avalanche of numbers. But behind these figures, we don't always know what culture we're talking about."

CONCLUSION

In this third chapter, the book explores the concepts of sustainable development, grounding them in theories and academic debates. It examines the links between sustainable development and cultural management, emphasizing management's role in promoting sustainability. Additionally, it highlights how culture, according to UNESCO, the United Nations, African perspectives, and others, can contribute significantly to sustainable development. However, some critics question whether the role of culture in development might be overstated or used as a decoy for other agendas.

CHAPTER 4
CULTURAL DIVERSITY

When a culture is denied in what it can bring to the universal,
Violence is never far away.
- Jacques Chirac

Section 4.1. Notions of national culture

4.1.1. Definition of national culture

4.1.2. National culture in management science

Section 4.2 Business Culture Concepts

4.2.1. Definition of corporate culture

4.2.2. History of entrepreneurship

4.2.3. Characteristics of the corporate culture

4.2.4. Business culture as seen by entrepreneurs and employees.

4.2.5. The culture between individual and collective conflict

Section 4.3. Culture and cultural management in some countries.

4.3.1. — Culture and cultural management in Morocco

4.3.2. — Culture and cultural management in France

4.3.3. — Culture and cultural management by UNESCO for 2030

Introduction

While culture plays a vital role in sustainable development, it also faces obstacles and criticism. A fundamental question arises: Does culture truly reflect a diversity of beliefs and truths, or does it risk creating conflicts? This diversity of culture does not reflect—it does not reflect a diversity of ways of living individually and collectively.

In other words, can we argue that these different ways of living do not clash — they do not clash with each other and do not risk creating individual or collective cultural oppositions? This is what the book attempts to explore in the lines of chapter four.

This chapter begins by examining cultural diversity through the lens of national and corporate cultures, before exploring aspects related to cultural conflicts. Indeed, the cultural dimension in private companies is part of a national culture within which the company establishes its own corporate culture. From this point of view, we explain the concept of national culture (41), before approaching the corporate culture itself (42). The book will then shed light on examples of cultural diversity and international cultural management, notably in Morocco, France, and UNESCO for its 2030 programme (43).

Section 4.1 Concepts of National Culture

4.1.1. Definition of national culture

It is therefore necessary to question the sources of national culture and its definition.

To do this, the book has chosen to show the sources of national culture reported by researchers and theorists. Among the researchers in the years 2006, Guy Arcand (2006) had treated the sources of the national culture in his doctoral thesis "Study of the role of national culture in the relationship between HRM practices and organizational performance: the case of banks from twenty-two countries in North America, Europe and Asia". Arcand (2006) notes a certain consistency in the sources of culture based on the work of Usunier (1992), who considers that the national component is not the main source of culture and proposes six sources of culture:

Nationality

The profession

The membership group

Religion

The family

The company

Other authors such as Daniels and Radebaugh (2001), on the other hand, later identified four sources of culture instead of six by excluding the profession, the group belonging to and the company in the work of its predecessors Usunier (1992), but adding the language:

Nationality

People who transmit culture (parents, teachers, social leaders, bosses)

The language

Religion

Griffin and Pustay (2005) four years later list five sources of culture by adding social structure, communication and values while removing nationality, the family in the definition of its predecessors Daniels and Radebaugh (2001:

Social structure : (social stratification, social mobility)

The language

Forms of communication

Religion

Values/attitudes

Comparison of these studies reveals that religion consistently emerges as the dominant source of culture across all three (Usunier, 1992; Daniels & Radebaugh, 2001; Griffin & Pustay, 2005). Language and form of transmission appear in only two works [Daniels and Radebaugh, 2001]; Griffin and Pustay, 2005).

Despite a subtle distinction in the terms of the three definitions, there is some homogeneity in the definitions relating to the sources of culture, including language, religion, nationality and education (Arcand, 2006). This approach to the sources of culture allows us now to address the notion of national culture. According to Arcand (2006), national culture is a hybrid concept combining the idea of culture with the legal notion of the nation-state. However, cultures often do not align perfectly with nation-states, as they can also be based on ethnic, linguistic, religious, or organizational identities—aligning with earlier work by Usunier (1992). Hofstede (1984) takes into account the concept of national culture, since he believes that citizens in each country react differently due to their distinct political entities, the value attached to the principle of citizenship, and the experiences they have had in this country. It is indeed this mode of organization of society that gave birth to the concept of the nation-state (Usunier, 1992).

Today, societies with a high level of organization are often called nations. Research indicates that the key differences in national cultures are rooted in societal values (Luthans, Welsh & Rosenkrantz, 1993; Schneider & DeMeyer, 1991; Schuler & Rogovsky, 1998). These values influence individuals' attitudes, which in turn shape their behaviors in various situations (Bergeron, 2001). These values that are perceived as beliefs will then define good and evil in society.

However, one should be careful not to want to relate everything to culture and that it is culture which influences the behaviour of individuals in a society. Indeed, Usunier (1985) believes that not everything is culture in the behavior of an individual and that there are two other levels according to Hofstede (2001; 1991) which influence the behaviors of people in a society apart from culture. Hofstede (2001; 1991 refers to the universal level and the individual level that are part of human mental programming. It considers the universal level to be a level of human nature found in every country in the world and which affects our physical and psychological functioning. The individual level, on the contrary, represents the actions of a person related to his own choices, his own tastes and his affinities that he does not share with any other individual.

Hofstede (1983, 75-76) states that citizens of each country react differently when it comes to national culture due to the distinct political organizations, value attached to citizenship and experiences in this country. Arcand (2006) attempts to explain societies or nations based on the definition given by Bollinger et al. (1987, 28): «a society is a social system characterized by the highest level of self-sufficiency in relation to its environment». Several studies cited by Arcand (2006) show that differences between national cultures can be traced back to societal values (Luthans, Welsh and Rosenkrantz, 1993; Schneider and DeMeyer, 1991; Schuler and Rogovsky, 1998). For Arcand (2006), the values of society will indeed influence the attitudes of individuals who will themselves adopt behaviors according to the situation (Bergeron, 2001). The researcher Arcand (2006), considers that several anthropologists and sociologists, the concept of national culture first, and that it took several years for management science to address the influence of national culture on management practices within an organization. Hence the need to seek to know, in the wake of this cross-literature relating to notions of national culture, how national culture is perceived in management sciences.

4.1.2. National culture in management science

In the area of human resource management, the book uses cross-studies by such researchers as Guy Arcand (2006), Fons Trompenaars (1993), Schuler and Rogovski (1998), André Laurent (1983) and others.

The first study addresses the role of national culture in the relationship between HRM practices and organizational performance. This is a quantitative study conducted by Guy Arcand (2006) among banking companies in 22 countries in North America, Europe and Asia. To develop his thesis, Arcand (2006) relies on several researchers of the previous century that we summarize in the following paragraphs. If HRM becomes a strategic element of the organization (McMahon, Virick and Wright, 1999), it is obvious to Arcand (2006) that companies must adjust their human resource management practices to the national culture of the country. Several studies have been conducted in this direction with multinational companies (Schuler and Rogovsky, 1998). Fons Trompenaars (1993) has looked at the relationship between cultural differences and management practices. Its study of fifteen thousand professionals across fifty countries has highlighted seven dimensions explaining the differences in management within companies around the world.

The seven dimensions of Trompenaars (universalism-particularism, individualism-collectivism, affectivity-neutrality, private-life, professional, achievements-social function, attitude towards time, will to control culture) closely resemble the dimensions of Hofstede. The French researcher André Laurent (1983) was interested in measuring the differences between managerial behaviour and practices in nine European countries and in the United States. His study revealed different patterns of behaviour from one country to another, based on three conceptions of the organization. The first concerns the hierarchical structure. The second refers to the political system, where it is more important to gain power than to achieve specific goals. The third is about the organization as a system. For Laurent (1983), it is cultural differences that determine the extent to which a manager will favour one concept over another. Ten years after Laurent (1983), Sparrow, Schuler and Jackson (1994) looked at the analysis of human resource management practices and the skills required for successful multinational enterprises in different countries.

Another study by Schuler and Rogovski (1998) aims to explore the relationship between Hofstede dimensions (Hierarchical distance, control of uncertainty, individualism and masculinity) and pay practices in twenty-four countries. This study shows that individual performance-based remuneration practices are perceived in countries with a high degree of individualism. Arcand. (2006) concludes in his thesis, relating to the role of national culture in HRM practices by this idea which he considers interesting, to validate the opposition between the universalist approach and the contingency approach by considering national culture as a factor of contingency. According to Arcand (2006), very few studies have been devoted to the relationship between HRM, performance and national culture.

Arcand (2006), comes to the result where it shows a significant relationship between an incentive pay practice in harmony with national culture and organizational performance. On the other hand, misuse of this incentive practice can lead to a significant decline in social, economic and financial performance. Building on the theoretical perspectives, the next section explores how culture is perceived and experienced within organizations—what is known as corporate culture. Companies are developing more and more links with cultural activities, and are increasingly interested in the notion of corporate culture that has emerged with charters defining the shared values of employees operating in the same company. It is through sustainable development and social responsibility strategies that companies can strengthen the image of their culture. The corporate culture, promoted by business leaders and sufficiently explained to employees and stakeholders, contributes significantly to the construction of a strategic cultural approach that will be further developed in the second part. How can we then define the corporate culture and identify its characteristics?

Section 4.2. Corporate culture

4.2.1. Definition of corporate culture

The concept of culture emerged in the 1980s, giving rise to what is now called corporate culture (Schein. 1985).

According to E. Schein (1985), the company culture is formed in part to respond to two essential problems. The first concerns the adaptation of the enterprise to its environment and raises the question of the survival of the organization. The second problem is an internal one, which concerns the establishment and maintenance of effective working relations between the members of the company. According to the author, corporate culture allows the company to deal with the uncertainty and complexity of the environment and respond effectively to employee integration.

The book describes the company culture at first sight, as a set of ways of acting and behaving in the same organization. The corporate culture corresponds to a system of values and rules shared by all the players in the company (Bournois, 1996). While there is an abundant literature on the notion of culture, the book has chosen in its remarks the description made by Godelier (2006), who considers that in the 1980s, the business world took over anthropologists' words such as “Culture”, “myths”, “rites”, "tribes", "family", "home", "team". Several academics, managers and consultants have sought to understand the concepts and practices of business, based on scientific criteria of sociology. It was not until 2006 that the notion of "corporate culture" emerged as a curiosity that Godelier (2006) calls "an exotic curiosity" and moves away from those who attribute to the notion of culture "management by values" or "intercultural management".

With globalization, corporate culture seems to have joined the long list of management modes according to Godelier (2006). Corporate culture is indeed regularly used in speeches by leaders such as the example of the president of Shell when he insisted in 2000 on the importance of culture in change, or the leaders of Rhône-AlpesPoulenc and Hoechst when they made culture an essential lever in the creation of the Aventis group. Godelier's book "The Corporate Culture" (2006) analyses how management has mobilized the notion of "culture" in order to bring order into the corporate community and prefers to define the corporate culture as follows: "all the principles, representations and values shared by the members of a society which organise their way of thinking and acting on their environment and themselves in order to organise their relations, that is to say the society". However, the author of the book wonders whether the notion of corporate culture does not constitute an artificial «alliance of two antagonistic terms». Because each company develops a specific and autonomous form of culture that distinguishes it from other institutions (state, political parties, family...) or other companies.

Corporate culture can act as a lever or brake on change, or sometimes merely serve as storytelling. According to Godelier (2006), it also embodies managers' practical concerns for maintaining social cohesion within the company. Corporate culture remains in the thinking of Godelier (2006), a notion that is not easy to grasp, because managers seem to ask too much from culture to be a lever for company action, or a means of social cohesion and ethics in the management of companies. Obviously, company culture can also sometimes appear in the eyes of Godelier as a miraculous way to settle the paradox of the integration of employees into the company; but eventually it becomes clear, through the observation of daily life, that there is a real gap between the cultural trends in favour of integration and actual human resource management practices. Should we conclude, asks Godelier (2006), that the notion of corporate culture is "unnecessary or even dangerous to the understanding of the company?"

The researchers in management sciences have indeed thought to rebuild for companies a form of sustainability supposed sustainable, continuous, permanent and perpetual. From this point of view, the company seems to represent an element of this sustainability. Godelier (2009) distinguishes between companies that possess a strong, coherent culture aimed at stability, and those with internal inconsistencies or tensions between subcultures. This dominant vision, inspired by American culturalism, conceives of culture as a conscious phenomenon sometimes as a set of folklore that limits the possibilities for evolution and innovation in companies. However, practitioners and some academic circles are thinking more about the sustainability and stability of values in companies. Thinking of culture as a resource for the sustainability of the company has become increasingly topical since the 1980s, this notion of culture in management was perceived according to Godelier (2009) as an attempt at ideological manipulation of employees.

A central debate concerns whether culture supports a company's longevity or, conversely, hampers its sustainability by limiting adaptability. This debate unfolds along two main lines:

The first concerns the objective of sustainability which shares with the notion of culture, creation and continuity in the company. The second is that the sustainability of the company must develop both paradoxical ways (to do and think a culture), which will allow it to produce and sell goods or services. This dialectical approach that characterizes sustainability and corporate culture allows us to understand the complex relationships between sustainability and culture. As a result, leaders and managers have sought to make culture and business sustainable (FGodelier, 2009). From this point of view, the practices of HRM often contradict the great speeches on the integration of employees in the capital of the company. Beyond the dialectical and paradoxical debate, the concept of culture, whether it is an opportunity or a limitation to the evolution of the company, needs to be explained in the history of the company through three metaphors.

4.2.2. History of entrepreneurship

Cross-disciplinary discussions on entrepreneurship are taught by researchers and practitioners. In the wake of this dialectical debate on the history of entrepreneurship, Godelier (2009) distinguishes three metaphors that have been used for 150 years by business leaders to legitimize entrepreneurship and employee integration. The first metaphor is that of the family. During the Industrial Revolution (1830–1880), many business leaders depicted the company as a large family, with the boss acting as the "father" of employees. The company resembles a natural and universal human organization called the family. Another metaphor has just been substituted in the speeches of employers.

The second metaphor comes from home

It was not until the end of the First World War that the “father” became the “home owner”. The company is presented as a “home” that surrounds, protects and unites its members. Far from disappearing after 1845, this house spirit continues to exist in many SMEs. It was not until the 1970s that the third metaphor took hold.

The third metaphor comes from the “sports” team

In the early 1980s, staff mobilization practices began to be inspired by sports competitions and their success criteria. But to be united in a team, competitors need a captain who is the company manager. It becomes both a symbol of collective cohesion and a form of participatory democracy. Eventually the business leader perceived as a good leader becomes an adventurer who shakes conservatism. For their part, employees, like champions, must be: flexible, responsive and dedicated to the team. The company/employee relationship is thus based on two pillars: on the one hand loyalty/fidelity to the organization and its captain, on the other hand trust delegated by the company. This latter metaphor is spreading rapidly according to Godelier (2009) at a time when western management has been looking for ways out of the crisis since the 1970s.

For Godelier (2009), corporate culture covers at least eight different metaphors during the 1980s:

1- A consensual vision of internal social relations;

2- A biological image that emphasizes the living and autonomous dimension of the company;

3- The difference, because culture allows for the specificities of each company compared to others;

4- A new lever of power that offers the leader a renewed technique of command replacing bureaucratic and hierarchical modalities. A brake on change when tradition seems to limit innovation

5- A more deterministic vision, to control and control the variability of individual behaviors;

6- A means of seduction and production of meaning that improves employee adherence, alongside the more conventional.

A social function of the enterprise other than the economic and technical function.

Thus, the relationship between culture and sustainability is aimed at how to sustainably regulate the behaviors and ways of thinking of company members. Ultimately, for a company to be sustainable, Godelier (2009) wonders whether it should rely on its own ways of doing and thinking, that is, on material and symbolic elements of its culture.

4.2.3. Characteristics of the corporate culture

For Godelier (2009), most definitions of culture in the social sciences emphasize certain essential characteristics. The first characteristic of culture results from a collective process of accumulation throughout history. The second articulates both material objects (techniques, practices, languages) and immaterial objects (ideas, representations, values). However, the notion of «values» is open to criticism in so far as it omits one of the two dimensions of culture that embody it. The third characteristic is that culture is a primarily collective phenomenon which is embedded in the unconscious of the members of a social group.

While Godelier (2009) studies the material and immaterial aspects of culture, Meier (2016) emphasizes the immaterial aspects of corporate culture, which are expressed through symbols such as logos, emblems, colors, and names. These symbols influence employees' social and emotional well-being. Preserving or questioning a symbol is indeed an action that reflects the role of corporate culture, depending on the option chosen (confirm or modify the existing values of the company). A company that wishes to enhance the culture of its «partner» will tend to preserve the name and brands of the acquired company (Peugeot and Citroën) or propose two brands with distinctive values: seriousness and tradition for Peugeot, technology and innovation for Citroën.

The company culture contains this particularity of valuing the common past and passing it on to new generations through rites and certain myths. The corporate culture can also be characterized by its internal coherence with a system structured around established values and rules. But this system of values does not mean that it is immutable and does not evolve with the events of growth and experiences in its environment. An example of cultural adaptation is the French family holding PSA, which, by 1973, had become the second-largest automaker in France after Renault. Its historical rapprochement (reorientation, rupture, success, failure, adaptation, change, transformation…) in 1974 with Citroën is a historic success, which has allowed it to become the equal of the Régie in terms of production. By acquiring Chrysler in 1978, the PSA group became the leading European car manufacturer. But the second oil crisis (1979), unprecedented since the Second World War, forced the new Group to carry out an internal reorganisation, redundancies, discontinuations of activities until the beginning of the fourth20 to launch internal growth and ad ho c alliances. The analysis of the characteristics of culture allows us to ask ourselves another question, which is the cultural analysis grid.

Building on Meier's (2001, 2016) work, a cultural analysis grid has been developed, comprising 11 key items:- The story;

- The job;

– Dominant values ;

- The development benchmark;

- Positioning towards the environment;

- Identification and membership elements;

- The type of structure;

- The decision-making process;

- Management style and sources of power;

- Human resources policy;

- Behaviour and attitudes.

According to Meier (2016), corporate culture, which embodies shared values and serves as a guiding reference for all members, consists of several components: - Standards when it comes to making choices

- Rituals when it comes to rituals around which the collaborators gather

- Myths that mean stories that have marked the company

– Symbols like a logo that makes the company stand out like the lion at Peugeot

- The company's history and its founders like Apple in a garage, or Facebook in a student room.

- The time and space of today, and tomorrow.

4.2.4. Corporate culture as perceived by entrepreneurs and employees.

Although the company culture is capable of generating values, it nevertheless runs up against the paradox that exists between the values announced by management and the values perceived by employees. If corporate values consider that each employee is a member of a "big family", while in reality managers never mix with employees, it is the value of "family" will be in contradiction with the perceived value and will therefore lead to a bad working climate (Meier, 2016). Often management is not aware that this paradox between speech and reality is quickly felt and experienced by the members of the company.

On this paradox between the speeches of business leaders and the realities experienced by employees, researchers such as Maurice Thévenet (2010) have pushed the reasoning to think about the temporary decline of corporate culture. The author argues that the concept of corporate culture has become commonplace in our vision, or a worn and outdated notion. Thévenet (2010), explains this observation by the fact that «many hopes that have been placed in the concrete scope of this notion of company have been disappointed» in the sense that culture has not always kept its promises».

In search of new ideas, some authors saw corporate culture as a source of performance, others as an explanation of the success of any organization. Culture remains a managerial recipe when the leaders of organizations have already tried everything (Thévenet, 2010). In spite of the paradox between discourse and reality evoked by Meier (2016), or the banal and outdated nature of the notion of corporate culture identified by Thévenet (2010), this one recognizes on the other hand that culture is not such an easy and banal concept as some think, but it tends to become a social science concept, and "is interested in similarities rather than differences, in all that is shared rather than what distinguishes, in all that unites within and makes a difference with the outside." The culture in the thought of Thévenet (2010) is ultimately imposed by its usefulness as a vision of organization and its ability to evoke "the time of history that brings the present closer to a past", although frozen and disconnected from contemporary reality. In other words, culture is "the strength of the moment relative to the richness of a past to honour a future".

Thévenet (2010) proposes to put an end to the notion of corporate culture if it continues to be seen as an instrument of oppression and a brake whose responsible will try to find scapegoats. Culture will indeed appear as the first brake for the success of a change and always a cause of failure, but rarely a reason for the success of the change. Thus, the first weakness of the corporate culture in the spirit of Thévenet (2010) concerns the methodology that highlighted values that were more relevant to the declared value than to the operative one. The second weakness is to generate policies that were ineffective and harmful. Finally, culture may have been a great disappointment and generated violent reactions beyond methodological and practical weaknesses, Thévenet (2010), finally asks whether the interest in culture is not justified by deeper reasons that relate to a collective vision of economic and societal development.

Ultimately, the doubts are not about corporate culture itself, but about the company. Without the company, the concept of culture would lack purpose. The company seems to be moving away from its collective vision of development and its collective agreement in favour of individual contracts. This individualistic dimension of the employment contract seems to be justified by the talent management (Dejoux and Thévenet, 2010) that appeared in the 2000s, which seems to focus more on the individual than the collective aspect. Indeed, researchers and business leaders recommend that employees should manage their own careers, and invest in their personal development within the company. Can we argue that the different ways of living one's culture individually or collectively, can clash with each other? Would cultural diversity, discussed above, be likely to create individual or collective cultural oppositions and conflicts? This is what the book tries to explain in the following lines.

4.2.5. The culture between individual and collective conflict

Raja Choueiri (2008) attempts to answer the question of whether cultural diversity reflects an individual or collective conflict by explaining two opposing notions: the cultural conflict and the conflict of cultures that the author describes as cultural shock and clash of cultures. The book used the term cultural conflict instead of culture shock. The first notion of cultural conflict is perceived from a psychological and personal point of view, while the second is understood from a historical and geopolitical point of view to serve as an interpretative grid for intercultural phenomena. The author wanted to demonstrate that cultural conflict (psychological and personal) is positive, inclusive, and progressive, while the conflict of cultures (geographic and geopolitical) is negative, exclusive, reductive, and regressive. Raja Choueiri (2008) argues that cultural conflict induces a process of discovery of the other according to a «living» memory, while the conflict of cultures closes itself to external influences according to a «dead» memory.

From this point of view, Choueiri (2008) gives the example of the psychology of children who are more predisposed to cultural conflicts related to their learning than that of adults who are overwhelmed by more diverse and diversified information. The personal cultural conflict resulting from the discovery of the other remains for Choueiri (2008), very useful insofar as it is associated with positive values of tolerance, moderation, adaptation, mental flexibility, openness, the challenge of inherited prejudices, self-criticism and consideration of other cultural points of view. Everyone is called to multiply their cultural conflicts through knowledge, reading and travel in other countries near and far. Choueiri (2008) has the merit of having made a comparison between the two antinomic notions: cultural conflict and conflict of cultures.

Dialectical comparison

In a dialectical comparison, Choueiri (2008) contrasts two related concepts: cultural conflict and the conflict of cultures. He argues that cultural conflict is constructive, whereas the conflict of cultures tends to be destructive. The first, for Choueiri (2008), is inclusive, the second is exclusive. The former is a driving force for change, while the latter acts as a brake on change. For the cultural conflict, the present is important which wants to associate all contemporary cultures; while the conflict of cultures legacy of the past determines all cultures, placed in divergent orbits. Moreover, cultural conflict resolves in personal subjectivity, in the process of discovery and often leads to the questioning of certainties, because it is itself synonymous with cultural discovery.

The conflict of cultures is essentially collective, demagogic that generates prejudices and promotes cultural conflict. For Choueiri (2008), the conflict of cultures fuels racism, colonialism, fundamentalism, fundamentalism, contempt for peoples and their culture, and reason in sharp divisions: bloc against bloc, which hardly tolerates self-criticism. Choueiri (2008) simplifies the comparison: cultural conflict pertains to the clash of ideas and ideals, whereas the conflict of cultures involves groups motivated by material interests. Cultural conflict is a curiosity willing to explore the culture of others, through a mental change of scenery. The conflict of cultures is the externalization and devaluation of the culture of others, by a mental enclavement. The cultural conflict is equated with a cultural eurêka, a cry of Archimedes: «I have found» to the extent that I came out of myself. Everyone is called to multiply his cultural conflicts by readings, trips and a change of scenery in the geographical and human sense. "The beginning of wisdom is a salutary shock," said civilization historian Arnold Toynbee (1951). If for Choueiri (2008), everyone is called to multiply its cultural conflicts through his readings, and his travels, the author gives the example of the classical education of the humanities that allowed Europeans to establish close relations with other worlds, other intelligences and cultures, putting their own culture into perspective. It is for the author, in the wake of the values of humanism, to seek the universal in each individual and that the particular can be rejected in favor of the universal. If the historian of civilizations Arnold Toynbee (1951) considers that "The beginning of wisdom is a salutary shock", it is worth considering whether the cultural conflict would be linked to religious data aimed at personal conversion.

Cultural conflict and religion.

It should be noted that religious cultural conflict differs from geopolitical cultural conflict in that the former does not admit relativism after conversion to the absolute truth to which it must lead, whereas the second would be an endless series of reconversions to truths always refutable and perfectible. (Choueiri, 2008). Choueiri (2008) believes, in the end, that everything that connects, comes under the cultural conflict wants to be creative pulling upwards, towards the new at the end of a process of maturation. On the other hand, everything that barricades is part of the conflict of cultures. For example, the Silk Road exemplifies cultural conflict, serving as an extensive multicivilizational communication route. In contrast, the Great Wall of China symbolizes the conflict of cultures—a geohistorical barrier and symbol of rupture.

Below is a comparison table outlining the key differences between cultural conflict and conflict of cultures:

Table of cultural conflict and conflict of cultures

Cultural Conflict	Conflict of cultures
Geo-cultural personal psychology	Geopolitical collective psychology
Self-inquiry mechanism	Mobilization mechanism against external
Living memory	Dead memory
Pragmatism and debate logic	Dogmatism and logic of struggles

"Negotiation", educational and inclusive	Confrontational, antagonistic and exclusive
Progressivism and ascendant dialectics	Downshift Stillness
(The dialectic between «me» and «the other» leads to a new, higher synthesis)	(the confrontation between «us» and «them», leads to a mutual tension
Engine for history (and synchronizing the present that unites cultures)	Brake for history and mobilising diachrony: diverging legacies
Forum for political moderation	Forum for political radicalism
The typical reformers: Lebanon, 17th century, Peter 1st of Russia, 18th century, Mohammad Ali of Egypt, 19th century, the Meiji era in Japan, 19th century, Mustapha Kemal of Turkey, 20th century.	The Conquerors militaristic types of East and West in history
Small coastal countries of the cultural interface (countries in "inter")	Large continental countries at the heart of linguistic identity (countries in "pan")

Choueiri (2008) points out that it is very easy to move from a cultural difficulty to a culture difficulty and vice versa, but history has rarely presented cases without mixing one type or the other.

Most often these are mixed forms that we observe in personal psychologies and international relations.

Attachment to one's own culture which does not exclude the good disposition towards other cultures would indeed be the very wisdom of cultures. From this point of view of the wisdom to open up to other cultures, the book discusses cultural management practices in France, Morocco, and UNESCO, illustrating different approaches to intercultural management.

Section 4.3. Culture and cultural management in selected countries

4.3.1. — Culture and cultural management in Morocco

Several works deal with this question of culture relating to the management methods of companies in Morocco. The book cites as examples, but not exhaustive, some 21st century researchers such as Benabdeljalil (2007), El Amrani and Chebihi (2003), El Aoufi et al. (2000) and those of the previous century as Ali and Wahabi (1995).

Benabdeljalil (2007), based his work on previous surveys carried out by Ali and Wahabi (1995) with 600 large Moroccan companies in the public and private sector located in Casablanca, Rabat, Marrakech and Mohammadia. Ali and Wahabi (1995) sought in their survey to analyse the extent to which cultural values influence the behaviour of the Moroccan companies studied. Their results show that the diversity of Moroccan society is reflected in the attitudes of householders, according to their income, country of training, region of origin, hierarchical level, age, seniority, social class, work of the father. From this point of view, Ali and Wahabi (1995) distinguish four typical profiles of managers in Morocco:

- the manager focused on his own interest and short-term profit, rather authoritarian and not very attentive to the feelings of others;

– the manager << manipulator >>, who has succeeded thanks to his network of relations and/or political maneuvers and who, at first materialistic, seeks gain and power;

- the manager << citizen >> and open to the environment who develops a pleasant working climate, shares the company's benefits with employees;

– the << tribal >> type manager, who centralizes decision-making and surrounds himself with the family for managing his business.

For these authors, the dominant profile would be that of the manager centered on his own interest. Comparing this trend with that of managers in other Arab countries, the authors conclude that the political and economic dimensions of the environment influence more the behaviour of Moroccan managers than cultural factors. Other cultural studies show trends in work behaviour and hierarchical relationships. El Amrani and Chebihi (2003) observe that the management mode in Morocco is characterized, by a great hierarchical distance, a domination of mascu lines values in the sense of Hofstede, a logic of opportunism, short-term and rent. They identify, however, values of solidarity and attachment to family and ethnicity.

Other work carried out on 87 companies from different sectors spread over the entire Moroccan territory, El Aoufi et al. (2000) , showed that the Moroccan company is characterized by a system of labour relations based on paternalism, dependency and even clientelism. Based on the above work, the surveys conducted by Benabdeljalil, N. (2007), through 54 interviews in 35 companies, revealed that the notion of work is associated with values of a cultural and symbolic nature. The cultural dimensions identified in the qualitative interviews conducted by Benabdeljalil (2007) explain the lack of initiative on the part of those responsible. The mode of education is at the origin of this passivity according to a leader in agri-food questioned by the author: there is no initiative. They can wait for a day if they are not told what to do. The workers are afraid of being wrong, this is not forgiven in Morocco. So they're not taking the initiative. It's a problem with basic training and the apprenticeship system. Delegation is difficult because of that: we spend 90% of the time managing things with low added value."

This education, which was not satisfactory in the eyes of the interviewees, could be explained according to the author by a lack of self-confidence and the low level of qualification of the workforce. For a majority of managers, these cultural perceptions reflected by business leaders reinforce their tendencies towards centralisation, control and non-delegation. If cultural dimensions explain the tendency of company managers to adopt a personalization of their hierarchical relationships and submission to authority; for employees, cultural perceptions translate into awork and a high sense of solidarity between workers. Benabdeljalil (2007), considers that the cultural values perceived by the interviewees are used, by some of them, consciously or unconsciously, as a lever in the management of companies that will be developed later.

4.3.2. — Culture and cultural management in France

Benjamin Pelletier (2010), who has lived and worked in the Middle and Far East as an intercultural management trainer, prefers to talk about French-style management in his interventions by relying on the sense of culture applied to business and geography.

Benjamin Pelletier (2010) discusses the relationship between national culture and corporate culture, asserting that the French tend to lack understanding and sensitivity towards other cultures. Because for him, for centuries, French culture has positioned itself in a contradictory dimension that is both universal and prestigious. The author relies on this point of view on Philippe D'Iribarne's diagnosis of French strangeness; "Caught between these two references, in a sort of symbiosis of conflict between the desire for greatness and the ideal of equality, today's France lives in a permanent contradiction."

However, if this contradiction affects the relations of the French among themselves, there is unfortunately, according to Benjamin Pelletier (2010), no reason why it should not affect the relationship of the French with foreigners. Benjamin Pelletier (2010) affirms this way of thinking of the universal, does not facilitate the understanding of foreign cultures and does not allow to create cooperation, because foreigners are required to adhere to our universal values while implicitly judging their culture as inferior to ours.

This contradiction that affects the relations of the French between them is reflected in the relationship of the French corporate culture with the national culture, because for Benjamin Pelletier (2010), each company must give a dressing, a physical and visual identity specific to its culture (history, symbols, myths, logos, etc.). The author thus gives the example of the reward of individual merit by a performance bonus that is not highlighted in the collectivist context. Moreover, according to Pelletier (2010), this generalization which aims at giving the international company a universal dimension is often accompanied by a particularization, either because of the products strongly rooted in a national culture foreign to the culture of the country of implantation, or because of managerial practices that must adapt to the local culture.

As a result, the author argues that the international company is constantly living in this identity gap which can be detrimental to the adhesion of foreign employees, especially in emerging countries where economic patriotism is booming. Consequently, international companies face a key choice: retain their national identity, adopt a universal approach, or fully embrace local adaptation without reservations. In recent years, the latter strategy has gained prominence. Pelletier (2010) illustrates this trend with the following examples:

Over a decade, the number of expatriate assignments has decreased significantly; for instance, out of 79,000 employees, Alstom now has only 700 expatriates and 2,000 on temporary assignments.

A wave of returns from expats from emerging countries (40,000 expats resettled in China in 2006 compared to 7,000 in 1999; among other nationalities, this movement also affects Indians strongly with 35,000 returns in 2006).

Companies are taking more initiatives to fit into the local landscape of their host country (partnerships with universities, sponsorship of local artists, humanitarian actions, etc.)

On the relationship between culture and geography

Pelletier (2010) does not speak here of the relationship to space (private/public space,), but to geography in our way of perceiving this space in relation to culture. Pelletier wants to make it clear that this geographical proximity does not necessarily mean cultural proximity. For him, geographical proximity accentuates the idea of cultural rivalry, because the proximity induced by the resemblance that leads to mimetic rivalry Pelletier argues that the reverse of this phenomenon is that the closer the other is to me geographically, the more I consider that it must enter my normative system. But since we are both close geographically, we consider that it is each other's job to adapt to ourselves. The author reveals two parallels that never meet and which are engaged in an absurd race of cultural speed. The author then wonders whether geographical distance would be able to facilitate cooperation. He immediately answers his question in the negative, because radical difference can lead to total strangeness, where there is no more necessary resemblance that allows the different actors to find this resemblance without sinking into cultural rivalry. The author concludes his speech with this significant example where he sometimes has less difficulty for a French to cooperate with a Japanese than with a German.

On the French management

To argue his thinking on management à la française, Pelletier (2010) is based on a document from a study conducted by the Observatoire international des Salariés of TNS/SOFRES. This study focuses on labour issues in major Western countries and China over the period 1997-2007. The document has the merit of drawing a comparison between French employees according to whether they work for a French company or for the subsidiary of a foreign company located in France. The result is final:

The document rightly points out that there is a real managerial problem in French companies: too much hierarchical distance, personal power taking precedence over the interest of the common project, difficulty in working as a team, reluctance to delegate, a lack of recognition of the work done, imprecision on objectives, coldness of human relationships. If French employees perceive differences between managing French companies within France and managing foreign subsidiaries in France, what about foreign workers employed by French companies abroad? Yvon Pesqueux (2016), believes that the introduction of culture in management sciences occurred when company agents were led to ask the question of the links that can be established between national culture and corporate performance.

Drawing on Hofstede's four dimensions of national culture, Pesqueux (2016) suggests that French culture is characterized by individualism, a high tolerance of uncertainty, a preference for hierarchical distance, and a more feminine approach to problem-solving. This would explain, in his opinion, the development and legitimacy of bureaucratic structures. Despite the criticism of Hofstede's work, Pesqueux (2016) considers that Hofstede's epistemological project is to build a culturalist sociology based on a statistical method. Pesqueux (2016), wants to specify that Hofstede makes culture a context of action where D'Iribarne makes it a context of meaning. Continuing the work of Hofstede, Pesqueux (2016), cites the Globe (Global Leadership and Organizational Behavior Effectiveness Research) project initiated by House (2001), to clarify the issue of "global competencies" in relation to "cultural groups" geographical and cultural homogeneity.

The GLOBE project, conducted by a team of 150 researchers, collected data from 17,000 managers across 951 organizations in 62 countries. It examines organizational culture and leadership based on nine cultural dimensions, expanding beyond Hofstede's original four:

– uncertainty control,

– hierarchical distance,

- collectivism I

- Collectivism II

- gender equity,

– future orientation,

- human orientation,

– self-affirmation,

– performance orientation.

The results distinguish the following groups which are sometimes constructed in a curious way:

– Anglo Cultures (Great Britain, Australia, the "white" component of South Africa, Canada, New Zealand, Ireland, USA),

– Arab Cultures (Algeria, Qatar, Morocco, Egypt, Kuwait, Libya, Tunisia, Lebanon, Syria, Yemen, Jordan, Iraq, UAE, Bahrain, Saudi Arabia, Oman),

– ConfucianAsia (Taiwan, Singapore, Hong Kong, South Korea, China, Japan, Viet Nam),

– Eastern Europe (Hungary, Bulgaria, Romania, Czech Republic, Slovakia, Poland, Lithuania, Latvia, Estonia, Serbia, Greece, Slovenia, Albania, Russia),

– Germanic Europe (Netherlands, Flanders, Austria, German-speaking Switzerland, Germany, South Tyrol, Liechtenstein),

- Latin America (Costa Rica, Venezuela, Ecuador, Mexico, El Salvador, Colombia, Guatemala, Bolivia, Brazil, Argentina)

– Latin Europe (Italy, Portugal, Spain, France, French and Italian Switzerland), Nordic Europe (Finland, Sweden, Denmark, Norway)

—Southern Asia (India, Bangladesh, Indonesia, Malaysia, Thailand, Iran, Philippines, Turkey),

– Sub-Saharan Africa (Namibia, Zambia, Zimbabwe, the “African” part of South Africa).

The results achieved in relation to 9 cultural competences (the orientation towards performance, towards authority, towards the future, towards individual respect, institutional collectivism, group collectivism, gender equality, hierarchical distance, relation to uncertainty) lead to 6 Implicit dimensions of leadership: (the orientation towards charismatic values, the orientation towards team spirit, the orientation towards self-protection, the orientation towards participation the orientation towards respect for others, autonomy in the perspective of building a grid for decoding a “globalized world”. While maintaining the methodological framework of. Hofstede other authors such as Schwartz (1997) cited by Piqueux (2016), claimed to exceed the four dimensions of Hofstede to prevail and retain in 1997, 10 items (» fulfillment, autonomy, goodness, conformism, hedonism, power, security, stimulation, tradition, universalism).

In response to this approach of action on the cultural dimension based on a statistical methodology, D'Iribarne advocates the development of management methods appropriate to the cultural context of each country by inscribing itself through its method of meaning in one based on the model of Japanese companies, without falling into an excessive particularism of cultural determinism, D'Iribarne (1989), argues that it would be necessary to contextualize management methods when it comes to building its point of view from the comparative analysis of three factories located in three countries: France, the United States and the Netherlands. D'Iribarne (1989), attempts to highlight an ideal of honour in France, where debates and conflicts of opinion are important, an ideal of fair exchange in the United States and an ideal of consensus in the Netherlands.

Ten years later, D'Iribarne (1998) studied a broader set of cases to validate his ethnographic approach beyond the concept of honor. These included management modernization in Quebec, Belgium, and France; face-to-face cultures such as France-Sweden, France-Slovenia, and France-Switzerland; and innovative management in developing countries like Mauritania, Cameroon, and Morocco. D'Iribarne (1998) defends the idea that contemporary anthropology favours culture as a context for interpretation, which justifies the fact that within a single culture, practices, issues and strategies do not have the same value. D'Iribarne (1998) proposes the use of «ultimate references» based on history and considers that national culture is also the reference that makes it possible to make intelligible identity conflicts more than organizational conflicts. D'Iribarne stands out for its multi-dimensional cultural approaches based on statistics (Hofstede, 1984; Schwartz, 1994; and House 2001), to propose two dimensions for distinguishing cultures:

- the relations to subordination which make it possible to approach relations with power and thus validate the variety of conceptions of the free man.

- the meaning given to the interpretation of sanctions and criticism and that given to failure.

In contrast to these different cultural approaches aimed at adaptation to the surrounding environment, a poor adaptation to a foreign environment in the context of an expatriation does not only risk to jeopardize cooperation with employees from other cultures, but it can also increase the causes of failure of expatriations.

Culture and difficulties of adaptation to the environment

Pelletier (2009) notes that, although expatriate loyalty increased from 9% to 17% between 2007 and 2010, disaffection remains high.

This underscores the need for companies to implement follow-up programs for expatriates after their assignments. In the case of cooperation, where there is no agreement or trust between Western managers and local workers, the impact on the company would affect its image in the country of establishment; and above all, its ability to mobilize local human resources to sustain its current and future activity.

In the wake of this idea of cultural adaptation, Pelletier (2009) gives the example of a Chinese Li He, specialist in 3G development, who has been working for several years for a Chinese subsidiary of a large international group based in Shanghai. He is now divided between the prestige of working for a large foreign group and the desire to join a Chinese company such as Huawei where he will find benchmarks in terms of management and culture. Indeed, the engineer explains: “A few years ago, I would never have considered working for a Chinese company. Wages were too low and career prospects were poor. With my experience working in a large international group, I realize that I am not always comfortable with my foreign hierarchy, and I tell myself that I might be more in sync in a company like Huawei.”

For Pelletier (2009 Chinese specialist Li He, developing 3 G’s, is hesitant not because of salary or benefits but because of cultural differences: "Simple things for a Chinese become sources of conflict in mixed teams. Time is wasted on endless management updates. I think I’d be better at Huawei, but there’s really a lot of competition for these positions.”

This example highlights that, despite efforts by developing countries to adopt Western management models, large international firms remain cautious, often preferring to operate within familiar cultural frameworks and avoiding past intercultural conflicts. Thus, Pelletier (2009) observes through this testimony that the use of expatriation will be less and less a solution, and that the challenge for large

Western companies is to find a point of differentiation and that intercultural management should no longer be a mere varnish of expatriation, but a priority of sustainable development strategy.

The goal of sustainable development, supported by the various theoretical approaches discussed, was reaffirmed by UNESCO's 2015 initiative for sustainable urban development 2030. The following sections outline the main features of this UNESCO plan.

4.3.3. Culture and cultural management as perceived by UNESCO for 2030

The 2015 UNESCO Agenda for Sustainable Urban Development 2030 initiative sets out in its introductory statement the commitments of heads of state and the goals to achieve sustainable development by 2030. The UNESCO initiative targets 91 commitments by heads of state and 17 key global goals to be achieved by 2030. The first UN commitment is: "We, heads of state and government and senior representatives, meeting at the United Nations Headquarters in New York from 25 to 27 September 2015 on the occasion of the 70th anniversary of the Organization, today agreed on new global sustainable development goals." Other UN commitments include the elimination of poverty in all its forms, the fight against inequality, and the creation of conditions for inclusive sustainable economic growth, recognize that the dignity of the human person is fundamental and applies to all, taking into account the different realities of civil society and other stakeholders around the world. It is also a matter for the United Nations to ensure full respect of international law based on the Universal Declaration of Human Rights and international human rights treaties.

The challenges and commitments outlined in major summits and conferences are interconnected and require integrated solutions to address a world where billions of people still live in poverty, face wealth disparities, inequality, unemployment, conflict, violent extremism, depletion of natural resources, environmental degradation, and freshwater scarcity.

The UN reports that the world has improved over the past 15 years, notably through increased access to education for both boys and girls. The diffusion of information and communication technologies and global interconnectivity have great potential to accelerate human progress and reduce social divides. As a result, the United Nations has developed 17 sustainable development goals with 169 associated and indivisible targets for the new 2030 agenda. The means to implement this ambitious agenda are public finances, both national and international. The United Nations wants to recognize, in the spirit of achieving this 2030 agenda, the role of the diversified private sector, ranging from micro-enterprises to cooperatives to multinationals. The United Nations affirms that it is responsible at national, regional and global levels for achieving the goals and targets over the next 15 years. “To foster accountability to our citizens, we will provide for systematic monitoring and review at different levels as outlined in this program and the Addis Ababa Agenda for Action.” The means of implementation and global partnership will facilitate this intensive commitment to achieving all the goals and targets set by the United Nations. The book summarizes the 17 goals of the UN 2030 agenda:

1. Ending poverty in all its forms around the world

2. Eliminate hunger, ensure food security and improved nutrition and promote sustainable agriculture

3. Ensuring a healthy life and promoting well-being for all and at all ages

4. Ensure inclusive and equitable quality education and promote opportunities for lifelong learning for all

5. Achieve gender equality and empower all women and girls

6. Ensuring the availability and sustainable management of water and sanitation for all

7. Ensuring access to affordable, reliable, sustainable and modern energy for all

8. Promote sustained, inclusive and sustainable economic growth, productive full employment and decent work for all

9. Building resilient infrastructure, promoting inclusive and sustainable industrialization and fostering innovation

10. Reducing inequalities within and between countries

11. Making cities and human settlements inclusive, safe, resilient and sustainable

12. Ensuring sustainable consumption and production patterns

13. Take urgent action to address climate change and its impacts

14. Conserve and sustainably use oceans, seas and marine resources for sustainable development

15. Protect, restore and promote the sustainable use of terrestrial ecosystems, sustainably manage forests, combat desertification, halt and reverse land degradation and stop biodiversity loss

16. Promote peaceful and inclusive societies for sustainable development, provide access to justice for all and build effective, accountable and inclusive institutions at all levels.

17. Strengthening the means of implementation and revitalizing the global partnership for sustainable development, recognizing that the Convention-The UN Framework on Climate Change is the main international and intergovernmental forum for negotiating the global response to climate change.

CONCLUSION

In this fourth chapter, the book attempted to present cultural diversity in its national and corporate form, and then to analyse the other culture relative to the cultural conflict. The book demonstrates that corporate culture is rooted within a broader national culture, within which companies develop their own organizational culture. It first explains the concept of national culture before examining corporate culture. The words of the book then chose to shed light on examples of cultural diversity and cultural management in Morocco internationally, especially in France, and UNESCO for its 2030 cultural programme.

CONCLUSION OF PART TWO

After establishing the importance of culture in Part One—characterized as a mosaic of traits interacting with science and the environment—Part Two explores the relationship between culture and sustainable development across two chapters (three and four). In chapter three, he dealt with culture and the notion of sustainability by explaining the notion of sustainable development in which cultural management cultivates a sustainable interaction. The book then attempted to answer the question of whether culture can contribute to sustainable development or vice versa, it is perceived by some countries, especially in Africa, as a decoy.

In Chapter Four, the book explores cultural diversity, highlighting differences between national and corporate cultures. It concludes with an analysis of cultural management practices worldwide.

PART THREE
CAN CULTURE SAVE THE WORLD?

Culture saves nothing and nobody,
It does not justify. But it is a product
of man: he projects himself, recognizes himself in it;
alone, this critical mirror offers him his image.
- Jean-Paul Sartre

7.3.1. Humanist cultural leadership.

7.3.2. Transformational cultural leadership

7.3.3. Cultural leadership is a pedagogical responsibility of management schools.

7.2.4. Practical cultural leadership is a responsibility of the leaders themselves.

Section 7.4. Comparative study between cultural leadership and power

7.4.1 — difficult choice of leaders to relinquish power.

7.4.2 - Difficult choice between positive and negative power concepts

Section 7.5. — Theoretical contribution of supranational cultural leadership

7.5.1. Contribution by knowledge management

7.5.2. Discussion of types of historical and contemporary leaders

7.5.3. The new paradigm of supranational cultural leadership

Introduction

In this third and last part, structured in three chapters, the book suggests to deal with culture and its influence in the world. It is a question in cross-literature whether the cultural dimension exerts a positive or negative influence on human behaviour (chapter 5).

In chapter six, the book asks whether culture can save the world based on the contribution of cultural intelligence, artificial intelligence and cultural change to create a new paradigm of cultural leadership that will save the planet.

In the final chapter seven on supra-national cultural leadership as savior of the world, we proposed to show that the observation of the field enriched by a management of the knowledge combined with the experiences of the researcher and his vision to advance the science and the sick world of the management, the emergence of a new supranational cultural leadership to save the planet.

The work of the book justifies the new supranational leadership in chapter seven, by a relation of influence and power that exerts a humanism transcending all other types of classical and contemporary leaderships. These latter types of leadership have not yet succeeded in achieving the conditions for living together on this planet, without suffering from exclusion, discrimination and endless conflicts.

CHAPTER 5
CULTURE AND ITS INFLUENCE IN THE WORLD

Culture makes absolutely no sense
if it is not an absolute commitment
to change the lives of men.
- Romain Gary

Introduction

In this chapter, the book proposes to deal with both the negative and positive influence of culture on human behavior based on a cross-literature. In the negative approach to cultural influence, he explains to what extent it constitutes a brake on sustainable development (51) based on studies and literature. The book then sheds light on the other positive approach to cultural influence, while showing that culture is seen as a vector of sustainable development by some researchers and qualitative surveys. (52)

Section 5.1. The negative influence of culture on human behaviour

5.1.1. Culture as a brake on sustainable development.

5.1.2. The negative influence of culture in literature

Section 5.2. The positive influence of culture on human behaviour

5.2.1. Culture as a vector for sustainable development in literature

5.2.2. Culture in the Arab-Muslim approach

Section 5.1. The negative influence of culture on human behaviour

We deal successively with culture as a barrier to sustainable development and the negative influence of culture in literature.

5.1.1. Culture as a brake on sustainable development.

While managerial discourse often praises respecting existing cultures or implementing new ones, Thévenet (2010) argues that culture is primarily a barrier to change and is frequently a source of failure rather than success. In addition to the perception of culture as a brake on change, it would also be perceived as a kind of collective doxa imposed on employees. Some company managers believe that it is enough to announce the values of change for employees to believe them, and adhere to them without murmurs or hesitations. The resistance to change by employees explains the illusion of business leaders to view culture from a purely mechanistic angle.

In other words, culture would be approached in a non-mechanistic approach, not as a theory that describes the real, but rather as a component of this real. In this reality, culture seems to exercise a certain power, a kind of oppression and intrusion into the intimacy of people. According to Thévenet (2016), culture can act as a factor of submission and dependency, hindering personal development in a context where individuals' efforts are often driven by obligation rather than genuine commitment. However, the importance of corporate culture remains an essential component of society in that the company must offer its employees not only material and financial benefits but, above all, intangible benefits. The goal is to bring teams together around cultural values aimed at true cohesion, empowerment and sustainable development. From this point of view, the company that defines the cultural values of its organization only reflects the true nature of the company and the personality of its founder.

Other researchers like Nadia Benabdeljalil (2007) prefer to adopt a more moderate approach compared to the thought of Thévenet (2016). Indeed the work of Benabdeljalil (2007) reveals that culture is useful, but insufficient to understand social relations in the company. In her qualitative research, the author states that she has adopted an intermediate position, considering that national culture is only part of reality and that it is necessary to be careful not to reduce everything to a national culture. Other dimensions related to the manager's profile (personality, training,) and individual cultures must be taken into account. Benabdeljalil (2007), nevertheless agrees with Thévenet (2016) in her thinking about the culture of submission, when she considers that the cultural constants she identified in her qualitative survey are related to a dominant paternalistic culture, submission to authority, low level of qualification, illiteracy and a high sense of solidarity among workers. For Benabdeljalil (2007), it is therefore important to relativize the place of cultures in the company, because the manifestations of cultural values are not absolute, but contingent on the situations and the environment, socio-economic.

Do different individual or collective expressions of culture coexist harmoniously, or are they prone to conflict? The following sections explore these questions. For Meier (2016), the corporate culture presents itself as a differentiating factor in relation to the environment (Allouche, Schmidt, 1995, p. 45) and constitutes a means of exerting an influence on human behaviors.

If Adam Smith was talking about the invisible hand that influences and regulates the market, is it fair to say that culture is an invisible force that influences and regulates human behaviour? There are indeed values in a culture that have a great influence on human behaviour; just as the strength of technology will force individuals to adopt a position of humility and cultural tolerance (Herskovits, 1950). In this perspective of influencing behaviour, the question is whether it is a positive or negative influence. The words of the book further explain the influence of culture on human behaviour and organizations. It proposes to present first the perspective of the negative influence of culture as a brake on development, based on two approaches: that of Godelier and Thévenet.

The Godelier approach (2009) on negative cultural influence

On the question of how culture negatively influences human practices and behaviour, Godelier (2009) asks in its own way whether the corporate culture can be seen as a source of continuity and sustainability or, conversely, a source of inertia and immobilism.

Godelier (2009) explains that, under the influence of American culturalism, culture is seen as either a source of stability and sustainability—when it is strong and coherent—or as a hindrance when inconsistencies and tensions exist within subcultures. This vision sees culture as a collection of folklore that would limit the company's opportunities for evolution and innovation. This import of the American culturalist vision was perceived, outside the management sciences, either as not rigorous or as an attempt at ideological manipulation of employees. Thévenet (2010), believes that the concept of culture is so trivialized and integrated into the company that one is tempted to relegate culture to obsolete and outdated notions.

However, Thévenet (2010) points out that many hopes placed in the scope of this notion of culture have been disappointed: culture has not always kept its promises. The author's second remark is about company concepts, which today are less suited to the notion of culture. The author wonders, however, whether culture retains some of the uses that the book develops later.

The Thévenet approach (2010) on the negative influence of culture

Thévenet (2020), develops in this perspective of the negative influence of culture two dimensions of cultural decline: a cultural decline of the enterprise and a collective decline of the enterprise.

The cultural decline of the company

Regarding the cultural decline of companies, Thévenet (2010) speaks of respect for existing cultures, creation of a new culture, overcoming old cultures. Culture appears to the author as the first brake on the success of change, and as always a cause of failure, but rarely a reason for success. The author sees culture as a kind of collective doxa imposed on people. Some business leaders thought that it was enough to spread collective values for employees to believe in, adhere to and change their behaviour towards the company. Some business leaders continue to ignore that change is not decreed, but must be prepared, accompanied and maintained.

Pou Thévenet (2010), culture has long been understood as a tool to create, manipulate, change or replace it, not as a theory describing the real, but rather as a component of the organization. For Thévenet, culture is an object that managers can manipulate to create or modify organizational culture. According to the author, culture has a first weakness that implies insufficient and misleading methodologies, and a second one that elicits vain actions of any change draining values and a concrete vision of the world. Thévenet (2010), considers that the so-called values were more relevant to the declared value than to the applied value and that public policies for human resources management were at best ineffective, at worst harmful. Thévenet (2010) gives the example of the «cultural revolution» which, according to him, consisted in imagining and imposing new references disconnected from the past and reality.

The culture associated with references to paternalism refers to this pejorative notion of paternalism that is expressed by the exercise of personal power, and direct or tacit oppression on people. Culture becomes for Thévenet (2010), a factor of submission, which prevents people from developing and leaving the circle in which the assistance of paternalism is paid in dedication. Criticism of culture or paternalism often triggers defensive reactions. Thévenet (2010) views the invocation of culture as a subtle means for organizations to resist the emphasis on individual autonomy and free choice.

The decline of collective bargaining

It seems, according to Thévenet (2020), that the company has moved away from the collective agreement in favour of individual contracts. The concept of talent which favours the individual over the collective aspect explains this individual tendency. Talent, the hallmark of a person's uniqueness and originality, explains why many people want to pursue their careers, invest in personal development and not expect anything from the company where everyone thinks they can decide for themselves. However, is it permissible to argue that forms of collective life have evolved rather than disappeared, with the growing importance of social networks? Indeed, social networks have the singularity of offering a form of collective life that is different from that of work in companies, because at the office for example you can not delete your colleagues from your list of friends. Thanks to social media, interpersonal relationships are now instant and real-time. Organizational systems appear increasingly provisional, with employees feeling that each project or restructuring is succeeded almost immediately by another. The ongoing questions of change no longer target the process of change, but rather fight against the brakes since the objective is no longer to change, but to change quickly (Miles, 2010). The present seems to be the only place of refuge for companies by removing the duration.

5.1.2. The negative influence of culture in literature

If culture is a daily affair (Thévenet, 2010), Norbert Elias (1897-1990), German writer and sociologist, in his book on the process of civilization, argues that «Culture is a dynamic of successive transformations revealing forces that coexist, repel and fuse together. Other work by Robert Stoller (1924 - 1991), an American psychiatrist and psychoanalyst, shows that forces of nature act on human attitudes and behaviors demonstrating that innate can influence acquired knowledge. In the same sense of Stoller, Thévenet (2010), believes that the strength of culture is ultimately imposed by its usefulness and its ability to evoke history and bring together the present a past. In other words, culture is for him "the strength of the moment in relation to the richness of a past to honour a future". From the perspective of the negative influence of culture, the book quotes in a non-exhaustive literature works and studies by some authors of the 20th and 21st centuries as follows.

Defrenne and Delvaux (1992) study on culture which kills progress

Defrenne and Delvaux (1992), do not favour the adaptation of culture, but rather go further than Bateson and Watzlawik (1972), in their analysis opposing adaptability to culture. For Defrenne and Delvaux, culture kills adaptability because it subjects individuals to resignation, protection and defence, while adaptability means progress. For authors, culture becomes synonymous with alienation and weakens adaptation. In view of this uncertainty, which makes the strategic decision very difficult, the historical tools of the strategy seem insufficient, and lead to the development of a strategy in a state of uncertainty, which has gradually integrated concepts such as market dynamics, the use of game theory. This strategy is in a state of uncertainty arising from a complex environment and the need to take decisions on increasingly distant horizons.

The view of Defrenne and Delvaux (1992) has been taken up in Anglo-Saxon literature by more recent scholars such as Wood (2002). This anthropologist at Boston University traces the evolution of cultural diversity, and the multiplicity of its senses based on ethnic, racial, or other physical characteristics. He argues in "diversity: the invention of a concept" that, rather than leading to greater unity and equity in American culture, cultural diversity is a traditional concept that undermines the principles of freedom, of equality and to reverse the trends towards racial division in society.

For Defrenne and Delvaux (1992), adaptability means progress, and progress signifies a better but uncertain future. They defend the idea of embracing uncertainty and the unknown. Building on this, researchers Mieszala and Sibony (2009), based on a survey conducted by McKinsey in September 2006 with 800 managers, found that only 45% were satisfied with the strategic planning process. Moreover, only 23% believed that major decisions were made within this framework. For millennia, man has sought according to Boyer (2007), in his editorial: Management and future to «guessed» the future in a religious way, or «scientific» as if man could not live in the present without looking at the future. Based on the reinvented foresight by Gaston Berger (1997): «The future is not created, it remains to be done». Looking to the future, Godet (2007) distinguishes four attitudes: the passive ostrich who undergoes change, the reactive firefighter who waits for fire to fight it, the proactive insurer who prepares for foreseeable changes, the proactive contractor who responds to bring about the desired changes.

The idea of a prospective to face fatalism fits perfectly with the problem of the reactive profile of business leaders in some developing countries who consider the future as inevitable. For example, Morocco and Turkey have the lowest future orientation score compared to comparable countries such as Egypt, Kuwait and Qatar (Kasabakal 2002).[6] This is why the notion of culture has been the focus of many studies in anthropology, psychology, organizational behaviour and international affairs.

---

[6] Kabasakal H. & Bodur M. (2002), «Arabic cluster : a bridge between East and West», journal of world business 37 (2002) 40-54.

Researchers in these disciplines have produced a large body of literature that deals with norms, values and behaviours in organizations and business relationships. Some work addresses the influence of national culture in business management. (Kenneth 2002). Others deal with cultural management and uncertainty (Defrenne. 1992), while some others discuss the influence of culture on the style of management (Kasabakal H. 2004), the link between religion and economy (Boubacar, 2004; Donna dieu 2007), or the diversity of the like and the different (Frimousse, and Peretti 2006).

Among the studies that support this notion of negative influence of culture which hinders the development of business management and the management of companies, it is worth mentioning Kabasakal and Bodur (2002) . These authors' work coinciding with that of Kenneth, who identified nine cultural dimensions influencing the management style of managers: 1) future orientation, 2) remote powers, 3) institutional collectivisms, 4) human orientations, 5) Successful orientations, 6) Family collectivisms, 7) Gender equality, 8) Affirmation, 9) Avoidance of uncertainty.

Kabasakal and Bodur's (2002) approach, culture hampers progress and the future. Studying a cluster of five countries: Morocco, Turkey, Egypt, Qatar and Kuwait, the researchers find that despite the common characteristics of these nations (religion, language, culture), the practices specific to each country, allow them to differentiate on certain cultural values, collectivism, individualism, attitude to uncertainty, and avoidance (Hofstede 1994).

While companies in the Arab group studied by Kabasakal and Bodur (2002) place little importance on planning for the future and score low on future orientation, due to the negative interpretation of the notion of fate over the future, the authors find that these countries rank differently according to the influence of the nine cultural dimensions (Figure 1). The study shows that Morocco and Turkey have almost identical scores in some cultural aspects. They lead the group in terms of family, collectivism (Turkey, and Morocco 5.88 - 5.87) and bondage (Turkey — and Morocco 4.53 - 4.52). They show the lowest avoidance uncertainty (Turkey - and Morocco 3.63 - 3.65).

In addition, Morocco (5.80) is ranked as the highest remote power, followed by Turkey (5.57). On the other hand, Turkey (3.94) had the lowest score for human orientation, followed by Morocco (4.19).

The high scores of Morocco and Turkey regarding family and power distance corroborate findings from previous analyses by Eddakir (2001), Al-Arkoubi (2004), and Abakouy (2006). Morocco (3.26) also shares the lowest future score with Kuwait (3.26), followed by Turkey (3.74). In terms of leadership, previous studies have indicated that leadership for this group is seen as an important concept, which is vital to the well-being of society and organizations.

Figure 2: Scores of cultural influence in the Arab pole (Kabasakal 2002)

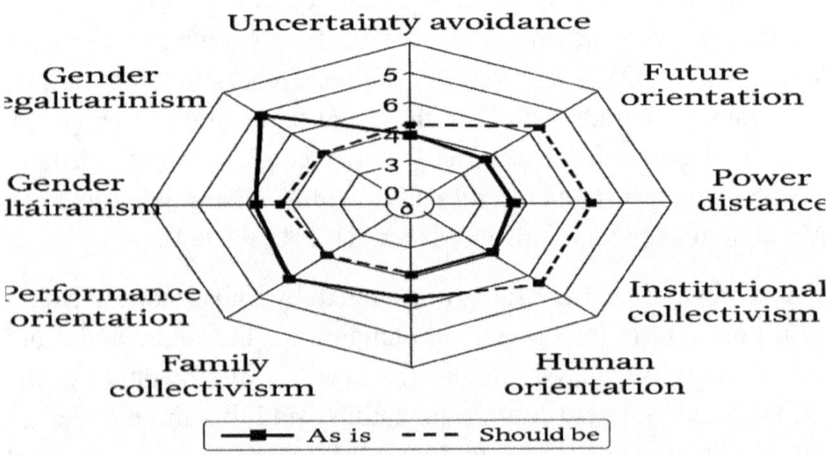

The researchers' study shows that helping family members is considered more important than being generous to others. Thus, Islam promotes and maintains kinship and family relations, creating a highly collectivist culture. The notion of "fate" in the culture of these countries can be seen, according to the authors, as a factor negatively influencing future direction. According to Kabasakal and Bodur (2002), the notion of destiny in these cultures is very complicated because there are also religious recommendations that explain the importance of human responsibility and choice of actions. While Morocco has the best ranking among the 61 GLOBE companies on remote power, on human orientation, Turkey (3.94) scored the lowest, followed by Morocco (4.19). On the other hand, Morocco (3.87) is the lowest in institutional collectivism, followed by Turkey (4.03). They are also the two very male companies.

Egypt has the highest score on human orientation (4.73), performance orientation (4.27) and future orientation (3.86). Egypt joins Qatar and Kuwait on institutional collectivism (Egypt 4.50, Qatar 4.50, and Kuwait 4.49). In addition to their high scores on institutional and collectivism, Qatar leads on gender egalitarianism (3.63), while Kuwait has the highest score on avoidance uncertainty (4.21) and the lowest on (3.63), forward-looking (3.26), egalitarianism and gender equality (2.58).

In terms of values, all the societies of the Arab group aspire to more results in future orientation, collectivism, humanity orientation. The contrast of values shows a significantly higher score in terms of collectivism and family, and a lower score for gender egalitarianism, avoidance uncertainty, and future orientation. Attachment to family seems to be a major feature of this group. The researchers find that individuals find their satisfaction in relationships within groups which may be family, neighbourhood, village, school of friends, or sect. What is interesting in the work of Kabasakal Eral (2002) is that individuals in the Arab group are more tolerant about uncertainty in the environment and do not need to make plans for the future.

Table 1 : Comparative table of the 5 countries studied

Cultural dimensions	Morocco	Turkey	Egypte	Qatar	Kuwait
Avoidance of uncertainty	3,65	3,63	4,06	3,99	4,21
The future direction	3,26	3,74	3,86	3,78	3, 26
Remote power	5,80	5,57	4,92	4,73	5,12
Institutional collectivism	3, 87	4,03	4,50	4,50	4,49
Human orientation	4,19	3,94	4, 73	4,42	4,52
Strong focus	3,99	3,83	4,27	3,45	3,95
Family collectivism	5,87	5,88	5,64	4,71	5,80
Gender equality	2,84	2,89	2,81	3, 63	2,58
The statement	4,52	4,53	3,91	4,11	3,63

Societies in the Arab group are continually experiencing the duality between east and west, tradition and modernity, religious and secular. They are simultaneously semi-feudal, semi-capitalist, semi-agricultural and semi-industrial (Barakat, 1993). These dualities create conflicting expectations on the part of the managers of these companies regarding the importance of relationships in the group on the one hand and the improvement of performance on the other. Business leaders are expected to behave in this way as "paternalistic" and provide employment opportunities and privileges for family members, relatives and their own employees.

In a cross-cultural study involving 10 countries, Turkey is very high on paternalistic values (Aycan et al. 2000). In a study on Danish investors in Turkey, Bodur and Madsen (1993) concluded that personal contacts with officials are crucial tools in finalizing decisions. Additionally, Kabasakal and Bodur (2002) highlighted the existence of a dual system of values—both Western and Eastern—that characterizes organizations within the Arab group studied.

The Kenneth (2004) study, a culture of relationships for business Joining the study of Kabasakal and Bodur, the work of Kenneth (2004) shows the importance of friendly Moroccan relations in the business world. Managers place more emphasis on personal contact and less on procedures. Building trust becomes an important factor in business partnerships when it comes to local and international markets. Shane (1993) had shown nine years before Kenneth that national cultures have an effect on the entry patterns of multinational enterprises. For companies considering entering Arab markets in this way, the entry mode would be very difficult due to lack of relationships and trust. The «negative» influence of culture on human resource management developed by Kabasakal (2002) has been defended by other researchers.

The book aims to recall some of them here, not because they studied the negative influence of culture in Morocco, but because their research on cultural influence is of interest to our question.

The Friedman approach (2005)

Closer to us, the book allows us to recall that Friedman (2005), analyzed above, rejects the influence of any culture, except for the dominant one resulting from the rampant globalization under American domination. Even more recently, Barabel and Meier (2008) defend this same idea by considering that HRM practices are increasingly crossed by managerial fashion phenomena which come mostly from the United States (coaching, 360 degrees, psychometric tests, Assessoraux Centers, Balanced scorecard, SIRH...). These modes are gradually imposed on all companies and multinational companies in the sense of Barabel and Meier (2008), often act as pioneers in the transmission of these practices.

In this perspective, organizations are "institutionally rooted and socially embedded" within their respective national contexts. Consequently, the view that culture negatively influences organizations and HR practices—advocated by Kenneth (2002), Kasabakal (2002), Wood (2002), Friedman (2005), and Defrenne and Delvaux (1992)—is not universally accepted. If culture had no benefits, it would likely have been abandoned long ago, given its role in providing stability and comfort to individuals and communities. Recent studies, such as the work by Georges BIDI and Mahamadou Falilou Bane (2021), suggest that cultural practices in the African public sector can, in fact, weaken organizational performance—specifically, the Senegalese General Directorate of Taxes and Domains.

Many researchers have argued that culture is a lever for development and progress.

Section 5.2. The positive influence of culture on human behaviour.

In contrast to the American culturalist vision, which is considered dominant and distinguishes between a good culture and subculture, and moving away from Thévenet's (2010) thought on the decline of corporate culture, Some researchers of the previous and contemporary century believe that culture can be a vector for sustainable development on the planet. Indeed, if culture is an everyday affair (Thévenet, 2010), Norbert Elias (1897-1990), a German writer and sociologist, argues in his book on the process of civilization that «Culture is a dynamic of successive transformations revealing forces that coexist, repel and fuse together. Other work by Robert Stoller (1924 - 1991), an American psychiatrist and psychoanalyst, shows that forces of nature act on human attitudes and behaviors demonstrating that innate can influence acquired knowledge. We cite other researchers who support the sustainability of culture, such as Godelier (2009), Defrenne and Delvaux (1992), Wood Peter (2003), Nouiga (2004), Demergon (2000), Trompenaars (1994), Pettigrew (1995), Schwartz (1994), Kasabakal (2002), D'Iribane (1989), Millot and Roulleau (2005) which the book attempts to analyse in the following paragraphs.

5.2.1. Culture as a vector for sustainable development in literature

The book explores here the different approaches to culture as a vector of sustainable development, starting with Maurice Godelier.

The approach of Maurice Godelier (2009) on the sustainability of culture

Godelier (2009), for example, considers at the beginning of this 21st century that culture is a managerial tool capable of overcoming the failings of classical doctrines and restoring a form of continuity within large private organizations. From this point of view, culture allows a company to last and not reduce its prospects for sustainability and change.

The link between the concept of "culture" and that of sustainability lies in the fact that the company seeks what is sustainable, continuous, permanent and perpetual. The company culture seems to be an element of this sustainability. Godelier (2009), wanted to show that the goal of sustainability shares with the notion of culture a common element which is: the creation and continuation of a social community in the company. Similarly, the sustainability of a company requires developing a culture, doing and thinking to be competitive in the market. Because often the practices of HRM contradict the great speeches on the mobilization of employees and theories of human capital.

From this bridge of vision, it is also essential to rely on the social sciences. Thinking about the relationship between culture and sustainability requires us to look at how we can sustainably regulate the behaviors and ways of thinking of company members. The company's long-term existence is ultimately based on its own ways of doing and thinking, on the one hand, and on the other on the material or symbolic elements of its culture. If culture means that it is what remains after having forgotten everything (Émile Henriot (1889-1961), it remains in the perspective of sustainability, the managerial recipe when one has already tried everything (Thévenet, 2006).

The Tylor (1996) approach to a dynamic and evolving culture

In contrast to earlier works that criticize culture—claiming it "kills adaptability" and fosters racial division (Bateson, 1972; Defrenne and Delvaux, 1992; Wood, 2003)—Tylor introduces the idea that culture is dynamic. He argues that culture is not static; it can add, modify, or eliminate elements that are then acquired by all members of the same culture. Tylor (1996) thus joins the supporters of culture considered rather as a dynamic dimension, by Ulrich (1989), Ketter and Hess Kell (1992) and later Spector (2007). In this respect, Nouiga (2004) refers to Thevenet, Demorgon and Hofstede to argue the dynamics of culture.

For Thevenet and Vachette (1992), culture is built throughout history in response to environmental problems and internal cohesion. Culture develops through a learning process, and changes throughout history as it confronts problems encountered in companies. For Demorgon (2000), a culture is an overall dynamic that combines the past, present and future. It explains this dynamic in the following terms: If cultures are now more present to each other than they have ever been, humans do not yet have the concepts that can contribute to their coexistence, which is always problematic but could be more evolutionary, dynamic and inventive."

Hofstede believes that culture is not a legacy, but an achievement that comes from the social environment of an individual, not his genes. Culture must be distinguished from human nature and individual personality even if the boundaries between the three concepts remain controversial by practitioners and experts. Hofstede is joined by Demergon, who shares his view that culture is not a product of the past in danger of extinction, but a matrix of actions and thoughts that confront the constraints of the moment.

On the same level, the coexistence of humans and cultures remains a problematic but dynamic and evolving issue (Demergon 2000). A problem cannot be solved with the same map as the one that created it, says Dilts, who agrees on this point with Albert Einstein: “Our ways of thinking create problems that cannot be solved by those ways of thinking.” For Dilts, the change process is therefore a problem-solving process. Regarding culture as an evolution in the environment, the founder of the European community, Jean Monnet, defends the dynamic and non-static dimension of culture, and joins previous research work when he states in substance: “If I had to face the challenge of European integration again, I would probably start with culture". Culture, says Trompenaars (1994), in the same vein, is "the context in which things happen. Outside of this context, even legal questions mean nothing."

Clark (1996) identifies four key factors influencing HRM practices in each country, one of which is the national culture. For instance, the European HRM model is distinguished by a more institutionalized cultural context compared to other regions, leading to specific HR practices (Barabel et al., 2008). Supporting this, Barabel (2008) argues that a company's competitive advantage is enhanced when it adapts its HRM practices to external factors, particularly cultural and socio-economic conditions.

These authors who highlight the influence of the cultural factor external to the company, thus join the fundamental idea of the contextualized theory of André Pettigrew (1995). Similarly, Tylor, Beechler and Napier (1996) Barabel reports that multinationals implement three different strategies, the most important of which is the local adaptation strategy taking into account local cultural specificities to adopt the best practices they from subsidiaries or head office.

In order to situate the importance of cultural influence on human resource management practices, the work of the book has chosen to undertake a comparative approach with other cultural specificities of countries from four continents. On this question of cultural specificities that distinguish countries according to their characteristics, the book referred to a researcher from the previous century (Schwartz, 1994), who positioned some countries (France, Germany, USA, China, Netherlands, Japan and Spain) on criteria such as conservatism, hierarchical distance, intellectual and emotional autonomy, and collectivism (see Table 2).

The choice of Schwartz (1994) is enriching for comparative research on the scope of the cultural dimension. This comparative research allows us to note that, what Schwartz did in 1994 by comparing a group of countries from Europe of America and Asia; the researchers Kasabakal and Bodur (2002) did so eight years later by comparing a cluster of countries in North Africa and the Middle East (Morocco, Turkey, Qatar, Kuwait, Egypt) explained in previous sections.

This comparative table by Schwartz (1994) makes it possible to see points of convergence and divergence between cultures and to identify «possible cultural shocks», in the words of Barabel (2008). Although these cultural blocs have significant differences (China leads on conservatism 3.97 and on hierarchical distance 3.70, France leads the block on intellectual and emotional autonomy; Spain on individualism 5.55).

Table 2 : National comparative analysis on cultural criteria

Pays	Conservatism	Hierarchical distance	Intellectual Autonomy	Emotional Autonomy	Individual ism
France	3,35	2,16	5,15	4,41	5,45
USA	3,90	2,39	4,20	3,65	5,29
Chine	3,97	3,70	4,27	3,32	4,49
Japon	3,87	2,86	4,68	3,54	4,79
Allemagn e	3,42	2,27	4,75	4,03	5,37
Espagne	3,42	2,03	4,90	3,97	5,55
Pays-Bas	3,68	2,26	4,44	3,51	5,45

Based on Schwartz 1994.reported by Barbados l (2008)

Some work has shown that the countries of these different blocs have much more similarities than differences in their cultural profiles. In one of the most recent and comprehensive literature review studies covering 98 US articles, 83 Japanese articles and 73 German articles (quantitative study with 232 HR managers including 107 Germans, 68 Japanese and 57 US); Barabel identifies twelve categories of socio-economic actors grouped into four categories that can influence a HRM policy:

1— Cultural factors: general characteristics of the country: Hofstede dimensions, Trompenaars dimension.

2— The socio-political factors: global economic system, social actors, demographic, educational system, industrial.

3— Economic factors: macroeconomic factors, market characteristics, relationships

4— Managerial factors: management principles, organizational structure, roles and significance of human resources for managers.

The HR policies of American and Japanese companies are at odds on many dimensions (recruitment and dismissal of employees, training, evaluations, promotion criteria, remuneration, communication within the company, decision-making, relationship between managers and their teams), whereas German practices are often between these two countries.

The Japanese model is characterized by potential identification during recruitment.

The French or Latin model that recruits its future leaders according to the notoriety of their studies.

The German model emphasizes professional experience and functional expertise

The multinational enterprise model is based on decentralized recruitment at the local level.

If in this same perspective, D'Iribarne (1989) talks about the distinction between three models of society, in his more recent work D'Iribarne (2006) returns to what he calls «the French strangeness» when he evokes the «employment problems, the school crisis or the difficulties of integrating immigrants». Thus, according to the author, each country, depending on its economic, cultural and social history, has very deeply rooted founding «myths» that weigh on the practices and behaviors of the different actors. In Benchmarking, Millot and Roulleau (2005) defend three broad «families» of models at the European level.

The Rhine model (Germany, Austria, Netherlands, Belgium, Sweden, Finland, Luxembourg...) characterized by a cooperative and partnership attitude of social relations.

The British model (England, Ireland, Cyprus, Malta, Denmark) is characterized by a weak role of the state

The Latin model (Greece, Spain, France, Portugal).

It should be stressed that Millot and Roulleau (2005) do not, however, speak in our opinion of the characteristic of the Latin model which is distinguished in the table by a strong implication of the role of the state and an indifference of public opinion, compared to other models. By contrast, the British model is characterized by a very weak role of the state and public involvement. (see Table 5)

The points discussed so far highlight the importance of the concept of culture in the conduct of HRM practices both in Morocco in comparison with other countries on the same continent as in other countries on other continents of the globe exaggerating the cultural differences between countries, because Brannen (1999), reacting to the idea of a culture considered static and impervious to change, states that a culture is evolutionary and homogeneous. Closer to us and in the same direction, Gelfand, Nishii and Raver (2007) speak of an open culture.

Tableau 3 les trois modèles européens de comparaison distinctive.

FEATURES	LATIN	RHINELAND	BRITISH
Union diversity	Plurality/Diver sity.	Unitary: Majority unions	Unitary
Trade Union Representation	Low unionization rate.	High rate of unionization.	Average rate of unionization.
Type of trade unionism	Activists/Ideol ogical Struggle.	Clients/ service.	Customer
Location of the trade	Interprofession al.	Branch / Region.	Business
Branch Orientation	Contractual.	Contractual.	Contractual
Mode of operation	The pre-negotiation strike.	Negotiation.	The negotiation
Nature of relationships	Conflictual.	Consensus / Co-management .	Compromise
Role of the state	Strong.	Weak.	Very low
Relations with policy makers	Low independence. Supposed hidden links.	Weak.	Strong average
Public Opinion	Indifferent.	Very involved.	Involved

Based on Millot and Roulleau, 2005, reported by Barabel (2008)

In the same year and in the sense of this open culture, researchers like Frimousse and Peretti (2007) not only confirm the importance of cultures from the history of different nations, different civilizations, or different religions, but enchant the meeting of these various cultures in nature to allow «hybridization and mixing» capable of «reconciling the universal and the particular». The authors of «La diversité ou la dialectique du semblable et du différend : Implication managériale» seem to position themselves as defenders of cultural diversity against any form of domination by one culture over another, supported by Friedman (2005) in Anglo-Saxon literature. Frimousse and Peretti (2007), have the merit of emphasizing the conciliatory character of the mixing of cultures, leading to the «discovery of the other» and not «reducing the other or subjecting it to domination». For the authors, some large prospective firms have already implemented this new form of cultural diversity management in their business strategies.

Frimousse and Peretti's work on cultural coexistence is somewhat similar to an earlier idea developed by Rosen (2003), about tribes that can coexist with other systems. Drawing on his experience as an anthropologist in Morocco, Rosen analyses several facets of the modem of Muslim society. For Rosen (2002), power can develop outside the barrel of a rifle. But it is considered legitimate only when the leader takes into account the primacy of social relations, especially tribal groups.

Rosen rejects the idea that tribes are only a stage in political evolution, but can coexist within other types of political systems. Rosen believes that Pipes was wrong to say in his 1983 book, The Way of God, that Islam, Islamic political power, and the expectations of good governance are set so high that no Muslim can reach. His assertion that "profound cultural change is not underway" in the Islamic world remains to be verified, but the author stands out for the audacity of his reflection — intuitive. The positive influence of culture on participatory management and HR practices is not only defended in French and Anglo-Saxon literature, but also in German literature.

Merkens' approach (1990). Franco-German study

The book references a Franco-German survey conducted by Merkens (1990), which appears in his article "Management interculturel." This research develops the concept of intercultural management based on an approach called "Learning by Doing." According to Merkens (1990), intercultural management aims to address or prevent issues arising from the diversity of native cultures influencing organizational decision-making. According to Merkens (1990), theories of future intercultural management would then have to articulate the components of «universal constructs» and «indigenous constructs», in a logic that he calls «Learning by doing». In other words, it will be a matter of reconciling the universal and the particular to take up the terms defended by Frimousse and Peretti (2007).

Among the defenders of culture as a vector of development and not a brake on, the book chose to quote Probst and Ulrich (1989), Rosen (2003). In a collective work thought global et management, the authors Probst and Ulrich note that companies have become complex and that management becomes also complex. Thus, according to the authors, the concept of comprehensive management allows for a change in attitudes and the image of a company perceived as an organization that only seeks profit.

Ulrich seems to be among the precursors who consider that the cultural dimension influencing the enterprise is a dynamic, evolutionary and not static, fixed dimension. He explains that businesses are the fruit of human values, intentions and actions. They are a cultural product. Crops are not static, but change more or less quickly. It is clear that we are witnessing a period of precipitated cultural upheaval. Probst and Ulrich confirm in this sense that: «The representation we have of the company thus bears the imprint of some previous experiences, acquired under other cultural conditions».

Joining the idea of Frimousse and Peretti on the coexistence of cultures for a hybrid management between the universal and the particular, Pras (2007) among the researchers who studied the relationship between business and the culture of Islam, use the term "harmonious coexistence" between the values of the company and those of Islam. Focusing more particularly on "the part of conviction" and that of "scientific analysis", in the academic works of some Muslim authors, Pras (2007), shows a "management vision" that evolves within the very ranks of Islamists (the militants), and the emergence of an «Islamist elite» more sensitive to modern management.

The contribution of the religious cultural dimension to the progress of management is demonstrated by Pras, in the successful example of the TQM (Total Quality Management) approach, conducted in Morocco by the company Thomson on behalf of «Islam et management, le rôle d'un univers de sens». The example of the Lafarge Group in Jordan has also succeeded in reconciling religious ideals and shared values.

Researchers prior to Pras (2007) had emphasized the importance of the approach (TQM). This is Iribane (2004), who had studied the approach (TQM) in Morocco, three years before Pras, and had also given the example of performance by the approach (TQM), in the Moroccan subsidiary STMicroelectronics. Performance in this subsidiary is due not to technical tools, D'Iribane (2004) specifies, but by moral precepts based on the good, honesty, exemplarity of the company director. "Good is all that is TQM, and evil is all that is not TQM".

In this undertaking, the researcher notes that "collective work does not prevent individualism" or that each person benefits from his own ideas. This management model based on the moral and religious values of Islam, and the exemplarity given by the company director, differs from the ordinary management of Moroccan companies where the hierarchical relationship reported by d'Iribarne (2004), with its interlocutors, is based on "mistrust and not shared values".

Nouiga's research work (2004), particularly on the cultural and contextual dimension that the book has willingly integrated into this chapter because of its epistemological importance, seems interesting to highlight. The most interesting contribution of Nouiga's work lies in his conclusion of the analysis of the different conceptual approaches. The staff is part of both the general (social and cultural) environment and the internal environment of the company. The focus is first on man in the organization and then on man in the environment. The general environment consists of culture, political system, economic system, technology (training, education and technology) and social organization. Among these components, "the culture is the most specific, and initiates the evolution that is slower and more difficult to change".

On the coexistence, conciliation between different cultures and different interests that Frimousse and Peretti (2007), Belkahia (2004)[7], chairman of the ethics commission and good governance, studying the confluence of corporate and state interests, proposes good governance as a system for reconciliation between government and business. Culture, religion, tradition and progress are widely used themes that have attracted the interest of many authors, researchers and theorists. The literature dealing with these subjects

---

[7] Belkahia R. (2004), "The accompanying measures for corporate governance in Morocco", international meeting on the theme: Corporate Governance, a lever for growth, 9 March 2004, at the Faculty of Law — Casablanca.

appears to be quite abundant. Research papers even talk about the intercultural dimension, diversity and international mobility of executives (AGEF Symposium, May 2007, at Casa).

In addition to French and Anglo-Saxon literature that deals with the importance of cultural influence on management practices, in a logic favourable or unfavourable to progress and development, an Arab-language literatureAfrican produces some research work on the cultural dimension in management. Researchers include D. Boubacar (2004), Eddakir (2003), Mohamed Nouiga (2003) and many others.

5.2.2. Culture in the Arab-Muslim approach

In his research work: Sociocultural factors and business creation in Guinea: doctoral thesis in administrative sciences, Boubacar (2004) refers to the influence of culture on Adler's behavior (1994). Boubacar considers that the common asset of the countries of dragons is in their trading traditions. However, not all societies with the same value system have reached the level of development of these countries. Among the many possible explanations is Weber's rationalism, which preaches a simple life on the social plane. This implies a large accumulation of capital, hence the savings that should not be used to lead a life of luxury, but rather to be reinvested for a continuous accumulation of wealth.

In his analysis of the foundational texts of Islam, Tribou (1995), in The Muslim Entrepreneur, identifies, based on surveys, a significant correlation between the religious ethics of Islam and entrepreneurship. Like Weber, Tribou draws several conclusions:

Islamic religious philosophy emphasizes individual freedom.

Islam promotes private property, encourages economic enrichment and the realization of well-being in accordance with religion.

Islam encourages industrial work as well as trade.

Islam accepts innovation, except in matters of religion, compensates for the prohibition of usury by the institution of Islamic banks in financing risk.

The Muslim entrepreneur in the sense of Tribou (1995), "finds in Islam the values, meaning and strength that animate it, spiritual nourishment for its economic activity." Boubacar (2004), which draws on the work of Wéber and Tribou (1995), considers that culture should not be seen as a handicap but rather as a structuring factor in organizational behaviour.

The work of theorists and researchers examining the influence of culture on HR management practices demonstrates that employees contribute a range of social, cultural, and religious knowledge to the organization as they participate in its development. In turn, the cultural dimension shapes employee behavior, which then influences HR practices. On this same question, the professor, teacher-researcher in Fez, Eddakir gives his reflections about the influence of culture on human resources management practices. Eddakir (2003), in fact highlights in an article entitled: «Study of the relationship between national culture and management practices: case of Morocco», that if the problems they encounter. Companies are the same all over the world, but the solutions offered differ from one cultural context to another.

It is precisely from the perspective of this cultural difference that Eddakir attempts to show that national culture influences management practices in a company. Eddakir considers that individuals "change businesses more easily than they do national cultures". The majority of empirical studies in this field (G. Hofstede, 1989; Rabanne, 1989) show that differences in attitudes and behaviour at work are explained by national cultural origins.

Based on the 1994 Hofsteth findings: living in a multicultural world, highlighting the four cultural dimensions (Individuality versus collectivism, large or small hierarchical distance, strong or weak control of uncertainty, masculinity versus femininity), Eddakir tries to show how these four dimensions are applicable to the Moroccan enterprise. He explains that the Moroccan culture is collectivist, masculine, with little control over uncertainty and great hierarchical distance, thus joining almost a year later the work of Kabasakal (2002) the influence of nine cultural dimensions on HR management practices.

In terms of entrepreneurship. Eddakir (2003) stresses that entrepreneurship has always been present in the Moroccan cultural context. Moreover, it is perceived by religion as "the foundation of human life activity". The author cites these verses in support: "Say, act, and God will see your actions, as well as the prophet and believers" (Sura Attawba, verse 105 Ayat). In the spirit of Eddakir, religion encourages action and initiative in all areas. He is joined in this by the work of Boubacar (2004). Unfortunately, and sometimes a misinterpretation of the Qur'an and tradition is the vehicle, according to Eddakir within companies, «negative» values such as the passive attitude towards future events. [8]

People think they have to endure the events as such because they are the manifestation of the divine will. According to Eddakir, this state of mind is embodied in the absence of any attempt to counteract unpredictable situations. This is what has enabled some authors (from outside the Arab-Muslim world) to support the idea that "the Muslim is subject to a particularly totalitarian religious law which restricts his freedom of action" (Tibou, 2004).

"We stress that this type of analysis is influenced by an ethnocentric (western) vision that attempts to interpret the sacred word (the

[8] B. Azzouzi, op. cit, p. 204.

Qur'an) without having the means or the necessary hindsight to do so." Wrote Eddakir (2003). In terms of the development of entrepreneurship within Moroccan society, Eddakir notes that its evolution took place in a quasi-annuity situation, under the paternalistic protection offered by the administration. As a result, this company could not be an entrepreneur (Oulalou 1998).

If the Moroccan company is perceived by its managers as a means of generating profit, neglecting other dimensions of the business, it would be inappropriate to speak in this context of corporate citizenship.

Overall, Eddakir highlights that Moroccan companies face several weaknesses—many stemming from conservative values and outdated beliefs. Unlike proactive, innovative leaders, traditional leaders tend to favor maintaining the status quo, which is perceived as more comfortable. This perspective on the influence of culture on HR practices is supported by other research, such as Nouiga (2003), whose doctoral thesis, Driving Change Through Quality in a Socio-Cultural Context, offers a detailed analysis.

CONCLUSION

The question of whether culture can influence global behaviour, the book has shown that culture can exert both a negative and a positive influence according to cross approaches in the literature of different English-speaking and Arabic-speaking researchers.

Those who advocate the negative influence of culture consider that culture and religion are often misinterpreted. The reactive profile of business leaders, and their passivity to take initiatives are obstacles that hinder economic growth and sustainable development.

In contrast to this current of thought, the proponents of the positive influence of culture on human behavior argue that culture is dynamic evolving towards human progress and constitutes a vector of adaptability to the world and its sustainable development

This positive aspect of the influence of culture makes it possible to base and defend further the emergence of a new paradigm of cultural leadership capable of saving the sick world from management.

CHAPTER 6
HOW CAN CULTURE SAVE THE WORLD?

The man of culture must be
an inventor of souls.
- Aimé Césaire

Culture and intelligence,
It's like parachutes.
When you don't have one, you crash.
- Dis La Rochefoucauld

Introduction

This chapter approaches cultural intelligence from a cross-literature perspective, highlighting how it can contribute to saving the world. The book discusses how both American and French approaches can shed light on this issue. Additionally, a multicultural approach enriches both anglophone and francophone perspectives. The book also emphasizes the role of artificial intelligence, whose interaction with cultural intelligence enhances our understanding of culture's potential to address global challenges. Finally, the chapter concludes with an analysis of cultural change, outlining three essential steps for successful transformation.

If culture can save the world, it is important to know how.

The book has the merit of analysing the idea that culture can save the world through cultural intelligence (61), artificial intelligence (62) and cultural change (63). These concepts are discussed in turn in the following paragraphs.

Section 6.1 — Cultural intelligence to save the world

6.1.1. Why cultural intelligence

6.1.2. Cultural intelligence in literature

6.1.3. The American approach to cultural intelligence

6.1.4. The French approach to cultural intelligence

6.1.5. Multicultural approach to cultural intelligence

Section 6.2 — Artificial and cultural intelligence to save the planet

6.2.1. The contribution of artificial intelligence to cultural intelligence

6.2.2. Interactions between artificial intelligence and cultural intelligence

Section 6.3 — Cultural change to save the world

6.3.1. The meaning of cultural change

6.3.2. Cultural change through innovation

6.3.3. Cultural change in stages

6.3.4. Cultural change through processes

Section 6.1 — Cultural intelligence to save the world

We propose to deal with the primary question of why cultural intelligence and what its contribution throughout the world (6.1.1) before explaining cultural intelligence in literature (6.1.2.). We then chose to exploit and intersect different approaches to cultural intelligence. We retain the American approach and show its characteristics (613). We then examine the French approach and its historical perception of cultural intelligence (614). Between the

Anglo-American and French-speaking approach, we sought to study a multicultural approach to cultural intelligence in order to have a global perception emanating from different civilizations on the cultural intelligence that could save the sick world of management (615).

6.1.1. Why cultural intelligence

To the question of why cultural intelligence and what its contribution is to human life, the answer offered by the book is that cultures are everywhere in the world (regions and countries and companies), to interact with individuals in their requests for sensitivity and adaptability. Earley and Elaine Mosakowski (2004) argue that people who fully embody the habits of their native culture may appear to be the most foreign when they enter another culture. On the other hand, people who are slightly detached from their own culture adapt better to the habits of a foreign guest because they see themselves as natural observers and feel more comfortable adapting to them.

In the context of this analysis, Earley and Mosakowski (2004) recommend cultivating cultural intelligence through a systematic process: first, assess one's strengths and weaknesses; next, undertake targeted training to address shortcomings; then, apply this knowledge to adapt behavior; and finally, reevaluate the effectiveness of the training.

Because the cultural intelligence that can save the world is part of a change management strategy. On the question of how to change culture, today's challenges require a culture that promotes anticipation and intelligence. What to do, for example, if your company approaches its current environment with delay and values from another era? What if your company continues to adopt inconsistent practices and behaviors in the face of a changing new strategy?

Non-intelligent organizations adopt counterproductive flat structures and clutter up with unnecessary hierarchies, slowing the flow of information, distorting decisions, and depriving general management of the reality of the field. On the other hand, intelligent organizations with pragmatism show an ability to analyse their environment, perceive weak signals of upcoming threats or new opportunities to seize, and design effective responses adapted.

This is a real change management problem, because change is part of the organization's DNA. Transforming a company culture to save the world requires deep reflection and mastery of change. The strategic approach, or strategic intelligence, to change must be based on a careful preparation to shake up employees' habits and change their way of being.

From this point of view of cultural adaptability, it would not be useless to suggest some simple practices towards others and their environment, which can help develop cultural intelligence (Sources : cultural intelligence, David A. Livermore, Grand Rapid, Michigan : Baker Academic, 2009):

. Go to a restaurant from another culture.

. Invite and visit people from other cultures.

. Walk into an international grocery store.

. Learn a new language.

. Ask how to greet in their culture of the other

. Attend celebrations and cultural events.

. Be aware of important issues in other countries.

. Look for the invisible. Ask the question: how is the.

Culture influencing this behaviour?

. Study the scriptures with people from different cultures.

. Beware of the cultural content of your language. Seek to know

if the other person understands the concepts and expressions you use.

. Observe non-verbal language.

. Find a cultural guide.

. Observe behavioral, interactions. Try to imitate.

. Join multicultural teams and groups.

. Travel abroad.

. Attend someone's wedding ceremony from another culture.

. Read the local newspaper when you travel.

. Ask, ask, ask.

In the light of the definitions provided by the Anglo-Saxon researchers Earley and Mosakowski (2004), there is a suggestion for a general definition of cultural intelligence that can be understood in its strategic dimension. It can be defined both as an exercise of intercultural skills and as the production of cultural information useful for sustainable development and the survival of the planet. On the one hand, however, it should be stressed that cultural intelligence is not merely a contribution of knowledge about cultures or cultural expertise, because cultural intelligence includes cultural expertise without being limited to it. On the other hand, cultural intelligence is not merely intercultural competence because intercultural competence does not necessarily imply the ability to produce strategic information for the organization. Cultural intelligence includes, but is not limited to, intercultural competence. The strategic dimension of cultural intelligence embodied by intercultural skills and cultural information thus contributes to the security, sustainability and sustainable development of the organization's activities. It is therefore appropriate to think that cultural intelligence meets somewhere here and there, economic intelligence in terms of security, surveillance and influence to the extent that economic intelligence cannot develop without cultural intelligence. Similarly, without economic intelligence, cultural intelligence loses its strategic dimension.

While intercultural skills are as important as language skills to work in an international environment, it should be noted that a linguistic competence does not necessarily mean an intercultural competence, as well as a technical competence can lose its effectiveness without intercultural adaptation. The cultural expertise that produces cultural information allows to decipher the particularity of a situation and the complexity of its environment, but cultural intelligence is not limited to knowledge and make people interact in an organization. Because the collection, analysis and processing of cultural information must follow a well-defined strategy. This conceptual framework can be visualized as the intersection of three key elements—economic intelligence, intercultural skills, and cultural expertise—as illustrated in Figure 1.

Figure 1 cultural intelligence at the intersection of the three concepts

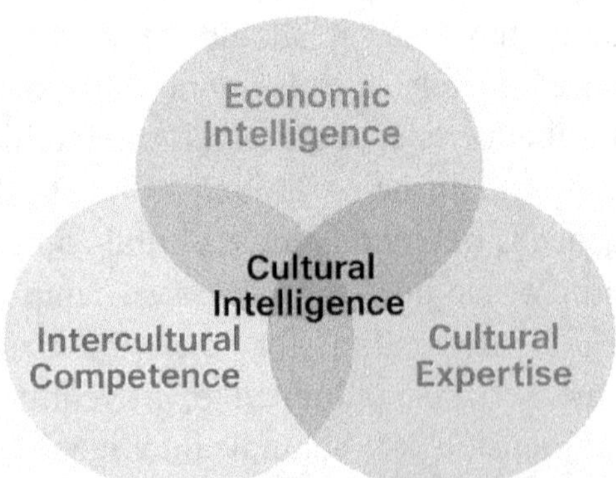

6.1.2. Cultural intelligence in literature

The book reviews various perspectives in the literature on the sources of cultural intelligence and explores whether culture can distort human nature. It then discusses a strategic approach to developing cultural intelligence.

Sources of cultural intelligence

American researchers Earley and Mosakowski (2004) adopted in the Harvard Business Review HBR three sources of cultural intelligence: head, body and heart. The cognitive head means learning about beliefs, habits and taboos of foreign cultures. The Body means acceptance of the world of other cultures. The Heart means that to adapt to a new culture, it is necessary to overcome its obstacles and delays.

Then, from an individual perspective, researchers Early and ANG (2004) argue that cultural intelligence would be the ability of an individual to adapt to a new or unfamiliar cultural environment. From an enterprise perspective, researchers Early and ANG (2003) believe that cultural intelligence would be a harmonious set of behaviours, policies, and procedures that allow managers to embrace cultural differences. One of the great challenges is to choose the cultural dimensions that aim to build a cultural competence within the company. Several intercultural experts have chosen these dimensions and proposed models to build a unique approach to cultural intelligence.

Hofstede's four-dimensional model is concerned, for example, with distance from power, distance from the community compared to individuality, distance from femininity compared to masculinity, avoidance and uncertainty, as well as short-term versus long-term. Lewis' three-dimensional model (1996) shows that humans are divided into 3 categories not according to their nationality or religion, but according to their behaviour. Having worked in more than 20 of the 135 countries he visited, Lewis (1996) concluded that the three profiles he established were linear, active, multi-active and reactive.

Meyer's model (2014) prefers to provide eight fundamental axes that constitute the source of intercultural conflict. Each of these axes, which make it possible to understand interactions in business, is described by Meyer between two diametrically opposite ends. The author wonders whether these interactions are simple and clear and require little context, or are they based on an elaborate context that conveys profound messages.

• On the evaluation axis, the author asks whether negative feedback should be given directly or indirectly and discreetly?

• On the axis of leading a team, are people from the same group equal, or do they prefer hierarchy?

• On the decision axis, the question is whether decisions are made by consensus, or on a top-down scale.

• On the trust axis, do people trust each other because they know each other well, or rather because they work well together?

• On the line of disagreement, the author wonders if disagreements are expressed clearly, or people prefer to - they avoid confrontations?

• On the planning axis, interactions in Meyer's (2014) model involve whether time is perceived as absolute linear points or as a flexible whole.

• On the line of convincing the other, the recurring question is whether people like to hear each other and tell situations, or prefer to receive detailed explanations

The eight axes outlined by Erin Meyer (2014) allow to set the different steps to be taken and develop individual and organizational skills in order to implement cultural intelligence. The first step is to develop awareness to understand similarities and differences. Understanding differences on the individual level can lead to a high degree of self-awareness and self-regulation, and a cultural approach that is not based on judgment.

Then, it is necessary to build a knowledge base, understand the norms, differences and cultural dynamics. Subsequently, communication and management skills must be developed in the context of these differences. In other words, it will be about developing the ability to change style, which can be a difficult skill to develop because it requires a great openness of mind on values and beliefs. This ability to change styles allows us not only to look at the problems that arise from cultural differences, but above all to reveal the potential forces that can arise from these differences.

Today, to learn how to navigate between cultures (Diateino, 2016), the map of cultural differences by Meyer (2014), offers a practical guide of 8 criteria, at the heart of an analytical grid that has proven itself in the field as:

1. Communication in a low context or high context?

2. Direct or indirect negative feedback?

3.Persuasion by theory or facts first?

4. Leadership, hierarchical or egalitarian?

5.Consensus decision or summit?

6. Trust by the head or the heart?

7. Confrontation disagreement or not?

8. Linear time schedules or flexible time?

The strengths inherent in cultural differences highlight the value of diverse perspectives, voices, and opinions. Many organizations recognize that such diversity can be a significant asset in problem-solving, developing new products, fostering innovation, and conducting international business.

Managers always ultimately need to understand human nature and personality differences for their business to succeed. Those in the 21st century need to embrace richer work styles, able to decode cultural differences in order to work effectively with colleagues, customers, suppliers and communities around the world. Hence the importance of cultural intelligence as one of the fundamental transversal skills on which todays and tomorrow's business should focus.

From this point of view, cultural intelligence can be stimulated by four levers:

1. Knowledge that aims at the understanding and challenge of cultural differences.

2. Interpretation that is the ability to interpret cultural signals and the degree of attention given to other cultures.

3. Perseverance to adapt to others and overcome intercultural difficulties.

4. Behaviour that allows for appropriate intercultural conduct with another culture. Each of the four levers stimulating cultural intelligence requires some pertinent questions, namely:

1. On Knowledge, the following questions should be asked

Do I speak any other language than French?

Do I know the basic cultural values of many other cultures?

Do I know how to deal with conflicts in another culture?

Do I know the roles and expectations of men and women from another culture?

Do I know the differences in beliefs of Christians from other cultures?

2. On interpretation, the following questions are interesting

Am I aware of what I need to know about a culture that is not familiar to me?

Am I aware of how my cultural background influences me in religion?

Can I determine what I need to know about a culture before interacting with people in that culture?

Do I compare my preconceived ideas about a culture with what I experience in my intercultural interactions?

Am I looking for appropriate ways to talk about my faith in an intercultural context?

3. On perseverance, the following questions should be asked:

Do I like intercultural interactions that are new to me?

Do I prefer staying with a local when travelling to another culture than staying in a hotel?

Do I prefer to eat local food when visiting a new place?

Do I enjoy spending time with people who are not of the same faith as me?

Am I confident that I could be effective in intercultural ministry?

4. On behavior, the following questions should be asked:

Do I change my way of expressing myself (accent, tonne, expressions) according to the Cultural context?

Do I use pauses and silences differently depending on the cultural context?

Do I display different behaviour according to the specificities of the local culture?

Do I change the way I greet (shaking hands, nodding, movement) according to culture?

Do I change the way I express my enthusiasm and empathy according to Cultural context?

The cultural intelligence stimulated by the four levers raised (knowledge, interpretation, perseverance, behavior) allows to face different situations of intercultural friction with actors of different nationalities. Culture thus becomes an analytical tool through which one person looks at and judges the other. The natural tendency of every individual is to understand the other in relation to his own culture, establishing a form of hierarchy between cultures. This hierarchy is the result of an intercultural comparison which tends to reinforce the cultural distance between individuals, groups and countries. Does this natural tendency to perceive the other in relation to one's own culture mean that culture is opposed to nature. In other words, culture can either serve man or distort man.

Can culture distort man?

The subject of cultural expertise refers directly to notions of nature and culture that are traditionally opposed. To nature as "what is animal in us"; is it permissible to oppose culture (which would make us human, which would differentiate us from animals), and all that comes under education and civilization (work, art, politics, language, religion...)? Culture, seen from this angle, can denature man as it is the process by which man draws him away from nature by denying his instincts and imposing rules of discipline and constraint.

However, is there really a nature of man that would oppose his culture? Is not man a whole, a mixture of nature and culture? What if the nature of man was to become a being of culture? Can culture distort man when the very idea of a human nature contains a cultural dimension? The book suggests explaining the two opposite notions.

The proponents of the first approach believe that culture only denatures man and removes him from his natural state, since culture is defined as the transformation of nature. Rousseau believes that, on the origin of the inequality of men, man was naturally good, culture has transformed him into a bad man, jealous, envious, greedy. Diderot describes the way of life of the wild man, close to nature, who lives in peace and out of any feeling of possessiveness. Thus women, the subject of discord in our civilization, belong to no one, marriage is only a cultural invention that plunges us into the illusion that the other belongs to us when by nature we are fundamentally free. For Rousseau and Diderot, we would be here in a nostalgia of a lost human nature, corrupted by the culture that is perpetuated by the transmission of education. Culture distances man from his true nature, and may even, as Nietzsche thinks, constitute the great misfortune of man, preventing his deep nature to express itself.

Conversely, Jean-Paul Sartre's existentialism posits that humans have no fixed nature; rather, existence precedes essence. For Sartre, qualities like shyness are not innate but are the result of individual choices and actions. If humans lack a predetermined nature, then culture does not distort them—it actively constitutes who they are.

So, man is only culture, because nature pushes him to eat, but the act of eating is completely soaked in culture created by the food industry and the customs of his country. Is it permissible to infer from Sartre's thought that the nature of man lies in his culture, because in reality man by definition opposes the animal, and differentiates himself by his culture which is part of man by essence?

Is it also permissible to say that man is naturally cultural and that, the more he is a being of culture, the more he conforms to his nature? The thought of Aristotle goes in the same direction of the existence of man who will allow to develop to become a cultural being.

However, if the nature of man is opposed to the animal, it should not be overlooked that the animal in us is also part of human nature, and that many perversions actually come from the culture that makes man can be inhuman.

Pascal's perspective highlights an inhuman aspect of human nature rooted in self-interest and hypocrisy. He argued that humans are fundamentally motivated by self-preservation and often act hypocritically to protect their interests, rather than following reason and virtue. However, Pascal believed that through virtuous friendship—an idea emphasized by Aristotle—individuals can transcend hypocritical tendencies and cultivate genuine moral relationships.

To this inhuman aspect that characterizes man by nature, wanting to protect his interests through force and power of domination, the book has chosen to write a chapter that will be developed at the end of the work. The book tries to show in this last chapter how to deal with leaders who exercise a power of domination over human beings. The book is distinguished by its merit of valuing the emergence of a new, more humanistic cultural leadership transcending all nations, and capable of safeguarding the human species and saving the planet.

A strategic approach to cultural intelligence

For Benjamin Pelletier (2012), intercultural management trainer and head of the economic war school, author of several literary narratives, cultural intelligence is a new notion that is quite floating and blurred. Between cultural intelligence, as the intelligence of cultures in its broad concept and the intelligence of cultural industries in its very narrow concept, Benjamin Pelletier (2012) proposes a general definition of cultural intelligence, addressing it in its strategic dimension. The author has defined it as both an exercise of intercultural competences and a production of cultural information useful to the activity of a public or private organization. As a faculty for deciphering the complexity of cultures, cultural intelligence is, according to the author, at the root of economic intelligence.

Cultural intelligence, in the context of strategic change, encompasses both cultural expertise and intercultural competence, serving the needs of public or private organizations. According to Pelletier (2012), the term can be understood broadly—as knowledge of cultures—or narrowly—as related to cultural industries.

Cultural expertise produces knowledge, information about the mental, societal, demographic, economic, political and historical context of an organization. This cultural information allows us to decipher the singularity of a situation and the complexity of its environment. As a result, cultural intelligence is not limited to the skills and know-how of people but responds to a specific need in order to achieve a certain result. Because the analysis and processing of cultural information must follow a well-defined strategy.

The author points out, however, that cultural intelligence is not merely a source of knowledge about cultures, but includes and goes beyond cultural expertise. Similarly, cultural intelligence is not merely intercultural competence but includes and is not limited to intercultural competence. Let us take up the three notions advanced by Benjamin Pelletier (2012), relating to the strategic dimension of cultural intelligence, intercultural competence and its expertise.

For the author, the two notions: intercultural skills and cultural information are included in their strategic dimension insofar as they contribute to the security of the organization. Cultural intelligence meets economic intelligence (security, surveillance, influence) in a relationship as essential as that of roots. Thus, economic intelligence cannot develop without cultural intelligence.

For the author, cultural intelligence must be perceived in close solidarity with economic intelligence. Both are two sides of the same coin. Without economic intelligence, cultural intelligence loses its strategic dimension. Similarly, without cultural intelligence, economic intelligence is uprooted from its operational dimension. Intercultural skills are as essential as language skills to work in an international environment.

Intercultural skills enable individuals to adapt their thinking and behavior, reducing the risk of cultural conflict. These skills often outweigh technical or language abilities, as proficiency in language alone does not guarantee intercultural competence, and technical skills may falter without intercultural flexibility. Pelletier (2012) asserts that intercultural competencies are central to international success—they must take precedence over other skills.

These non-technical skills are neither a varnish nor an accessory more in the perception of the company internationally: it is necessary to think and consider them in their essential and fundamental dimension, whatever the degree of technicity of the activity pursued.

6.1.3. The American approach to cultural intelligence

In the American approach, cultural intelligence refers to the cultural quotient to the extent that it is known as the cultural quotient (QC) (cultural quotient). The concept of cultural quotient was developed through research by Ang Soon, Linn Van Dyne and Christopher Earley at the beginning of the new millennium (2002-2003). In his book Research in, Organizational Behavior, Earley (2002), he defines cultural intelligence as “the ability of a person to adapt when interacting with other people from different cultural regions.”

In a 2004 article published in the Harvard Business Review, Christopher Earley and Elaine Mosakowski attribute to cultural intelligence "the seemingly natural ability of a stranger to interpret the unknown and ambiguous gestures of someone like her compatriots." From this perspective, it is possible to argue that the cultural quotient (QC) "measures" an individual's ability to function effectively in a multicultural environment. "Employers and organizations use QC as a means to foster tolerance and enhance intercultural interaction."

Cultural intelligence abroad can be a decisive factor in the success of public or private enterprise transactions, for example. From this point of view, the question that now arises is whether cultural intelligence (QC) is just a fashionable business concept. Does cultural intelligence, which is the cultural quotient, not come from another quotient called intellectual quotient (IQ) and another quotient called emotional quotient (EQ)? While cultural intelligence is the ability to adapt to different cultural contexts, failure of a transaction means that in 80% of cases the fault lies with a cultural misstep. For example, the long-standing use of Intelligence Quotient (IQ) tests can help an individual in an organization measure their ability to solve problems that are often related to intelligence. On the other hand, the emotional quotient EQ would be the ability of an individual to empathize with another to adapt to his environment.

The book proposes to explain the contributions and criticisms of this American approach to cultural intelligence based on the work done by Benjamin Pelletier in 2013. Cultural intelligence, or cultural intelligence (IQ), has become a fashionable topic in the United States for about ten years. The expression was popularized by Christopher Earley and Soon Ang (2003), in their book Culturale Intelligence: Individual Interactions Across Cultures, then later by other authors, such as David Livermore (2009) in Leading with cultural intelligence; the new secret to success.

This US approach aims to emphasize the concept of Cultural Quotient (QC), as well as the Intellectual Quotient (IQ) and the most recent Emotional Quotient (EQ). Each of these quotients is used to measure the degree of intellectual, emotional and cultural intelligence. Cultural intelligence would thus be the third and final term of a triangle structure to assess an individual's ability to cope with the complexity of the world. Cultural intelligence is thus conceived, in a cross-over between cognitive psychology and cultural anthropology.

The main idea is to measure (the quotient) of cultural intelligence on a scale comprising several degrees and scientific tests to determine the individual's cultural quotient. This quotient determines a person's ability to use their intelligence in a foreign cultural context. That is, to measure its capacity to adapt to its complex environment.

This capacity for adaptation is evaluated, measured, put into quotient on a scale, analyzed with scientific rigor. But from the definitions quoted above, it seems difficult to grasp the difference between cultural intelligence and mere intercultural competence. The work presents the cultural intelligence produced by the triangulation of the three quotients: intellectual, cultural and emotional in the following sketches.

Sketch of the triangulation of cultural intelligence.

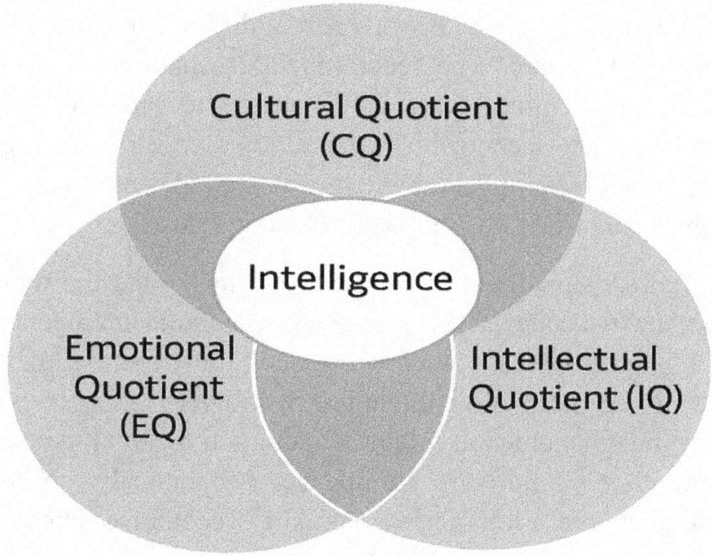

The criticism of the American approach to cultural intelligence is that it has reduced cultural intelligence to its psychological dimension in the sense of the intellectual capacity of the individual in a foreign context or with strangers. This is a very reductive view of the sense of intelligence that also refers to intelligence. Seen from this intelligence angle, intelligence would also be the ability to collect rare and useful information in the interest of a public or private organization. Information is used to protect the state's security against terrorism, for example, and to exploit information obtained illegally by intelligence services (interceptions and espionage).

Intelligence may in this sense correspond to the ability to collect, analyze and communicate rare and useful information. If this utility has an economic purpose, then it will fall under the economic intelligence. Rather than reducing intelligence to the faculty of the mind, it is appropriate to first discuss the dynamics of economic and cultural issues together. Then the intellectual capacity will intervene to integrate this dynamic. However, it is difficult to think of both economy and culture. The reason is that economic intelligence specialists lack cultural knowledge or fail to integrate cultural factors into their technical analyses. Also, cultural intelligence specialists lack economic knowledge, or are only interested in the economic issue when it is related to cultural industries.

The purpose of intelligence is to be able to initiate the dynamic between the two concepts of intelligence: economic intelligence and cultural intelligence. In other words, cultural expertise makes it possible to reach economic intelligence, without seeking to explain an economic phenomenon solely by a cultural factor (for example: «the countries of northern Europe are economically successful because they are Protestant»). Similarly, economic intelligence allows for the integration of cultural expertise, without seeking to reduce cultures to economic issues (for example: "We must abandon cultural practices that have no economic value"). Cultural intelligence would thus become the meeting point between economic intelligence and cultural expertise. After this essay on the US approach to concepts related to cultural intelligence (cultural quotient, intellectual quotient and emotional quotient), the words of the book explain what adaptation of cultural intelligence means in the French approach.

6.1.4. The French approach to cultural intelligence

The book attempts to justify here, in what extent the French approach of cultural intelligence differs from the American approach, based on the work done by Benjamin Pelletier in 2013.

According to Benjamin Pelletier (2013), the French approach to cultural intelligence is based on the meeting between theorists and practitioners of economic intelligence, but in a French way. The French approach interprets cultural intelligence through France's unique cultural and historical lens, within a legal framework. Unlike the American focus on psychological profiling and measurement, the French perspective, influenced by anthropology and ethnology, emphasizes avoiding essentialist stereotypes and the risks of rigid categorization inherent in overly scientific approaches, as noted by Pelletier (2013). This French approach is, however, facing two challenges:

1 — to overcome the pre-existing in France between the world of economics and that of the humanities.

2— (Re), to value useful information through the dissemination of information exploited in colonial times, and sometimes despised by disinterested knowledge, It should be noted that economic intelligence was inspired by the concepts and tools of the intelligence services and then developed its autonomy and specificity. In the same way, cultural intelligence has developed by drawing on concepts and tools from the military field, thus giving useful information its full meaning.

However, it must also be stressed that cultural intelligence is nourished by intercultural management in order to broaden its field of action to the strategic issues facing companies. However, in these two areas (impact of culture in military operations and intercultural management), Pelletier (2013) noted a lack of visibility in research. Indeed, the reflection on cultural and intercultural issues in military operations experienced a slowdown after the colonial era. Moreover, according to Pelletier (2013), no French researcher in this field of international importance has emerged who is more visible in terms of research and innovation in the Netherlands or in North America. Pelletier (2015), gives the example of General Dominique Gérard, Head of the Department of Cultural Intelligence and Economic Information Research at the Ministry of Economy, Finance and Industry (MINEFI), on the problem of cultural intelligence through different experiences with African countries and especially Senegal.

n 2015, Pelletier examined the concept of intercultural competence, referencing the report by France's interdepartmental delegation for economic intelligence (D2IE) titled Analyse, intelligence culturelle, un pas en avant pour l'intelligence culturelle. This report, building on previous versions from 2011 and 2012, highlights that "intercultural incompetence is a major risk factor in international relations, whereas understanding a partner country's culture is an effective means of prevention," especially in the context of economic security

This report, according to Pelletier (2015), is a first step towards valuing intercultural competence in the same way and rank as technical skills in risk management. However, the author notes that there is unfortunately in France an imbalance between technical and non-technical skills, favouring the former to the detriment of the latter. According to the author, this discrepancy is explained by the weakness of the French universalist model which continues to neglect the importance of cultural factors and thus displays a poor intercultural culture. The publication of the new benchmark for economic intelligence came to correct the mismatch between cultural and technical factors. The new framework aims to enhance the recognition of cultural intelligence by recommending the institution of a specialized master's degree on cultural intelligence. The objective is to control the activities of international companies and the risks associated with intercultural issues.

The cross-cultural issues introduced in economic intelligence training should not be limited to management alone, because according to Pelletier (2015), intercultural management is too restricted to include security issues, monitoring and influence of economic intelligence. The author proposes the use of an expression that is both broader and more precise: cultural intelligence. The ability to identify, collect, analyse and disseminate cultural information for an economic purpose. For example, according to

Pelletier (2015), this new benchmark allows a more than complementary approach to economic intelligence. Indeed, to speak of economic intelligence without the cultural dimension means to reduce economic internationalization.

Similarly, talking about cultural intelligence without security and economic development would amount to reducing the cultural dimension as a simple general culture. For Pelletier (2015), this is a first step towards cultural intelligence because economic intelligence specialists must develop intercultural skills, and experts in intercultural management must integrate economic intelligence issues. The author thus recommends three ways of measuring cultural abilities to improve cultural intelligence, through three levels of understanding:

1. Knowledge that aims at a general understanding of the culture for example, know how to greet, how to negotiate and communicate with the interlocutor to adapt to local customs and avoid offending partners.

2. Skills that are used to find ways of building cultural bridges with the interlocutor:

3. Attitudes that mean taking an interest in the partner's culture and discovering his country's history make it easy to build long-term relationships.

Also, the centre of cultural intelligence. (Cultural Intelligence Center) , as the authority figure for training and certification of cultural intelligence (CQ), proposes an updated definition: "Cultural intelligence is an essential part of standing out in today's globalized world of artificial intelligence, machine learning and innovation. It is the ability to build relationships, work effectively with people from different cultural backgrounds and project beyond existing notions of cultural sensitivity and awareness. Through cultural intelligence, you will be able to use cultural differences strategically to propose more innovative solutions."

The Cultural Guidance Centre describes the cultural quotient in four principles developed by Ang Soon and Linn Van Dyne (2008) in their book entitled: Handbook of Cultural Intelligence:

- CQ Drive or motivational cultural quotient: this is a person's level of interest, persistence and confidence to function in diverse cultural contexts.
- CQ Knowledge or cognitive cultural quotient: this is a level of a person's understanding of the similarity and difference of cultures.
- CQ Strategy or metacognitive cultural quotient: this is a measure by which a person plans, remains conscious in practice, and verifies his or her multicultural interactions.
- QC Behavioural action or cultural quotient: this is the flexibility and ability of a person to use a wide range of behaviours and skills appropriately in multicultural encounters.

6.1.5. Multicultural approach to cultural intelligence

The book highlights four main aspects of cultural intelligence: multiculturalism, which is nourished by diversity, communication and leadership.

Multiculturalism, emerging from the rise of new technologies and globalization, now crosses borders at an unprecedented pace. This phenomenon results in a unique blend of cultures that fosters mutual learning and coexistence as a shared human species on Earth. Essentially, multiculturalism is the art of living in peace and understanding, promoting fraternal relationships rather than conflict. It is widely acknowledged that understanding other cultures improves work efficiency, influences conflict resolution, and shapes the future. Cultural intelligence (CI) is a skill set that combines knowledge, attitudes, and behaviors, enabling individuals to accurately interpret cross-cultural situations and engage effectively within diverse environments. Successful cross-cultural collaboration requires careful management to prevent misunderstandings and frustrations both within teams and with external partners.

The diversity that nurtures multiculturalism at a personal or professional level allows us to learn something new and cultivate an exchange between different people. As a factor of progress, cultural intelligence helps us understand how to diversify our environment and get out of the comfort zone. In a world of ever-widening horizons, the globalization of trade and technological advances of recent decades have fostered an era where cultural differences have become vitally important for leaders, directors and managers. Each has characteristics coloured by its nationality which can alter the fusion of corporate cultures. As business environments have changed, organizations have had to create multicultural teams made up of people from different nationalities.

Communication, strengthening multiculturalism, remains an indispensable element of cultural intelligence. Because talking to each other and listening to the other becomes the effect, the pillar of cultural intelligence. The multinationals integrate this aspect of communication of cultural intelligence into that of their corporate culture. Coca-Cola, for example, has already integrated cultural intelligence into its new activities. Google uses it to evaluate the most qualified candidates around the world. McDonald's trains its executives to expand business abroad, in accordance with the principles of cultural intelligence.

Leadership rooted in multiculturalism is vital to the development of cultural intelligence, especially for entrepreneurs and multinational corporations. Members of such organizations often experience a sense of belonging akin to family. Their productivity increases under humanistic, inclusive leadership capable of guiding teams toward shared goals and values. This aspect of humanistic and transcultural leadership, capable of safeguarding humanity and the planet, will be explored further in the final chapter.

Taking up the updated definition of cultural intelligence proposed by the Centre de l'intelligence culturelle (Cultural Intelligence Center), the book quotes in its first paragraph that: "Cultural intelligence is an essential part of standing out, artificial intelligence, machine learning and innovation."

This definition shows that the use of cultural intelligence makes it possible to stand out from artificial intelligence in a globalized world. It is therefore necessary to analyse the content and issues of artificial intelligence in relation to cultural intelligence.

Section 6.2. Artificial and cultural intelligence to save the planet

In this section, the book try to show the contribution of artificial intelligence to cultural intelligence (6.2.1) and explore the interaction between the two intelligences. (6.2.2).

6.2.1. The contribution of artificial intelligence to cultural intelligence

The importance of artificial intelligence was highlighted by a study conducted by Oracle in 2020. In this study, Andrey Armyagov and shutterstcok (2021) consider that employees would trust robots more than their managers. From this point of view, it is to show the contribution of artificial intelligence to intelligence cultural and to explore the extent of interaction between the tow intelligences.

Artificial intelligence helps to build a smart business. It enables them to automate their operations, drive innovation and make the right decisions safely. Faced with the impact of the pandemic on the world of work in terms of stress, isolation, and work/life balance,

76% of people surveyed by Oracle (Oracle AI@Work Sudy 2020) believe their employer should do more to protect their mental health.

40% of them report that they face daily stressors in their work, such as pressure to meet performance standards, routine and tedious tasks. 35% of teleworkers say they work 10 hours more per week than before. 85% of employees say that their mental health problems at work have had an impact on their home life. In the end, 40% of employees say their productivity has decreased and they are making worse decisions at work. The Oracle study shows that 82% of employees surveyed think robots will support their mental health more than humans.

In general, the Oracle study is a continuation of weak signals that have been perceived for some time. The interest of the study lies in why employees believe in the potential of robots. Indeed, employees prefer to talk to robots about their mental health problems because their opinion is not biased and the robots provide quick answers to their questions. The fact that a robot does not judge employees and keeps its secrets for itself is seen as an advantage over a human being, because what matters to employees is having answers to their questions about their mental health.

In terms of innovation, Olivier Ezratty spoke in 2011 in «Les dessous de la bataille entre Apple et Google», a very detailed comparative analysis between the management systems of Apple, Microsoft and Google. Different axes are reviewed: the personality of the leaders, the mission of the organization, the product, research and development, acquisitions and recruitment. The personality of the head of the firm is present throughout the organization and management.

Both at Apple and Microsoft, senior employees are nostalgic for the past decades when they had more facilities, initiative, autonomy and risk-taking. The nostalgic phenomenon does not seem to interest

Google, a company younger than the other two with only a dozen years of existence against 35 and 33 for Microsoft and Apple.

	Apple	Microsoft	Google
Revenue (last 12 moths)	47389	59 544	24,916
Employees (estimation)	40 000	90 000	22 000
Revenue / employee ($m)	1,18	0,66	
Executives	Steve Jobs	Steve Ballmer	Eric Schmidt, Larry Page, Sergei Brin
% R&D of revenue	2,82%	13,70%	12%
Patents filed (USPTO)	3 206	15227	405

At Apple, for example, company director Steve Jobs had integrated all dimensions of the products, and assumed the role that Bill Gates played when he was head of a business before 2000, but the latter was less complete than Steve Jobs and lacked affinities. On the other hand, Steve Jobs in search of perfection focused on a value system that allowed him to refuse a sale to the Pentagon. People who disappoint him (from the technician to the top manager) can be fired for the slightest breach. The big question is how a company evolves after the departure of its founder and how to create leaders within its company.

At Microsoft, the company director Steve Ballmer who replaced Bill Gates in 2000 was very attached to Microsoft more than Bill Gates and showed great charisma and empathy. Steve Ballmer was not a product man, but rather a classic business leader of the «Corporate America» who mastered more numbers and sales than supply strategy. The quantitative, like the Excel spreadsheet and the quantitative dashboards considered as the daily lot of any manager, prevailed over the qualitative.

At Google, which has the most balanced profile of leaders, the business leader is considered a "business" that avoids autocracy syndromes and promotes a cultural dimension within Google where it seems to be good to live together. Google's corporate culture seems to be moving closer to that of Microsoft as the recognition of technical value, the appreciation of initiative and taking risks. 20% of free time is allocated to employees for all innovative projects.

6.2.2. Interactions between artificial intelligence and cultural intelligence to save the planet

While artificial intelligence facilitates the development of smart businesses through automation, effective leadership also requires the integration of cultural intelligence—combining both AI and intelligent enterprise. In essence, the ideal entrepreneur fosters the emergence of cultural intelligence alongside technological tools. From this perspective, "intelligence" becomes the common denominator linking artificial intelligence, cultural intelligence, and the broader concept of an intelligent enterprise.

The question is whether there is a significant relationship between intelligent enterprise, artificial intelligence and cultural intelligence. The triangular relationship between company, business leader and intelligence reflect this performance challenge sought by the three actors of power in the company, to achieve sustainable development for current and future generations.

The interaction that exists between artificial intelligence and cultural intelligence shows that cultural intelligence is not static, immutable, closed and isolated, but opens on the change in the world and binds itself to the contribution of science, new technologies and artificial intelligence. Similarly, artificial intelligence can not prevail, apart from the cultural intelligence that fuels technology by certain universal values immutable to live together. Artificial intelligence or the robot makes it possible to concretely realize the values of equality of objectivity by saving the world from any discrimination and all other human weaknesses of subjectivity.

Contrary to the widespread idea that robotization dehumanizes human relations, a digital world appears rather in a world that brings people together and allows us to do more together. A study by Adam Conner-Simons | CSAIL published on 21 August 2014 from the MIT (Massachusetts Institute of Technology) laboratory, shows that humans prefer to receive their orders from robots rather than managers. The robot makes it possible to de-passionate working relationships. He has his own rationality, does not react to the head of the client, is not suspected of favouritism or wanting to pull the cover to him, and has no moods. In absolute terms, it should be recognized that the robot ultimately makes fewer errors of judgment.

In 2015, Bertrand Duperrina writes that it is the time of robots, and that hell is others. It shows in a study (Odoxa, the Syntec Numérique and 01 Business) conducted on workers in a factory in France that the French welcome the arrival of robots in their daily lives. Workers are enthusiastic about living with them. The survey population voted on the issue of the advent of robots especially in the areas of robot assistance in domestic work (86%), assistance in everyday activities for people with limited autonomy and for difficult, technical or dangerous tasks (84%) and finally for cars without drivers (36%).

As stressed workers increasingly turn to artificial intelligence for support, AI may serve as a tool to strengthen individuals' connections to their cultural and professional environments. To understand this trend—favoring robot assistance over human managers—Oracle partnered with Workplace Intelligence to survey over 12,000 employees, managers, HR leaders, and executives across 11 countries in 2020. The findings revealed that 68%

preferred discussing stress and anxiety with a robot rather than a manager. As organizations adopt more technology solutions, AI is becoming a key instrument for enhancing productivity and fostering a positive corporate culture.

The survey shows that 30% of respondents believe that robots do not judge employees. They are impartial and provide quick answers to questions. 88% of survey respondents prefer AI solutions because of the following benefits:

• provide quick answers and information (63%)

• Automate administrative tasks (59 %)

• Recommend new skills to learn (50%)

For example, AI tools reduce stress levels by providing the information needed to do the job more effectively (31%), reducing workload to avoid burnout (27%) and helping prioritize tasks (27%). Core benefits of AI increase employee productivity (63%), improve job satisfaction (54%), improve overall well-being (52%), help workers shorten their workweek (51%) and take longer vacations (51%).

On the other hand, other researchers (Lindebaum, 2015) do not see positively the benefits of robots, and consider that technology supersedes humans in most activities and mechanizes human values, whereas materiality should be "subordinated" to values (Hinings & Greenwood, 2015). Lindebaum (2015) analyzes the different degrees of value mechanization, which can lead to better or worse practical consequences. Lindebaum in fact recognizes that the technique or technology can be used for pro-social purposes or, conversely, cause individual and societal harm if it is not controlled.

Lindebaum's analysis highlights two key implications: first, a tendency toward the mechanization of values, which shifts focus from ethical ends to technical means (Selznick, 1957). Second, an overemphasis on technological efficiency risks treating techniques as neutral tools, capable of serving any purpose, which can overlook underlying ethical considerations.

On the other hand, Selznick (1957) offers a similar warning when he draws attention to the drift that constitutes the tendency to detach oneself from the aims of institutional and community life. However, removing the "ends" from the theory leads to creating the conditions of "the tyranny of means and the powerlessness of ends" (Krygier, 2015: 38). The means can indeed exercise this tyranny when we confuse cause and effect. The cause of hypertension, for example, is defined in the biological field using technology, when in reality hypertension is a social effect. Therefore, structural socio-economic conditions as causes of hypertension should be addressed. For Lindebaum (2015), confusing causes and effects is not just a matter of non-information. , but requires the need for social scientists to know empirical data.

Having examined how artificial intelligence can support cultural intelligence in addressing global challenges, the book now turns to the second key concept: cultural change aimed at saving the world.

Section 6.3. Cultural change to save the world

First, culture is not visible and yet it exerts a strong influence on everything that happens within the organization. It is built throughout history through rites, beliefs and events forming the DNA of the organization. It is precisely on the DNA of the organization that we can act to change, heal and save the organization as it is just as conceivable to act on the DNA to transform and destroy the organization.

It should be noted that human behaviour is built on values forming the DNA of the organization, which imposes a certain cultural conduct starting with the leader himself. Advocating the change that will save the organization cannot really lead to the desired change if human behaviour remains the same as in the past. The organization's values define the direction of its strategy. The values then create types of behaviour within that organization and form the basis for the rules of operation of any organization's management system in the world. The values thus adopted facilitate employee engagement by giving meaning to their actions. To establish their strategies, organizations choose to formalize the values and disseminate them to teams.

Choosing and asserting one's values is an asset of differentiation strategy compared to the competition. Even if the value system is built to last, it should be updated, reviewed regularly, and checked that it is always in line with leaders' vision and defined missions. We must be careful not to want to admit that transforming, changing or saving the organization can be done with a snap of the fingers, but by a firm daily will to accompany the statements and follow them with concrete facts. Because the weight of the years has deeply anchored practices and reflexes in the DNA of the organization. Acting on the organization's DNA to change culture and save the world is a proven cultural intelligence. Other authors think in this perspective of a cultural change to save the organizations of planet Earth.

The book considers that cultural change is not decreed, but created and built to help save the world from all the chaos engendered by discrimination, exclusion, inequality and various forms of violence and human rights abuses. This vision of saving the world through change means a cultural change that can be declined by the anthropological meaning given to cultural change (631), by innovation that would induce cultural change (632) and the necessary steps that must be taken to achieve cultural change (633). The aim pursued by cultural change obeys in fact to the relevance of a process of change that the book explains and justifies further on (634).

6.3.1. The meaning of cultural change (foundations of anthropology)

Experience and observation consistently demonstrate that change is a universal aspect of culture. Anthropologists have documented this phenomenon even within conservative groups. For instance, few cultures escape the common refrain of elders lamenting the distancing of youth from traditional values. Older generations across societies often say, "In our youth, things were different. We showed respect for elders and worshipped the gods. Today, young people refuse to listen, follow, or learn from us." Conversely, younger generations often criticize their elders for a lack of understanding of their needs. Yet, elders seldom recognize the effectiveness of youth or realize that opposing change may be futile.

Change can be demonstrated in another way by looking at its results in regional groupings of the same culture. All local groups in a given region lead a very similar lifestyle, but differ from their neighbours in some details of traditional behaviour. Local dialects provide an example of this observation in the sense of Herskovits (1950), who believes that many changes have occurred over the years through the accumulation of minimal differences transmitted in one locality rather than another. The author notes that these small differences introduced into a culture come from outside and can easily be integrated into the lives of borrowers. The example of maize shows that it was in America that this plant was domesticated, and exported to Europe, then to Africa where it brought about changes in the diet and economy of the natives, despite the food conservatism of most peoples.

Today, corn is not only an essential food, but it has invaded a second aspect of culture which is the realm of ritual that also resists change. Another example of cultural borrowing is clothing, language, which has changed a lot since the 16th century due to these contacts between America, Europe and Africa. Indeed, for Herskovits

(1950), groups living in close contact have more opportunities to host mutual innovations than societies further away. If cultural change appears universal, it should be considered as meaningless unless confronted with the opposite phenomenon called conservatism.

Yet scholars have been more interested in the study of change than in the analysis of the stability of conservatism, for two reasons. One stems from the historical development of the notion of conservatism of "primitive" peoples. The second reason is the method. Because it is indeed easier to study a dynamic change than a negative conservatism characterized by a phenomenon of stability. Both concepts must be taken into account, says Herskovits (1950), if one is to understand the dynamic problems of culture. To give an example of the distinction between cultural change and conservatism resistant to change, some fairly old anthropologists such as Herbert Spence (1820-1903), English philosopher and sociologist, emphasize the need to study change within primitive cultures in the following terms:

Primitive peoples are often characterized as highly conservative. Even when different social groups or races interact, the less developed tend to be the most resistant to change. Introducing new methods or innovations among common folk is challenging; they often reject new foods or practices outright. Uncivilized or simpler societies tend to have less neurological flexibility, making them even less receptive to new behaviors. They exhibit both unconscious and conscious adherence to established customs and traditions.

It was therefore important to emphasize the universality of change and to reject claims that people of a "lower" order did not accept changes in their lifestyles. It should however be shown that the «primitive» man is not an automaton. Because the «primitive» societies had undergone changes, despite their remote habitat, their mass, their technological resources. Since change is everywhere in culture, the work of the book then questions why anthropologists have generally been less interested in studying conservatism as cultural stability. While it is permissible to accept change as always present, it is justified to conceive conservatism as resistance to change.

Certainly, any study of change reveals resistance to change, at least by deduction. But the book shows that people notice only slight differences between local groups of Eskimos, or between different hordes of natives in Australia, Bushmen in South Africa, or various tribes in Tierra del Fuego. These slight, albeit small, differences compared to the local differences in the uneducated world; however, they provide a kind of continued resistance to change. Where uneducated groups are in contact with writing peoples, it is possible to notice indeed elements of refusal. For now, let's just note that the study of resistance to change, that is cultural stability or cultural conservatism, is only one aspect of the study of cultural change itself. The question is whether one culture can be perceived as conservative, while another may be sensitive to change.

On the other hand, contemporary culture, which is seen as "progressive" and open to change, reveals resistance in the aspect of social life. The book also notes that change differs over time when looking at the study of cultural dynamics and structure. Indeed, cultural conservatism and cultural change result from historical and psychological factors of the environment. In some cases, habitat will be a significant example of resistance to change. In other cases, it seems that groups living in the most remote regions of the globe are considered to be the most conservative societies. However, the reverse is not true. Far Eastern civilizations are an example of cultural conservatism, yet they are not isolated. Eskimos may be considered conservative because they are isolated or because a specific habitat imposes limitations and changes on them.

Indeed, linking the natural environment directly to cultural conservatism or change is complex. It is essential to distinguish between inherent cultural tendencies—rooted in how a society is organized—and external factors, such as historical accidents, which are unforeseen events that impact a culture unexpectedly. This distinction raises a key question: does cultural change primarily originate from internal innovations driven by internal dynamics, or from external, unpredictable events?

6.3.2. cultural change through innovation

From a general point of view, the book identifies two categories of phenomena in cultural change. The first concerns change induced by inno-vat ions coming from within society. The second relates to change from outside society.

The recurring question, discussed above, concerns the acceptance or rejection of an innovation, whether it comes from inside or outside society. In addition, it is difficult to identify innovations that reduce resistance to change due to the complexity of the phenomenon of change. Indeed, the change that is a constant in any system of custom, is the product of discoveries and inventions. If the invention appears as an acquired aptitude, not as an innate instinct, it is on the basis of being known to be acquired that man can in fact reason and verify whether the result of the experiment is a confirmation of the theory or a true discovery. The well-known proverb: "Necessity is the mother of invention" is therefore only a partial truth in the material dimension of culture.

However, the reverse of the proverb: "Invention is the mother of necessity." , is not always true according to the American economist and sociologist Thorstein Bunde Veblen (1857 —, 1929), or as Agatha Christie (1890 — 1976), a British woman of letters would say: I do not think that necessity is the mother of invention. The invention, in my opinion, results directly from idleness, probably also from laziness to save oneself from boredom." The need thus explains the invention or discovery of a large part of culture by stimulating the minds of specialists who invent new objects. In other words, the change of culture results from changes produced from within by the accumulation of small pre-existing changes.

Therefore, a distinction should be made between large and small changes. Tom Harnett Harrison (1911-1976), reported by Herskovits (1950), speaks of "mutations" and invention in the development of material culture. The «mutation» results for him, of a selection made more or less at random by man in his environment that he is led to develop. If cultural change results from mutations and innervations in the sense of Harrison (1911-1976), is it permissible to speak of culture as a reference point of belief, as explained above, but also as a reference point for innovations, Is it a model of social innovation? In other words, is culture a social model?

While for some anthropologist's culture can be seen as a reference point of beliefs, for others culture would be a model of social behaviour, because all cultural behavior follows patterns that shape collective habits. Models that generate laws of individual behavior have an unconscious character in the sense that the individual obeys the models without having a clear awareness. The cultural model appears from the point of view of Lévi-Strauss (1967) as a «superorganism, a set of relations and institutions».

However, objectivists and subjectivists differ in their conception of the cultural model. For the subjectivists of the «Culture et Personnalité» school, the model should mirror empirical reality—what people actually think and do. Conversely, objectivists see the model as an abstraction created by the researcher to understand culture. Herskovits (1950) emphasizes that the question is not "does the model reflect reality?" but rather "is it the best way to understand reality?" He notes that, while both perspectives recognize the complexity of cultural reality, this complexity is visible only in certain aspects of culture, not universally.

The author calls this aspect of cultural reality a cultural focal point, or in other words the theory of the «cultural focal point» which concerns only the dynamic aspects of culture allowing cultural change. For Herskovits (1950), no individual knows all aspects of the life of his social group even in the most stable and conservative cultures. Similarly, no individual dominates his or her culture and no group is equally interested in all aspects of the life of its group members. Similarly, two individuals do not have the same interests and perceive culture differently to satisfy their different interests.

Herskovits (1950), summarizes these remarks in the following terms: «the dominant interest of a people can be conceived as the focus of its culture». He gives the example of the Maya Indians who live in the territory of Quintana Roo in Yucatan (Mexico) and who attribute to the cross, the role of a sacred symbol: The cross is the most sacred symbol of the group. It acts as an intermediary between God and man, for wherever there is a cross there are the eyes of God. The cross, however, does not communicate directly with God."

Sociologists and ethnologists thus discern groups, communities, societies as well as their boundaries through the symbols of participation provided by the conduct of people. Culture thus takes on the character of a vast symbolic social ensemble.

This symbolic social aspect of culture gives it a distinctive character. The collective demonstrations are thus understood as symbols of communication. Respect for cultural patterns symbolizes members' adherence to values and belonging to a given community. The solidarity between members of a society, felt as a reality, is in fact expressed through referentials of symbolic participation attached to their externally objectionable behaviour.

From this point of view, culture can therefore take the form of a symbolic whole, of psycho-social realities essential to the collective life of a society. This symbolic meaning of behaviour means that the members of a community must distinguish between members and non-members, between citizens and foreigners, between saints, faithful and unfaithful. Not attending meetings, for example, or signing a petition may be explained by a tendency to withdraw symbolically from the group, party, or association.

The social-symbolic aspect of culture must be distinguished from its objective and instinctive dimensions. Objectively, members of a community form tangible links—such as properties, buildings, or monuments—that constitute shared material assets. This aspect of culture aligns with Durkheim's concept of social solidarity or Auguste Comte's notion of societal consensus.

Instinctively, Rocher (1993) believes that to speak of culture means to situate it and compare it with the instinctive aspect of an individual in a specific community. The first distinction between culture and instinct, is supported by Ronald Fletcher (1957) when he defines the word instinct as «essentially congenital and not learned», whereas «culture is necessarily non-hereditary and learned».

The opposition between instinct and culture appears radical in this definition by 20th-century British sociologist Ronald Fletcher (1910–1996). The second distinction between culture and instinct lies in the fact that instinct is endogenous and inscribed in each organism inducing an instinctive non-social behavior for all species of a same family. Culture, on the other hand, is social in nature, characterized by a collective good.

For Rocher (1993), culture and instinct are not only opposed in their hereditary and social character, but both converge towards a function of adaptation to the physical environment. Indeed, culture fulfils for man the same function of adaptation to oneself and the environment as the instinct does in animals. It is the animal's instinct that allows it to adapt to and control the environment, says Rocher (1993).

Similarly, the author argues that culture enables humans to adapt to their physical and social environments—much like instinct does for animals. As humans seek to control their surroundings, feelings, and impulses, culture has gradually replaced instinct as the primary means of adaptation. This shift reflects the increasing importance of intelligence and symbolic reasoning in human development.

6.3.3. Step by step cultural change

This is an approach that uses a method called the "gap analyzed" method which means the transition from the current situation to the projected situation. The principle of the gap analysis method (gap analyzed) is based on the comparison between the current situation and the projected cultural change situation. The desire to identify the levers and tasks of cultural change aims to close this gap. The analysis of the gap and the levers requires, in fact, the use of methods, diagnostic tools, and problem solving.

It is therefore necessary to use the method and definition of the problem to be treated before solving this problem. Nor is it a question of confusing the problem with its symptoms. The problem should be posed in order to understand all its dimensions and involve the various collaborators in order to broaden the point of view on the problem. Then we must look for the causes and origins of this problem.

However, in trying to identify the causes of the problem, one must be wary of the origins of the problem which may appear at first glance as obvious. Then, we must find a solution. Because finding a solution means wanting to look for that solution using tools such as brainstorming, and then using decision support methods such as the decision matrix or the decision tree developed by Laurent Granger, responsible for the GO site manager updated on October 19, 2023. The choice of solution must take into account various criteria such as ease and speed of implementation, cost, skills to be mobilized, risks of side effects. It should be pointed out here that the solution with the greatest impact is not necessarily the one chosen. In any case, experimentation will always be an excellent way to verify the relevance of a decision.

Finally, it is necessary to implement the solution chosen after a good preparation. It is a matter of implementing the solution chosen and maximizing the quality of the deployment of the action while setting objectives to ensure the effectiveness of the actions. The solution chosen deserves continuous monitoring of its effectiveness and implementation. It is important in these remarks not to confuse the effectiveness of actions with the effectiveness of the solution chosen. This reminder of the problem-solving method helps to explain the implementation of the gap analysis method between a current and projected cultural situation. The method of analysis of the gap between a current cultural situation and the projected cultural situation can be done chronologically in three stages:

Step one. Take a photograph of the situation in line with the defined problem, based on the characteristics of the initial state and using conventional tools (brainstorming, interviews, group meetings, company dashboards).

Example of initial diagnostic scheme

Where are we?	Where do we want to be?	How to get there?	How to get there?
		Factors explaining the gap	Levers of action

Only 65% are satisfied with the change			

Step 2. The projected situation (objectives). Where do you want to be?

It is necessary to be in the factual and not only to state an intention. For example, avoid saying "we want to be #1", but rather "we are aiming at 30% market share within 2 years". Therefore, an overall goal should be broken down into several objectives in order to make it more operational.

Where are we?	Where do we want to be?	How to get there?	How to get there?
		Factors explaining the gap	Levers of action
Only 65% are satisfied with the change	80% satisfied within 1 year		

Step 3.

Identify the levers to go from current state to target state - how do you get there?

For each deviation, the factors explaining this difference should be identified. They can be both quantitative and qualitative, although in many cases it is possible to quantify a qualitative variable. Given these factors, it is then important to identify the levers that can be used to reduce the gap between the current state and the desired state. From the latter, it would then be possible to implement relevant actions with the objectives set. Without this thinking, the trap is to take the wrong action and see the current situation unchanged.

Where are we?	Where do we want to be?	How to get there?	How to get there?
		Factors explaining the gap	Levers of action
Only 65% are satisfied with the change	80% satisfied within 1 year	Listens to discussions on the quantitative and qualitative value of change	By - the motivation – the study of change in stages using a consulting firm

Now let's look at how To do it:

The first step is to analyze the characteristics of the current culture by examining the company's history, personnel, trades, missions, symbols, values, and behaviors. This diagnostic phase is crucial for understanding the present situation.

Next, it is necessary to define the desired new culture based on strategic analyses. The goal is to align culture with strategy. This may seem paradoxical, since naturally, strategy is often developed considering existing cultural values, rather than the other way around.

Finally, it is necessary to define the changes to be made and develop a relevant action plan. It is in this phase that good change management is important by putting the human being at the center of this project. The goal is to use appropriate techniques to raise staff awareness of the need for change. It is also important to establish indicators for assessing the effectiveness of actions. Olivier Ezratty offers us a very detailed comparative analysis between the management systems of Apple, Microsoft and Google. To make the change happen, Olivier Ezratty reviews different areas such as leadership personality, mission of the organization, product, R&D, acquisitions and recruitment.

6.3.4 Change process and its management

In order to manage the change towards the expected success, Raphaëlle Granger (2021) proposes to ask the following questions: 1 why and how to accompany the transformations?

2 What are the stages of the change process? 3 What tools and methods need to be mastered?

First question. Why and how to support the transformations?

Technical aspects often take precedence over human concerns in the context of transformations. However, success depends on accepting the new situation and the new tasks attached to it. It is essential to prepare and support change through a willingness to support employees during transformations and manage the resistance that may appear.

Deciding on a transformation without worrying about the impacts at all levels and being surprised that it does not work, that employees do not adhere appears more frequent in organizations. This is the typical example of an unprepared change not properly accompanied. The result of such an approach is clearly a failure. On the other hand, a complete management of change, from reflection to communication and implementation of support, would be the key to success. Thinking ahead of action facilitates the success of change by enabling, inter alia:

• Analyze the drivers of change to measure the impacts of the project on the entire organization.

• Examine the different forces in front of it to better understand the change and accompany it, and correct if necessary the shot or abandon it.

• Establish cause and effect relationships in the transformation process to articulate the project intelligently.

• Identify resistance to change in order to better understand and overcome it.

• Adapt as naturally as possible to the changing world,

Second question. What are the phases of the change process?

Every transformation is made up of different phases that are essential to the success of a change project. The German social psychology researcher Kurt Lewin (1951) defines three main stages, symbolized by the metaphor of a block of ice:

• "Unfreeze" — "Thaw": this is the essential step in preparing for change. The objective is to make employees aware that a transformation is inevitable, then convince them that the organization has no other way out than to do otherwise. Resistance appears from this first stage.

- “Change” — “Change”: this phase represents concrete change. As the minds are ready for the new thanks to the sense of urgency created by the previous step, new practices are defined. This step is broken down into several sub-phases that it is interesting not to overlook.

- “Refreeze” — “Freeze”: once the changes are adopted, the objective is to stabilize and consolidate the new organization, the new ways of working. If this phase is ignored, the project can quickly fail with a return to the old situation.

This model, sometimes referred to as simplistic, however, outlines the broad lines of any transformation and lays the foundations for a successful change management strategy.

Third question. What are the tools for change management?

Among the tools, methods and models that can be used in a successful transformation, Raphaëlle Granger (2021) four examples are suggested, described as follows:

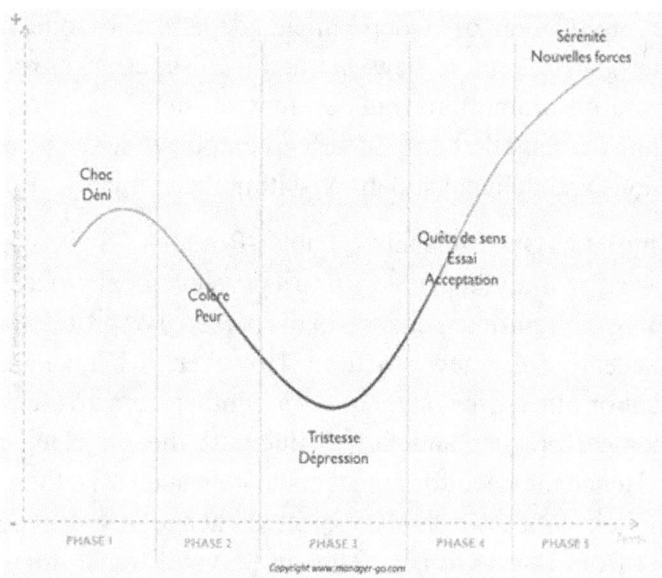

The mourning curve,

The Leavitt Diamond,

The Burke and Litwin Model, and

the wheel of the future Future Wheel

1st example: the mourning curve

For Raphaëlle Granger (2021), passionate about human relations and site manager go, the mourning curve schematically represents the different stages intrinsic to any change that each individual experiences before accepting the new situation and living it fully in a relationship shock/ denial, anger/ fear, sadness/ depression, search for meaning and serenity. Raphaëlle Granger (2021) states that any change, whether desired or not, is intrinsically linked to the loss and end of something. The passage through the mourning phase remains an immutable process mandatory to hope to live serenely the future and succeed the transformation projected in the future (reorganisation of the company, cultural change, change of premises, relocation of a department, departure of one or more colleagues, arrival of a new hierarchical superior, takeover by another entity, promotion, transfer, new challenges). These are all professional events that can disturb an employee and cause him or her tensions and delicate situations within the company.

According to Dr Elizabeth Kubler-Ross, a Swiss-American psychiatrist, an individual enters into a psychological process during a mourning or significant change in his personal or professional life, before accepting the new situation. However, it happens that this individual or others, for one reason or another, remain stuck in this psychological process and fail to integrate the projected cultural change. Hence the need for managers to help and assist these people stuck in their path towards the expected change in order to prevent this grief from lasting longer. Thus in terms of transformation and cultural change in business, whether at organizational, hierarchical, human or geographical levels, Raphaëlle Granger (2021), advises to master this concept of the bereavement curve in order to best support its employees on the path of change and avoid additional costs and total indifference related to change.

According to Raphaëlle Granger (2021), the mourning curve includes five felt stages that must be passed as quickly as possible in order to accept the change and project serenely into the expected future.

The mourning process is not strictly linear; individuals may move back and forth between stages or remain stuck in one phase, which can lead to anxiety and tension within the organization. When a blockage occurs, managers should intervene to support employees in progressing through each stage. As Granger (2021) explains, the stages of the mourning curve are as follows:

Shock/Denial Step

Following the announcement of a upheaval in the life of the company and the individual, unprepared, the latter appears at first surprised by the news and refuses reality. He seems paralyzed by his emotions and appears frozen by the announcement. Raphaëlle Granger (2021), believes that this individual is incapable of reasoning and reacts spontaneously as follows: "It's not possible !" "Is that true?!" "Is that a joke?!" For Raphaëlle Granger (2021), this step will be achieved more quickly if the change is minor or "expected". Thus, it would be easier to move quickly to the next step when it is a positive announcement for the individual or desired by the latter (promotion, transfer requested for some time, new position, etc.). However, during waves of layoffs, for example, or relocation or sale of the company, or cultural change, some employees may have difficulty realising the news and remain stuck in stupor (Raphaëlle Granger, 2021).

Anger/fear step

Once the shock has taken hold, the news leaves room for anger or fear of the unknown. It is an anger or a fear of losing something, caused by the unknown of the new situation. This is a period that will mark the beginning of revolt and resistance to change." I am totally opposed to it! "; " It won't be like that! "; " It's totally stupid!"; "It's not fair!" ";" How are we going to do it?". During this period, employees can sometimes say much tougher words.

Sadness/depression stage

This is a period characterized by great questions raised by employees such as: "It's no use" ; "It's fucked up for me"; "I'll never make it"; "We're going straight into the wall"; "I'll never be up to it"; "This colleague was so nice". This step is crucial in the path to change, because once it has been taken, there are some positive signs for the success of the change process. It seems essential for Raphaëlle Granger (2021) to help employees to overcome this phase and move towards the desired future for the company and the employee.

Sense Quest/Test/Acceptance Step

This step marks an optimism displayed by employees who will stop looking to the past and turn to the future. Employees show a motivation to abandon the old situation and explore the benefits of the new potentially promising and constructive situation. To support the beginning of this new dynamic of acceptance of the new situation, Raphaëlle Granger (2021) quotes some phrases from employees: «OK, but give me a little more time»; «OK, but under such conditions»; «Good... Since it is so... » ; "I have no choice anyway..." ; "Finally, I can maybe find my way there"; "I'm willing to try, but if it doesn't work, we start again as before."

Step of serenity/new strength

This final stage of grief shows that employees have understood and integrated the change. The employees adapt to the new situation and seek to know each other better, in order to achieve a collective framework of solidarity in the company. For Raphaëlle Granger (2021), all these stages of the bereavement curve leading to overall and individual performance vary in intensity and are not necessarily noticeable by an uneducated person.

2 — Leavitt's Diamond

Developed in 1965 by Harold J. Leavitt, an American work psychologist, the Diamond is an interactive approach to change that allows you to understand the mechanisms of a transformation and study its different impacts on the organization as a whole. (Raphaëlle Granger, 2021). Leavitt defines 4 intrinsic components to any organization, in order to draw a most relevant action plan and fully succeed the change management:

- Individuals
- The tasks,
- The organization,
- Technology

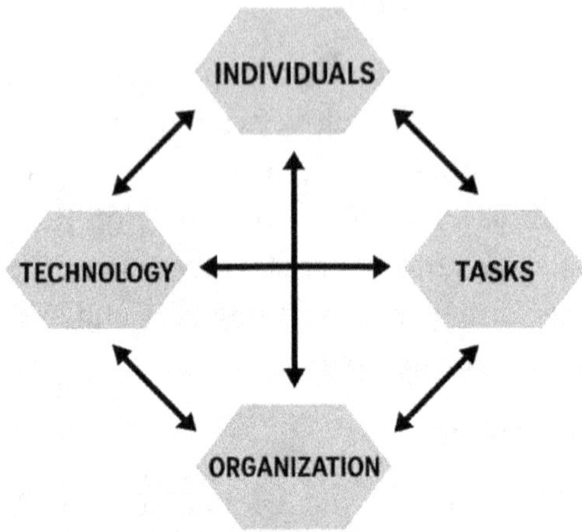

The objective is to identify the existing interactions between the two components and to analyse the effects of change in a global way in order to fully manage this change.

3rd example the Burke and Litwin model

Raphaëlle Granger (2021), indicates that this model sometimes called the causal model of organizational performance and organizational change is a tool for managing change and behaviors, developed in the 1960s by its two founders, Warner Burke and George H. Litwin, change management consultants. It is a relatively complex tool, which aims to assess the organizational and environmental dimensions necessary for successful change, Identify the cause-and-effect links between these different dimensions and make any adjustments in order to improve performance.

It is divided into 3 main groups (transformational factors, transactional factors and performance factors). It is built around 12 interconnected organizational elements. Any change in one of them has an impact on one or more other elements and even on all the elements.

1— External environment

2 - Mission and Strategy

3 — Leadership

4— Corporate culture

5 — Structure

6— Management practices

7 - Systems

8— Working atmosphere

9— Assignments and individual competencies

10 - Individual values and needs

11— Motivation

12— Individual and collective performance

4th for example the model of the future wheel “Futures Wheel”

4th for example the model of the future wheel “Futures Wheel”

According to Raphaëlle Granger (2021), this tool was designed by a prospective expert, Jérôme C. Glenn in 1972. It allows to visualize, analyze and collectively explore the direct and indirect consequences of a change. But change also brings risks. Due to a lack of anticipation, the consequences that result from the change are likely to have a negative impact on the decisions taken. If in the sense of Raphaëlle Granger (2021), the wheel of the future “Futures Wheel” remains a practical tool to help protect against this risk, the primary purpose of this tool used in a brainstorming session is to build a graphic representation of the consequences of change.

The objective is to decide whether or not a cultural change project can be launched despite the expected consequences, or to think about redefining the scope of the objectives.

The description of the wheel of the future «future Wheel» takes the form of a graph composed of bubbles whose center indicates the change studied and around the consequences established at several levels. The first level of consequences represents the most direct positive or negative impacts, and the most obvious ones.

The second level indicates the possible consequences that can possibly be broken down into a 3rd circle and so on. Despite its advantage of being used in several problems, this model of tool remains subjective and does not eliminate all risks. To enhance the relevance of its analysis, this model needs to be coupled with other analytical methods such as the impact assessment cited above.

The book takes here an example of a graph reported by Raphaëlle Granger (2021), as a simple didactic illustration whose title of change would be the impact of a reduction in the training budget.

Example of a "Futures Wheel" graph

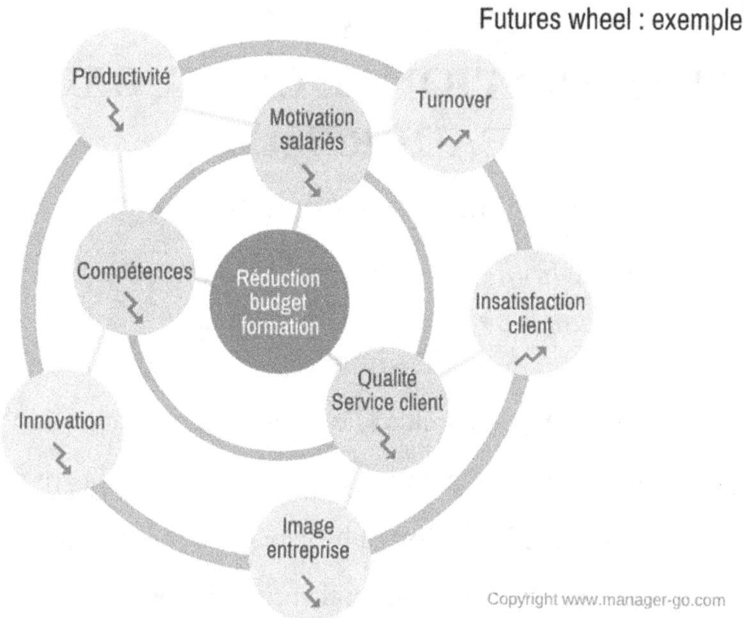

CONCLUSION

In this chapter, the book discusses how cultural intelligence can save the world by means of performance indicators and a cultural intelligence quotient that is perceived differently according to the American and French approaches. He finally showed the different aspects of cultural intelligence that can be present in the perception of researchers and decision-makers. This chapter has the merit of showing that culture cannot succeed in saving the world without the contribution of artificial intelligence which is developing more and more in this century. The idea of saving the world ultimately means a cultural change that can only be achieved through the contribution of a decision-maker with a supranational vision. This cultural change by a more humanistic and supranational leader will be addressed in the following chapter.

CHAPTER 7
SUPRANATIONAL CULTURAL LEADERSHIP

SAVIOR OF THE PLANET

He who has never learned to obey
can't be a good commander.
Aristotle

Innovation makes the difference
between a leader and a follower.
Steve Job

Introduction

If we are witnessing a multiform crisis: financial, economic and managerial, it can be perceived as a surprising event (Hermann, 1963 ; Shrivastava et al. 1988), or a harmful threat (Weick, 1988 ; Reilly, 1993) or a situation outside the usual framework (Combalbert, 2005). In response to this crisis situation, decision-makers have asked themselves whether cultural leadership can be acquired and can it achieve sustainable development and save the world? If the logic of cultural leadership implies knowing what kind of leadership would be able to save the planet and fulfill the expectations of present and future generations, the book is proposed from this point of view, to analyse the transformational theories of cultural leadership.

Cultural leadership's power is seen not only as a vertical dimension that enforces obedience but also as a relational concept, distinguishable from ideology, which seeks to instrumentalize the worldview of the dominated. The question of the century is whether decision-makers can exercise strategic thinking and acquire a universally recognized leadership profile in different cultures. The profile of decision-makers influenced by the cultural dimension can indeed be more humanized within a logic of altruism and dynamic learning psychology. Based on its independent character, the cultural leadership targeted would be supranational humanist.

The humanism evoked, is not only a thought, but also a new way of seeing the world that will influence and change the whole society. The supranational humanist cultural leadership whose contours can be shaped in management schools, would it be able to save the management of planet Earth in the face of a hypothetical crisis or an extraterrestrial threat? Do we need an extraterrestrial crisis or threat to think of a humanistic cultural leadership that saves the planet and transcends a classical leadership with a limited vision reduced to a population category or country, or continent?

In order to elucidate these ideas and answer the questions, we have chosen to first deal with the relationship between leadership and culture (7,1), before addressing the cultural leadership underpinned by power (72). We believe that the leader can be seen as a savior of the planet through humanistic logic (73). We propose to carry out a comparative study between power and cultural leadership (74) in order to evaluate our theoretical contribution regarding the emergence of a new paradigm of supranational cultural leadership (75).

Section 7.1. Leadership and culture, what influence relationship?

Peter Northhouse: Leadership. Theory and practice, published in 2018 by SAGE, was chosen for its reference on leadership in the Anglo-Saxon world, but remains little known in francophone research. What is interesting in the book of Peter Northhouse is the chapter devoted to the relationship between leadership and culture. In the wake of this report on leadership and culture, a global research programme has been designed to identify the cultural specificities that exist in the practice of leadership.

The question is how culture can influence leadership practice. With globalization, this question has become recurrent, as the confrontation with other cultures reveals misunderstandings about how organizations operate. Understanding how culture influences leadership practices is not merely an academic curiosity but also a critical step toward analyzing its impact. The GLOBE project studied nine cultural dimensions and explained how cultural differences influence the selection of leaders.

The GLOBE research programme, initiated by Robert House in 1991, involved more than 160 researchers and used quantitative methods to analyse the responses of 17,000 managers and leaders around the world. More than 950 organizations and 62 different cultures were targeted. Data were collected through questionnaires, interviews, focus groups, and press analysis.

The GLOBE project has the merit of showing nine cultural dimensions, thus expanding Hofstede's model (1 control of uncertainty, 2 hierarchical distances, 3 institutional collectivisms, 4 group-internal collectivisms, 5 gender egalitarianism, 6 assertiveness, 7 orientations towards the future, 8 orientations towards performance, 9 humanistic orientations). The Globe project then divided data from the 62 countries studied into ten regional clusters, based on common linguistic, geographical, religious and historical elements.

The primary objective of the GLOBE programme is to determine how individuals from different cultures perceive leadership, based on the theory of implicit leadership. According to this theory, individuals have beliefs and convictions about the attributes that distinguish leaders from non-leaders, as well as good leaders and ineffective leaders. To show how cultural differences affect the selection of these leaders, GLOBE researchers have identified six general leader behaviours:

1. Leadership based on charisma that reflects the ability of the leader to inspire or elicit motivation and adherence to performance based on strong values.

2. Team-oriented leadership emphasizes the leader's ability to build and maintain a united and coherent collective.

3. Participatory leadership indicates the degree to which the leader invites others to participate in decision-making processes.

4. The humanist leadership characterizes leaders who are listening and ready to support their collaborators, with generosity and benevolence.

5. Autonomous leadership refers to independent and individualistic leaders who stand out for their uniqueness, personality and charisma.

6. Self-protective leadership refers to behaviors that secure and legitimize the position of the leader in the group, such as formal procedures or a code of honor.

Referring to the characteristics of clusters in Latin Europe and Germanic Europe, researchers around the world find that Latin Europe values leadership based on charisma, while Germanic Europe values autonomous leadership. All other categories of behaviour are also desirable, with the exception of self-protection which is only moderately valued. Among the leadership attributes universally approved and valued by the 17,000 people from 62 countries, are 22 of the most universally desirable behaviours:

- 1 trustworthy.

- 2 Foresight

– 3 Positive

- 4 Instills confidence

– 5 Intelligent

- 6 Provides win-win solutions

- 7 Administratively competent

– 8 Focused on excellence

- 9 Fair

- 10 Proactive, anticipatory

- 11 Dynamic

- 12 Motivating

- 13 Decisive

– 14 Communicative

- 15 Coordinated

- 16 Honest

- 17 Encouraging

- 18 Inspire patterns

- 19 Reliable

- 20 Effective negotiator

- 21 Informed

- 22 Team Builder

In contrast, the GLOBE researchers identified a list of eight universally undesirable behaviors recognized as obstacles to leadership efficiency.

1— Solitaire

2— Irritable

3- Ruthless, severe

4— Asocial

5- Opaque, not very explicit

6— Dictatorial

7- Uncooperative

8— Self-centered

These tables, drawn by the GLOBE researchers, reveal a fairly clear picture of the qualities and shortcomings of universally recognized leaders across all cultures. The strength of the GLOBE project lies in the impressive amount of data collected, and the rigorous quantitative method. The analysis of the GLOBE research has the merit of being global and broad based on a macroeconomic approach, but it is limited to the extent that the study only covered the cluster of Latin Europe and Germanic Europe.

This study should be supplemented by work from other continents, including the North, Europe, Africa and Anglo-Saxon.

A 2006 PhD thesis supported in Metz by Guy Arcand examines the role of national culture in organizational performance. The study specifically focuses on banks across twenty-two countries spanning North America, Europe, and Asia, aiming to demonstrate how cultural factors influence organizational outcomes.

On the African continent, the words of the book are aimed at the work of Moroccan researchers who have analyzed leadership and cultural influence. On the leadership register, the Arabic word for leader Za-im refers to a mystical image expressing a value-based relationship of emotional authority (Camau 2011). According to researcher Fadoua Tahiri (2021), the Moroccan leader uses trust as an essential value that reflects a strong «glorification» of leadership (Al Arkoubi, 2008), thanks to which he can obtain results from his followers.

In Nigeria, recent work (Oruh and Dibia, 2020) has investigated the link between cultures and employee stress. The authors from the University of London found that employers can identify stress symptoms in employees through effective communication with them. The authors point out, however, that it is the cultural dynamics of the environment which determine the effectiveness of the working relationship and above all make it possible to solve work-related stress problems. These dynamic interventions differ between authors due to cultural differences (Hofstede, 1980; Aycan et al., 2001) which may lead to cultural friction.

In the Anglo-Saxon literature, a survey by on a questionnaire sent by researchers (Aycan,Z., and all, 2001), to 1954 employees of commercial organizations from 10 countries, indicates that the social and cultural environment influences human resource management practices in the company. On 57 questions measuring managerial perceptions of four socio-cultural dimensions, the authors revealed three sets of variables (fatalism, fidelity, paternalism):

- the first was managers who described their environment as fatalistic also assumed that employees were not malleable by nature.

- The second, for managers who value high loyalty, assumes that employees must fulfill their obligations to each other.

- The third relates to managers who perceived paternalism and high power distance, assumed responsiveness of employees and did not bring empowerment to jobs.

Focusing on culture does not mean ignoring institutional factors related to HRM practices. Culture is not independent of institutions, but evolves and shares common values with them. Contingency models allow management practices to be aligned with societal culture (Aycan et al. 2000). Other authors (Stefan Lagrosen, 2003) based on a questionnaire survey in 30 countries explain that the cultural dimension significantly influences the quality of management.

In the wake of these ideas developed by different researchers at the macroeconomic level of leadership and its influence relationship with culture, the work suggests an approach to supranational cultural leadership that will be justified by power and humanism.

Section 7.2. Power-based cultural leadership

Cultural leadership is linked to the power that aims at the obedience of men. Even if power and leadership may at first glance have similarities in the idea of obedience, the differences appear more accentuated in a perception considered to be short-term in power and long-term in leadership. The book aims to provide decision-makers with critical reflection and insight into the differences in perception and choice that exist in the concept of power and leadership. Power, the management capacity of men, most often contains an implicit threat of passage to the exercise of binding power. However, power cannot produce its effects without the consent of management stakeholders who exercise their freedom to obey or not a power, because there is no power that does not run into a challenge. Although the origin of this challenge often comes from the law, some thinkers even consider power not as a vertical relationship but as horizontal. From this point of view, the exercise of power in the management of men and organizations, concerns different horizontal relations related to the fields (political, economic and ideological), in which power can be embodied, or challenged. The book also proposes to analyse these areas of political, economic and ideological power (7.2.1) as well as recent theories related to it (7.2.2).

7.2.1. — Cultural leadership underpinned by economic and ideological political power

First, the nature of political power including economic power in all organizations has its origin in the difference between the absolute will of decision-makers and the absolute making of executors.

Political and economic power

The power of cultural leadership is perceived not only as a compelling vertical dimension aimed at the obedience of humans, but a relational concept, which deserves to be distinguished from the ideology that aims to instrumentalize the worldview of the dominated. They become victims of a perverse power of the dominant management. Even if power and cultural leadership may at first glance have similarities to save human management by merging into the idea of obedience, the differences appear more accentuated in a perception considered in the short term in power and in the long term in cultural leadership.

Political and economic power means the will of a ruling class which, in order to safeguard its strategic management, exercises its dominant power over a dominated class in a form of obedience to command (Worms, 2013). If power is exercised by men over other men, the purpose of cultural leadership is to be obeyed, to achieve managerial efficiency and mastery of the management of employees' rights and duties. For Max Weber (1959), power in management is not reduced to violence, of which the state has a monopoly and coercion. “The strongest is never strong enough to always be the master, if he does not transform his strength into right and obedience into duty” (Rousseau, 1712-1778, du Contrat social). Power therefore seems to need coercion, authority or legality, for obedience presupposes recognition and freedom. In ancient Greece, the free man had the privilege of being a producer or citizen. Obedience to the law or military discipline only made sense if each could, in turn, command or obey.

In addition to the meaning of obeying the law of dominant management, the other role of commanding the dominated was defended by the German theorist Jurgen Habermas (1987), who supports the idea that man seeks in management to command and control the other through speech. The art of talking to others, the power to control the audience and convince by speech, and by telling a story, was taken up about ten years later by Denning (2000) in the method of storytelling. The power of storytelling discourse has indeed become the new paradigm at the service of dominant management. The exercise of the power to master the techniques of speech and use of the verb, criticized by Socrates, deserves however to be distinguished from propaganda and ideology. Certainly, in both cases, it is a matter of witnessing the exercise of a power to influence the management of a reality represented by the dominated. But the ideology is distinguished by its desire to instrumentalize the perception of the management of the dominated who become victims of the perverse power of the dominant.

Ideological power

More than ideological alienation, Foucault (1976), a fervent French philosopher of twentieth-century social criticism, has studied the different technologies of power and the mechanisms of discipline and surveillance installed within organizations. These different ways of exercising managerial power lead, for Foucault (1976), to the more or less imposed collaboration of the employees who are engaged in it. Foucault believes that the worker, whose work is measured by the dominant management system in place, does not really have the choice to avoid the productivist demands of the managerial power of the dominants.

Foucault's philosophical thought (1976), relative to this ideology of the dominant capitalist system, although little studied in French literature, served half a century later, for the emergence of an abundant Anglo-Saxon literature. It is appropriate to cite authors such as Barney and Rangan (2019), who believe that the legitimacy of dominant capitalism as a political and economic system seems to be increasingly questioned because the system develops some negative aspects, social inequalities, political and economic corruption, precarious employment and the degradation of natural environments. Other authors (Lazzaroni, 2021 ; Reinecke and Ansari, 2021) go in the same direction of this paradox of the dominant capitalist management system, suggesting the idea that capitalist societies need to be reinvented.

Other authors even closer to us, such as Aguilera, Aragón-Correa and Marano (2022), have attempted to respond to this paradox by drawing on philosophical precepts that call for concepts of societal progress and justice. The authors consider that social progress and justice are based on moral logic rather than profit. As a result, the authors intend to introduce new ideas and perspectives to rethink the role of power and leadership in safeguarding management and sustainable development within companies and society.

It should be noted that in the thinking of Foucault (1976), Barney (2019), Lazzaroni (2021), Reinecke (2021) and Aguilera (2022), the dominant ideology of capitalist societies increases the managerial power of the ruling authority. Weber (1959), the predecessor of the above-mentioned authors, considers that the authority of an individual, amplified today by power, rests on the legitimacy of this individual. Weber thus distinguishes three types of legitimacy: the charismatic legitimacy of power based on the exceptional character of the chief, the traditional legitimacy based on the absolute power of the chief and the legal legitimacy based on laws and regulations. These three types of legitimacy of power can, however, move from one type of legitimacy to another. European monarchies, for example, have moved from the legitimacy of traditional power (the power of the king) to the legitimacy of legal power. In a democratic society, governments based on the legitimacy of legal power may accept that the charismatic power of the president or prime minister is legitimate.

These three types of legitimacy of power can, however, be at the same time driving, saving and disrupting men's management. This dual role of power, both saving and disrupting, simple and universal, elusive and multiform according to Crozier and Friedberg (1977), is one of the most fundamental aspects of management of people and organizations. Several thousand years after Moses and Pharaoh, the debate about power as a savior or agitator remains. If the pyramids were built on the banks of the Nile symbolizing the absolute power of the dominant chief, they still remain relevant in the organization charts of companies, to symbolize the continuity to dominate those who work there. The mentioned history has given us two types of leadership embodied by Pharaoh and Moses.

The first, praising his power and might, enslaves, conquers, dominates others. The second acting as savior, practices right action and transmits meaning. Power in this historical perspective can be seen in cultural leadership, as a relationship of exchange between two individuals (positive conception) or as a constraint on the other individual (negative conception).

Finally, the work consulted provides a critical view of how policy-makers have failed to control abuse of power due to their limited skills and capabilities. At the organizational level, Risse and Wollner (2019) analyze how the abusive selfishness of managers seeking only profits generates an abusive discrimination against employees.

The emergence of the phenomenon of cultural leadership underlaid by political, economic and ideological power makes it possible to question the recent theories of power that underlie cultic leadership. Beyond the approaches of Habermas (1987) on the control of the other through discourse, of Foucault (1976) on the different technologies of power and of Weber (1959) on the types of legitimacy of power, other theories called modern (Bourdieu, 1970 ; Lukes, 1974), emphasize the reproduction of social hierarchy, the power of symbolic violence and the relationship of moral and physical forces

7.2.2 - Cultural leadership in modern power theories

The work of this book has chosen from this register of modern theories, two approaches, one of which is a replacement of Bourdieu (1970) and the other developed by Lukes (1974), which aim to influence men's management through domination of power relations and symbolic violence.

The approach of Pierre Bourdieu (1970)

Pierre Bourdieu (1970), one of the most important French sociologists of the second half of the 20th century, established a theory of symbolic class struggle and found in his book Reproduction, that the education system transmits knowledge similar to those existing in the ruling class. The school is considered by Bourdieu as neutral and its knowledge as independent, while failure or success in school are regarded as «gifts» referring to the nature of individuals. The ideology of gift in Bourdieu's conception plays a decisive role in the acceptance by individuals of their educational destiny (dominated and constrained) and their social destiny that follows from it (dominant management).

Bourdieu (1970) establishes a theory of symbolic class struggle and considers that in their symbolic struggles, the dominated classes can only lose, without ever reaching the level of the dominant. Continuing his reflection of social criticism in the management of men, Pierre Bourdieu develops a theory of reproduction of social hierarchies.

In his book La Reproduction, Bourdieu (1970) tries to show for example that the education system exerts a «power of symbolic violence», which contributes to give legitimacy to the relationship of force at the origin of social hierarchies. This process of legitimation, reinforcing a dominant management, comes from two beliefs. One is that the school is considered by Bourdieu as neutral and its knowledge as independent. The other is that academic failure or success are considered as "gifts" referring to the nature of individuals.

Bourdieu's theory has been criticized by other sociologists who consider that the nature of management brought by Bourdieu is rigid, simplifying and comes under a critique of «determinism». The French philosopher and rationalist Bouveresse (2004) who received in 2019 the grand prize of philosophy of the Académie française, recalls that «Bourdieu has been regularly accused of proposing social analyses that can only lead to nihilism and a feeling of impotence more or less radical». However, Bouveresse (2004) recognizes that Bourdieu's merit was to have sought the opposite of the criticisms mentioned, namely a "form of realistic idealism based on knowledge rather than desires, dreams, great ideas and good intentions".

The approach of Steven Michael Lukes (1974).

Lukes (1974, 2005 and 2021), developed his power theory in his book Power: a radical view (1974) and recently discussed it again in the second edition of the book Power: a radical view second edition (2005). Steven Lukes (1974) is notable for synthesizing recent developments in power theories. His work discusses the 'three dimensions of power,' relating to the theories of Bourdieu, Foucault, and gender studies. In a simple system, power in the management of men and organizations can only be a relationship of forces (moral or physical) according to Lukes (1974). But for him, human societies are so complex in their management that there exist in the management of men, reciprocal obligations that bind people and force them to behave in a certain way. Thus, the theory of Steven Lukes is that people are dominated and controlled by three types of power: (1) the power to impose a decision; (2) the power to choose topics on the agenda; and (3) ideological power. This last ideological dimension, studied by Habermas (1987), Foucault (1976), and Weber (1959), is based on the power to influence people's thoughts and wishes without them noticing.

For Lukes (1974), this influence in fact exerts in the management of men a power of domination so powerful that employees end up performing in their public or private organization, things contrary to their interests. In a so-called family business, the power of influence is explained by the relational links of the family shareholders considered by contemporary literature (Ben-Shahar, Carmeli, Sulganik, Weiss, 2022), as a soft power that manages to influence the hard power of other shareholders in order to dominate decision-making.

Faced with the various issues related to this exercise of dominant power abuse that favours profit, at the expense of the three dimensions of sustainability (social, economic and environmental), certain philosophical approaches come to the aid of decision-makers to promote strategic management of companies. Authors such as Risse and Wollner (2019), for example, advocate a philosophical plea for a new global contract (New Global Deal) between employers and employees, while Elizabeth Anderson (2017) prefer to analyze how employers regulate the lives of employees and why no one talks about it. Other authors (Kitcher and Keller, 2017), go so far as to denounce the dominant power of certain decision-makers over future generations regarding climate change and suggest in their work, six ways to save the planet (The Seasons Alter: How to Save Our Planet in Six Acts).

Risse and Wollner (2019) want to conceptualize the abuse of power by companies in terms of injustice «injustice by power». They provide a useful roadmap for understanding how multinationals often use their power to cut back on wages and security conditions at home and abroad. The multinationals allow themselves to settle abusive agreements with local subcontractors. On the other hand, workers with limited bargaining power can only accept their working conditions that reflect an arbitrary and irresponsible use of leadership power.

The reviewed literature offers a critical perspective on how policymakers have failed to curb abuse of power, often due to limited skills and capacities. At the organizational level, Risse and Wollner (2019) examine how managers' selfish pursuit of profits can lead to discriminatory practices against employees. In this ideological dimension, power is no longer seen as the property of a single individual. Instead, Steven Luque (year) conceptualizes power as an ideological construct shared among various social groups.

In the approach of Bourdieu (1970), "power of symbolic violence", or of Worms (2013) "implicit threat of coercive power" or of Lukes (1974) "power to impose a decision", managerial power whether it is highly dominant or low disruptive, may indeed destabilize the organization that calls for help from a cultural leadership savior of the organization. The cultural leadership appears thus the strategic management par excellence savior of situation which is shown as the light of an effective management. The emergence of the phenomenon of leadership raises the question of whether we should rather strengthen the management of the planet by a transformational humanist leadership logic.

Section 7.3. Supranational cultural leadership underpinned by humanism

In the context of management of men and organizations, leadership, a universal phenomenon that has worried academics, politicians for centuries, has always been identified as playing an essential role in the success or failure of organizations. Some surveys that attributed up to 45% of an organization's performance to the quality of its management team have shown a strong correlation between leadership behaviour and subordinates' performance. In relation to management, leadership takes over from management.

In contrast to management, leadership reflects the view of Kouzes and Posner (1991) that “leadership begins where management ends...” According to Bean (2001), an effective leader may not be a good manager. While the leader is defined by Carlzon (1986) as a person who creates the conditions for effective entrepreneurship, Kotter (1990), sees that leadership manifests itself in growth and change. In relation to humanism, human capital, leadership relies on humanism to change the management of the world and save the human species.

In the wake of the rise and change advocated by leadership and humanism, the book endeavoured to analyse for the reader, the humanistic cultural leadership that is a savior of the human species, which should be promoted in the various academic institutions and management schools (7.3.1). The book then studies transformational cultural leadership that could save the management of planet Earth (7.3.2). Finally, it highlights the shortcomings of management schools in offering practical leadership training that effectively humanizes human resource management and bridges the gap between theoretical instruction and real-world application (7.3.3). By relating the responsibility of management schools, the book tries to demonstrate that responsibility is shared and also rests with the leaders themselves (7.2.4).

7.3.1. Humanist cultural leadership.

Although the word “humanism” comes from the Latin “humanitas”, which refers to the study of the ancient languages of Latin and Greek, originally the “humanists” were engaged in translating these ancient texts. The humanism that appeared as an artistic literary movement is not only a thought, but a new way of seeing the world that will influence the arts and the whole society. The humanist affirming his faith in the human being that he places at the center of everything, evolves with culture, science, nature and religion. Thus the term humanism has entered today in common language as a certain form of altruism and benevolence. "Happiness is born of altruism and the misfortune of selfishness," said Bouddha, later taken up by 92-year-old French journalist Philippe Bouvard. "Indifference is a sign of selfishness. Wickedness is a form of altruism."

From this point of view, the link between humans and the centre of the world, and the profile of human-based cultural leadership, seems to be clearly established. The cultural profile of leaders can indeed be humanized in a logic of altruism and dynamic learning psychology. The humanization of leaders, seen through a psychodynamic approach, can be achieved, according to an expert on leadership development (Petriglieri, 20 112 015), by learning in management schools. But this learning psychodynamic conceptualization of humanized leaders in management schools, does not mean the acceptance of dominating others by means of leadership power as explained above. While the use of humanized leadership power is at the core of "power and influence" theory, other theories and concepts related to philosophy and psychoanalysis are equally concerned with the humanization of cultural leadership and abuse of power, Management schools.

The book quotes in his remarks, the philosopher and psychoanalyst El Meligi (2007), who, a few years before Petriglieri (2011, 2015), examines in his work (direct. A humanist vision of leadership), influence models and the use of abuse of power and leadership. Based on a study of behavior and the phenomenon of obedience, the author analyzes the psychological and cultural foundations of obedience, models of obedience and collusion in abuse of power between leaders and followers. Instead of imposing an ideal model of dominant leadership, El — Meligi (2007) lays the philosophical foundations that enable institutions, including management, to choose themselves the models most appropriate to their historical circumstances or values and those of students, future leaders. Alongside management schools, as a psychodynamic guide to humanized leadership learning (Petriglieri, 20 112 015), the book by El — Meligi (2007) is intended as an interdisciplinary and multicultural guide for those interested in the training of managers and future leaders.

The researchers El — Meligi (2007) and Petriglieri (20 112 015), seem to aim for a humanized leadership that respects and takes care of humans and the planet in a long-term perspective. The leader targeted by the authors must, beyond skills and performance, take responsibility in his evolution as a complete human: physically, mentally, emotionally and spiritually. It is this deep conviction which, according to the researchers, gives birth to a humanist leader with meaning at the service of all. Closer to home, Ashton (2021), a leadership expert and writer in US newspapers, considers that human leaders do not need to wait for any crisis to show up and realize the value of human capital. For Ashton (2021), human-leaders are able to recognize the mistakes made in exercising their power and show a willingness to make up for them to ultimately demonstrate their duty of care towards all stakeholders in the organization. The exhaustion of our economic, social and ecological systems justifies for the author, the need to resort to humanistic leaders. The health crisis linked to COVID-19 has revealed more than ever, the need to transform this world for a more humanistic world.

If the Old World collapsed because of the adoption of yesterday's solutions that are no longer adapted to today's issues, the New World does not seem to be visible enough for humans. The world, which is in a phase of transformation, is always looking for a humanist leader who carries within him the beginnings of the transformation of the world by setting up a new vision, new systems of thought, and new solutions. What animates the humanist leader is not only altruism, but above all a deep need to heal the world that is sick of management (Gaulejac, 2005). In the same sense, Lecomte (2016) considers that a new philosophy of management is beginning to emerge that allows humanist companies to be stronger not by a logic of calculation, but by a voluntarist choice to change the world.

Rodary (2019), expert in Leadeurship and Transformations, joins the idea of Lecomte (2016), considering that transformation by humanistic enterprises is underway and that it is human rather than technological. “Who says Leadership problem says Leaders, Leaders and Vision problem”. Thus, the 21st century has a strong need for leaders of a new scale, that is to say, humanistic leaders, in the sense of Rodary (2019), capable of drawing up a vision for aspiring to a New World. For Rodary (2019), a New World requires a new leader who would be able to seek to transform current organizations.

However, the terms leadeurship and humanist can be opposed if they are interpreted in their excesses in the sense of Pascal Ponty, consultant en accompagnement de stratégie et de leadeurship (2007).

Indeed for the latter, leadership means anticipation, charisma, but expressed with excess, it can pour in harshness, and narcissism.

Similarly, humanism that signifies respect for people and kindness can drift into overprotection and immobility if expressed in excess (Figure 1).

Graph 1: Humanism and leadership in excess Leadership

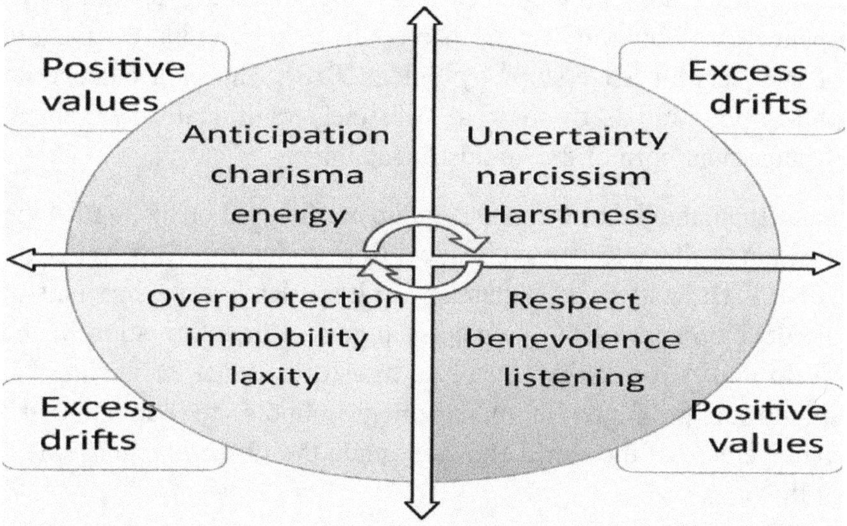

Humanist

(Inspired by Pascal Ponty, 2007)

The normal acceptance without excess of the terms leadeurship and humanism, aims instead to reconcile the positive values of leadership and humanism. In other words, according to Pascal Ponty (2007), it is a matter of seeking without giving up either, a synthesis, not a soft compromise, but a true dynamic synergy between demand and benevolence, between commitment for the vision and attention to people, between concern for the other and the energy of action. Thus the humanist leader sought to heal the world leads everyone in a positive dynamic, at the service of a legitimate vision and values expressed with kindness.

In the same way of thinking researchers El — Meligi (2007) and Petriglieri (20 112 015), Vernazobres (2016) researcher at the Université Paris-Est, showed that leadership based on behavioural character has evolved towards a more «humanistic» and «democratic» leadership based on field practices. Vernazobres

(2016), defends the idea that the leader is interested in the search for meaning and something greater than oneself, adopting an attitude of openness and humility rather than control, thus joining the posture of the "servant leadership" by Belet (2013). This is a managerial philosophy opposed to that of the traditional hierarchical management born of the «industrial age».

Since then, the literature on leadership has focused on distinguishing the human characteristics of leaders from managers (Deffayet et al., 2010). The analysis of humanistic cultural leadership that aims at the development of the human, change and transformation of the world makes it possible to call on transformational leadership that should be promoted in management schools, to humanize the management of the world and strengthen the strategic management of the planet.

7.3.2. Transformational cultural leadership.

According to researchers such as Bass (2002), most leaders adopt a transactional or transformational management style. Any manager who favours transactional leadership keeps their organization on track and delivers little results, because it is attached to the past and cannot project itself into the future to meet the expectations of present and future generations. Strategic management, in this transactional leadership, cannot be saved from the grip of the past. On the other hand, one who exercises transformational leadership obtains great results from his followers by appealing to their highest values and ideals. Transformational leaders who are able to imagine the future, have a vision and challenge employee values. (Figure 2).

Chart 2: Transactional and transformational leadership

(Based on Bass, 2002)

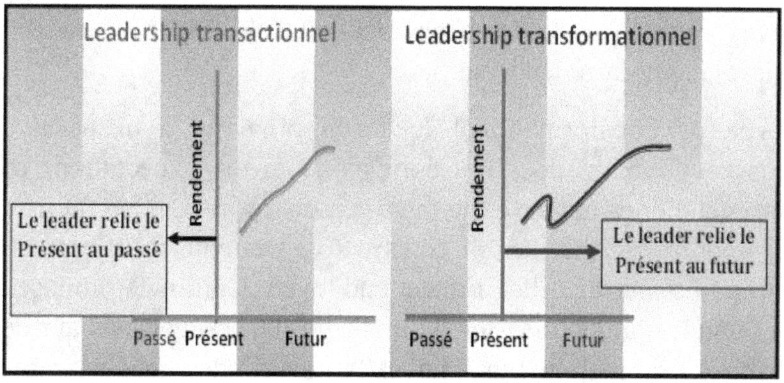

Transactional leadership struggles to achieve sustainable development because it is confined to the status quo and remains anchored in past practices. Conversely, transformational leadership emphasizes projecting strategic management into the future, aiming to preserve and adapt management practices for the benefit of both present and future generations. It should be noted, however, that if the transformational leader is coveted in some nations, it appears unacceptable in others. Kuchinke (1999), a professor at the University of Illinois in Urbana-Champaign, USA, who studied leadership styles among American and German managers, noted that transformational leadership was particularly accepted in the United StatesUnited in the 1980s and 1990s, but not appreciated in Germany because of its resemblance to certain aspects of Hitler's Third Reich.

Also, transformational leadership is not always constructive towards followers, but can reveal negative destructive behavior whose causes may come from, according to Bardes and Piccolo (2010), characteristics of the leaders themselves-even, such as anger hostility selfishness or an exaggerated and dysfunctional need for power. Later, concepts of the same connotation appeared, including "toxic leaders" (Lipman-Blumen, 2005) and "crazy bosses" (Bing, 1992). In the same vein, Einarsen (2010) describes destructive leadership when the leader misbehaves on at least one of the following forms: tyrannical behavior, disloyal support, deranged behavior, laissez-faire leadership.

The type of transformational leadership, having a destructive noxious connotation, does not correspond to the expectations of followers and does not save the management of men, in so far as it cannot appropriate the idea of constructive strategic management. Rejecting the heroic, illegitimate and even legitimate imposed leader often leading to disaster, Mintzberg (2008) suggests that true leadership is earned in what he calls "distributed leadeurship", shared among several people (Luc, 2010). The author rejects the obsession of individual leadership which is the cause of the world's problems and considers that we are the solution to the world's problems, because we need not only better leadership but also less leadership.

This raises the question: where can we find the leadership capable of transforming the world, and how can we train such leaders? Today's leaders often fall short of their humanist mission due to weaknesses in skills, personality, or a distant humanist vision. Is leadership an innate trait—something one is born with—or can it be developed? If it is not innate, how can it be acquired?

Leadership can be acquired through the knowledge and skills imparted in management schools. The book focuses on leadership acquired in management schools to shed light on the reasons that prevent participants in management training from actually practicing what they have learned about leadership. From a critical approach to management schools, the work of the book examines the extent to which management schools show weaknesses in pedagogical vision regarding the practice of humanistic cultural leadership.

7.3.3. Cultural leadership is a responsibility of management schools.

It should be considered that the responsibility for teaching humanistic cultural leadership lies with the management schools to the extent that these institutional institutions merely teach theoretical knowledge about leadership, neglecting to target the Foundation of values and humanism that characterise the personality of responsible leaders. Universities and business schools do not sufficiently integrate the real needs of the company and society in terms of internship practice and long-term stays to enable the learning cadres to touch fingers and practice cultural leadership more humanist.

The confrontation between management schools and field practice requires researchers to intellectuals and decision-makers leaders to explore appropriate solutions and reflect on programs and practical modules of cultural leadership for the benefit of a new generation of leaders practicing in deeds and facts humanism including the present and future world needs. Some Anglo-Saxon researchers, particularly in the UK, have already begun to think and study the gap between learning leadership in management schools and practicing leadership on the ground.

Amal Ahmadi, lecturer on organizational behaviour at the Henley business school in the UK and Bernad Vogel, director of the Henley leadership centre, presented a study in 2022 on the gap between leadership (conceptual knowledge) and lead (applied knowledge). For these researchers, what managers learn is not always used in their practice within organizations. The Anglo-Saxon literature on leadership learning defines this phenomenon as a transfer problem that occurs when managers do not apply knowledge, the skills or abilities acquired through return-to-work learning.

Although there is increasing interest in the evolution of humanistic cultural leadership—aimed at supporting managers in their leadership practices, as Vogel (2021) highlights—management schools tend to focus more on imparting leadership knowledge than on fostering its practical application. Certainly, managers can accumulate knowledge of cultural leadership through various sources, such as books, audios and videos, work experiences, programs or leadership development practices, such as 49-degree feedback, Coaching, mentoring, networking and action learning.

But their knowledge of cultural leadership remains, however, in the terms of Quinn (2012), inactive and potentially internalized, thus limiting their ability to manage men and organizations (Boyer, 2006) in the direction of desired humanism. Researchers Ahmadi and Vogel (2022) describe this potential as dormant and under-utilized, which means that decision makers are making fewer actions and changes in their organizations.

Also, overall, the literature on leadership seems to be based more on how to learn (how and what to learn) from leadership, than on how to apply leadership teachings and experiences in the sense of McCall (2010) of the University of Maklahoma. It would be wrong to think, according to researchers at the University of Michigan (Derue and Ashford, 2010), that holding leadership positions in organizations could be enough to intrinsically convey leadership behavior.

Similarly, the pedagogical methods of current management education do not favour more active pedagogy based on exchanges between learners allowing them to talk to each other, listen to each other and better understand each other througheven to understand their world that some learners would be called upon to lead. For example, the design of learning spaces must evolve and move away from traditional confined classrooms to more open spaces (round tables, exchanges outside walls, team buiding, meetings on a beach or at sunrise, in the mountains or in the sand dunes). The aim is to offer learners a global awareness and synergy of their worldview in relation to nature and humanistic and philosophical values that allow them to live together on the same planet. In the sense of a perspective to help management schools overcome their weaknesses, design a new vision, and respond to the emerging needs of organizations for leadership practices, It would not be impossible to consider a specialized Master's degree for leadership (in initial or continuing training).

The modules taught would relate to the history of leaders through time (successes and failures), philosophy, different constitutions and political regime (advantages and disadvantages), cultural and religious management (affinities, discord and conciliation), general culture, universal values of humanism (justice, equality, equity, respect for human rights of nature and ecology), international law, the UN, strategy (foundation, purposes and applications), conflict management, and other appropriate matters.

This specialized Master's degree in leadership could begin with a month at the management school dedicated to curriculum design, pedagogical preparation, and logistical arrangements. The subsequent months would involve immersive fieldwork—such as global travel to conflict zones or areas of social tension—allowing students to apply leadership principles in real-world contexts. Some managers, researchers, leaders and decision-makers might describe this new Master as utopian and impossible to implement. The first reason put forward by opponents of this innovative master, lies in the singular originality of this Master that goes out of the usual classical framework, opponents showing a fear, a reluctance to change, prefer a current comfort situation that is based on a transactional leadership content with the present and not the future. The second reason that could be advanced by opponents of the realization of this specialized Master lies in its significantly high cost. It must be recognized that the creativity and pedagogical innovation required of schools and organizations has a certain material cost.

Nevertheless, this pedagogical innovation is invaluable for training future humanistic, transformational leaders—those capable of guiding the world toward greater material and immaterial wealth, ultimately benefiting future generations. Living under the aegis of humanism has a cost, but does not have a price as health has a cost, but no price. The recommended master leadership is all the more important because most of the current leaders have a similar level of baccalaureate plus three (law degree), or technical school training, and rarely a master's or thesis training. Current leaders who are only legitimate by a slight majority of voters or a minority whose majority remains abstentionist are more concerned with the renewal of their election than with the renewal of more humanistic strategic approaches for the whole planet Earth. Consider a new master's degree in leadership, helps bridge the gap between theory and practice of leadership for a long time and train leaders who create a world that allows us to live together and not a world of domination, of war, and endless conflicts.

With the current leaders, the world has instead become a gigantic graveyard according to the expression of Pope Francis, reported on September 16, 2022, by the Italian newspaper Corriere della Sera, immediately after his visit to Kazakhstan: "The West has become a graveyard of humanity", "the Western countries are following the wrong path. They are no longer role models."

Other attempts to bridge the gap between theory and practice, which the management schools are encountering, have been approached by some researchers. It is for the latter to provide a solution by valuing in the eyes of practitioners, knowledge developed in relevant research such as the PM approach "Prospective Métiers" (Boyer and Scouarnec, 2009), the action-research approaches (Argyris, 1995; Eikeland, 2006), committed research (Van de VEN and Johnson, 2006), and research based on the relational integration between practitioners and teacher-researchers (Bartunek, 2007). The aim of these approaches is to bring an obvious interest for practice (David, 2007), because researchers Kieser and Leiner (2009) always question the legitimacy of a management science that does not bring scientific knowledge relevant to managerial practice.

We consider that the traditional types of research (quantitative or qualitative) seem obsolete, and no longer meet the practical needs for employability of current generations and companies. The surveys conducted by these types of research target only a very small representative sample (from 20 to 1000 people) infinitely smaller compared to a city, region, continent or planet. These superficial searches, often of convenience, not reflecting the concrete reality of the field, are often only used to fill in an old form or a rigid canvas to meet a classical academic and methodological form.

It should be pointed out that the reflexivity and innovation required of business must also be demanded of management schools and research teachers to help bridge the gap between school and business, between theory and practice, between science and non-science, between the true and the false. Kieser and Leiner (2009), proponents of the impassable gap between theory and practice, explain that the gap in question lies in the paradoxical fact that scientific knowledge always works on a logic of true/false. In this conception of science integrated into a positivistic epistemological paradigm, knowledge is only plausible hypotheses. They are not considered as rules, but simply as heuristic guides intended to stimulate reflection on the problem posed.

From this perspective, it is important to reconsider the responsibility of management schools and address the gap between theory and practice. According to Avenier (2009), closing this gap requires involving practitioners in assessing knowledge and research. Moreover, management educators are not entirely autonomous; they operate within institutions—public or private—that are often overseen by governmental or international bodies. This underscores the crucial role of decision-makers and leaders, who are primarily responsible for initiating organizational change and implementing transformational leadership.

The aim is for decision-makers to make it possible to implement the teaching of strategic management in management schools for the benefit of future generations. The involvement of responsible decision-makers in knowledge thus makes it possible to relativize the responsibility of management schools and to ask whether this responsibility does not fall on the decision-makers themselves who fail to implement the lessons learned. Is the behavior of decision-making leaders who do not practice humanistic leadership not justified by reasons of selfish psychology or context of a constraining hierarchical environment? The book first explains that cultural leadership is a responsibility of leaders before dealing further with that responsibility is shared between management schools and learner leaders.

7.3.4. Cultural leadership is the responsibility of leaders.

The recent qualitative study conducted at the Henley Leadership Center by Ahmadi and Vogel (2022) explores how and why decision-making managers experience gaps between their knowledge of leadership and their actual leadership. The analysis of interviews with 22 managers in managerial positions at different organizational levels in the UK presents this gap as a multifaceted, dynamic and complex problem involving individual, cognitive, affective and behavioural elements.

According to Ahmadi and Vogel (2022), this gap encompasses interactions among cognitive, affective, and behavioral factors at both individual and contextual levels. Cognitively, becoming aware of this gap often involves feedback from others and self-reflection. Such interpersonal feedback can prompt managers to recognize discrepancies between their knowledge and their actions, fostering greater self-awareness. Previous studies by Conger (2013) at

Clarement McKenna College in California show that 360-feedback can improve self-awareness and help an emotional experience.

Participants interviewed in the survey of Ahmadi and Vogel (2022) did target negative, but temporary, affective disorders. At the behavioural level, researchers find that managers either think to determine a future response to the gap (cognitive element) or adopt leadership to bridge the gap in the moment (behavioural element).

In planning how to bridge the gap between knowing leadership and doing leadership, reflection remains an important process that demonstrates that leadership meaning is complex and time-consuming, Forcing leaders to think and seek answers to a future challenge. The extent of the gap between these different situations can be shaped by managers' motivation, prioritization and trust, which in turn can also be impacted by hierarchical conditions, and organizational priorities (Ahmadi and Vogel, 2022). Thus, while managers may strive to apply their leadership learning, the demands of work may in effect take precedence over the application of their newly acquired knowledge, as defined by Hirst (2004), research fellow in group psychology at Aston University, Birmingham.

The analysis of both concepts of humanized leadership and dominant power allows a discussion on the differences in vision and perception between power and leadership.

Section 7.4. Power versus leadership study

We propose to elucidate the differences that characterize the two concepts of power and leadership. If power appears to be one of the most multiform and imprecise concepts according to Aubert (1998), the works devoted to power are «formidable» for anyone who tries to explain its different stakes and meanings. In power, the dominant influence (the influence of the one who dominates the relationship) is generally recognized, but rather more or less tacitly suffered.

In the case of leadership, the influence exerted by the leader is deliberately accepted or even sought with enthusiasm by the one on whom it is exercised. The book first attempts to explain the difficult choice of leaders to relinquish power (741). The book then sets out the positioning of leaders that should be identified either in the positive conception of power or in the negative conception of this power (742).

7.4.1. — Difficult choice of leaders to relinquish power.

Renouncing power would mean renouncing authority, because the notion of authority is more ambiguous, and contains according to Aubert (1998), both concepts of power and leadership. In a sense of power, authority means a type of power conferred by law or regulation to the person occupying a specific position. The authority in this case is of a temporary nature since at any time the rules may designate another person for this position. On the other hand, in an acceptance of leadership, authority comes close to leadership and refers to this natural quality of easily obtaining the adherence and obedience of others. Authority, in this second case, reflects an influence that is legitimized not by the rules, but by the qualities of the person who exercises it.

Also, power emanates from a position of authority whereas leadership does not require power. Leadership inspires its followers and followers while power forces people to follow orders out of fear. Power deprives itself of the creativity of others, while leadership bases its authority on the creativity of others. If today, authority has difficulty in imposing itself within the family, company or school, leadership on the other hand is easily imposed. The leadership that is created more over time composes with followers, while an authoritarian manager composes with subordinates. Similarly, to be authoritarian, it is not necessary to have charisma, but to be legitimate. The authoritarian manager is considered a leader, while the leader manager is respected and seen as a collaborator.

Historically, the adage 'Power tends to corrupt, and absolute power corrupts absolutely' highlights the dangers of unchecked authority. Leaders who seek to personally own and control their organizations risk detachment from their roles, which can lead to their downfall. John Randolph (1773–1833) famously remarked, 'You cannot separate property and power; they merely change hands.' Napoleon Bonaparte (1769–1821) noted that 'the art of governing is not to let men grow old in their posts,' reflecting the perils of excessive attachment to power. This enduring theme underscores how literature and history have long explored the destructive potential of disproportionate power.

Towards the end of the previous century, Enriquez (1991), cited by Aubert (1998), made a brilliant study in his book "les figures du maître" on attachment to power based on the myth of "Totem et Tabou" by Freud (1913). For Professor Enriquez, who studies imaginary functions and the social unconscious, especially the deadly aspects of power, it is difficult for the father to give up his power as it is impossible for the sons to accept it. For power remains sacred, "the divinized father is not tamed". We will then try to appropriate the power of the father by thinking either of sharing the rules, or as shown by Hegel, through the use of violence.

In any case, through an ideal of the father, one will seek to be «the father, the strongest, the one who has the right to compel others to conquer a recognition of a divinized power similar to that of the father». Enriquez (1991) points out in reference to this thought that all religions, and all ideologies brave the role of the Father: the dictator is the father of the nation. The dream lived by every man is to be the only father, the only holder of the Law: "The Law is me" (Enriquez, 1991, pp. 11-12).

Moving away from the founding myth of father power, Aubert (1998) believes that in the economic field, the work space in an organization thus gradually becomes the place par excellence where relations of dominance and power are lived. Indeed, as soon as men find themselves dependent on information and the rules of conduct imposed by business leaders, they become increasingly dependent on those who have the power to dominate the company.

More recently, at the beginning of this century, José Gaby Ababa Ekula (2007, p. 82) states in his book "Le leadeurship et le phénomène du pouvoir dans l'organisation" that power sometimes generates fear, sometimes the self-assertion that explains why some leaders reserve the right to talk about it. José Gaby Ababa Ekula (2007), wanting to emphasize the self-affirmation in the notion of power, aligns itself somewhat with the thought of Freud (1913) who explains that the exercise of power is reflected in analytical psychology, and in the affirmation of a compensation for a feeling of inferiority experienced in childhood.

Fifty after the work of Freud, Adler (1966) established in the sense of this compensation of Freud, a thesis that he calls the phenomenon of mental compensation starting from the observation that, on the bodily plane, the inferiority of some organs often results in compensation for other organs. Adler (1966) transfers this observation to the psychic and managerial sphere, and interprets the will for power and power as a necessity of overcompensation of a feeling of inferiority and therefore insecurity. This overcompensation according to Adler (1966) is a reactionary form that has been reinforced in the context of a «western civilization built on the domination of the powerful and the crushing or exploitation of the weak».

In the same sense of Adler (1966) and even before him, other authors such as Lasswell and Kaplan (1950), or Erich Fromm (1900 -1980), cited by Lester C. Lee (1963), have shown that the search for power in management presents itself as a compulsive defense against anxiety and self-depreciation.

7.4.2. — Difficult choice between positive and negative conceptions of power

The concept of power as a defense against anxiety and self-depreciation developed by Lasswell and Kaplan (1950) is later considered by Aubert (1998) to be a positive conception of power, building on its predecessor David McClelland (1970). Indeed, twenty years before Aubert (1998), David McClelland (1970), known to be at the origin of the theory of needs that act on the basis of human motivation, showed the two sides of power in management and distinguished the face personalized (negative conception) and the socialized side (positive conception) of power.

In the personalized side (negative side of power), the choice of a tendency to personal power would encourage the individual to engage with others in a win-lose exchange relationship. That is to say, any gain acquired in the company could only be at the expense of the other. According to McClelland (1970), this form of power seeking would involve selfish individuals who show a certain psychological immaturity on their part. In the second case of the socialized face, the choice of the social power tendency (positive face of power) would instead push the individual to favor a win-win relationshipwinning, that is to say, any gain obtained by the individual in a company is considered to benefit also the other members of the company. From this point of view, it can be argued that David McClelland (1970) was at the origin of what strategic management today calls the win-win approach, advocated by researchers, decision makers and practitioners of management in public and private enterprises.

In this provocative debate concerning the difficult choice between positive and negative powers and between power and leadership, the humanistic and logical temptation that results from this dialectical comparison makes it possible to encourage people to give preference only to leadership, But it would undoubtedly run up against another dif ficile logic, so much so that social life is organized around power and power relations. The book proposes to quote on this question of preference for power or leadership, the shared opinions of some management practitioners, presidents of companies also producers of knowledge and knowledge, which Girin (1989) calls «ordinary scientists», producers of theories.

Testimonials of company presidents on the choice between power and leadership.

Some CEOs (decision makers: strategy, finance, and law - April 2011) support the acceptance of leadership preference as follows:

Bill George, Harvard professor and former CEO of Medtronic :

« Only leaders who will remain focused on their values while identifying

Market developments can be seen as true leaders. »

Pierre-Étienne Lorenceau, CEO of Leaders League :

« It is time for the company to become a place of fulfillment and respect mutual, based on leadership rather than power and subordination. »

Pierre-Étienne Lorenceau, CEO of Leaders League and CEO of Harvard Squared :

« Leadership is a system of governance, and values, based on membership. »

Other CEOs, on the other hand, focus on the pre-eminence of power over authority and leadership whose opinions are underlined as follows:

Matthieu Courtecuisse, CEO of SIA Conseil :

« Power is different: it's a series of levers placed in the hands of an individual who may be totally without authority! »

– Yves de Chaisemartin, CEO of Altran :

« One can have a lot of power and not have any quality of leader »,

– Xavier Moreno, President of Astorg Partners :

« Power can also be in the hands of individuals without true leadership »

On the other hand, several other CEOs adopt a conciliatory position between the two concepts of power and leadership, as follows:

– Chiheb Mahjoub CEO of Kurt Salmon :

« Power without leadership is reduced to a balance of power and may be ephemeral »,

– Louis de Gaulle, founder and partner of the firm de Gaulle Fleurance & Associés: "It is possible to pass on power, not leadership",

– Francis Rousseau, President of Eurogroup Consulting :

« The role of a good leader is to know how to position the explicit/implicit cursor in the right place. »

The diverse opinions among company presidents regarding the difficult choices between positive power, negative power, and leadership highlight the importance of viewing leaders as producers of knowledge and theories—an idea rooted in the work of former CNRS research director Girin (1989), which was later echoed in Anglo-Saxon literature. For example, Zellweger and Zenger (2022), advocating a pragmatic view of entrepreneurship, argue that entrepreneurs are more than mere scientists; they actively seek to understand their environment and create value by solving various organizational problems.

The researchers believe that this pragmatic perspective of entrepreneurs is part of an epistemological debate between the notion of creation and discovery, and explain that entrepreneurs simply seek to discover a future that already exists in the present. This means that entrepreneurs seek to produce value in uncertainty (Zellweger and Zenger, 2022), and that overall they explore the adequacy and usefulness of their beliefs to guide and justify their actions (Bremner and Eisenhardt, 2022).

The word pragmatism means in the thinking of Zellweger and Zenger (2022) that entrepreneurs are pragmatic scientists who use a quasi-scientific process to act, solve problems and produce value in uncertainty. Indeed, it is precisely in contexts of uncertainty, or "unknown" contexts, that the scientific approach adopted by entrepreneurs is particularly interesting and useful. In the same sense of the epistemological debate between creation and discovery, other contemporary researchers such as Sergeeva, Bhardwaj and Dimov (2022) believe that entrepreneurs are theorists of discovery and that "future opportunities" are already exist and are just waiting to be discovered.

For these authors, the pragmatist perspective aims at learning that is anchored in a "determining future". They oppose the logic of discovery with their alternative perspective in which the future is not only «unknown, but unknowable» and where the future «emerges as a result of actions». Contrary to the thought of Sergeeva, Bhardwaj and Dimov (2022) on the future opportunities that already exist in the present and that it is enough to discover, researchers Zellweger and Zenger (2022), respond by stating that it is not the future solutions that exist in the present, but rather the problems that exist in the present, and that following a scientific and creative process, Entrepreneurs invent solutions and new products in the future.

Section 7.5. — Theoretical contribution of supranational cultural leadership

The book presents for the reader, in the paragraphs of this section, the conceptual justification of our theoretical contribution (751). He then discusses the types of leaders in contemporary and ancient history (752) that he confronts in favor of a new alternative type of cultural leadership more humanistic and supranational savior of planet Earth (753).

7.5.1. Theoretical contribution by knowledge management

Cultural leadership is called upon to deal with a crisis of strategic management (Beaumont, 1993) and knowledge management (Brown, 1999). In the context of a society in crisis with management problems (Gaulejac, 2005), the distance between the experts who design management tools and the agents responsible for their implementation is growing. Management knowledge seems to be more oriented towards the construction of operational tools, than towards a real understanding of the experience of organizations and people who work there (Gaulejac 2005). The coherence between experience and discourse, between prescribed and feasible is «cruelly lacking» in managerial enterprises where the prescription of the ideal sets up a universe of requirements without limits (Gaulejac ; Mercier, 2012) in which "the employee is guilty of never doing enough"?

Leaders increasingly recognize that effective knowledge management offers a competitive advantage and are attempting to shift their behavior from power-based approaches to ones rooted in ethics, meaning, and coherence between words and actions (Porcedda & Lapierre, 2008). In response to corporate crises caused by neglecting core values, Gehman et al. (2013), in the Academy of Management Journal, advocate for an ethical approach that moves beyond merely understanding values as abstract principles. Instead, they promote viewing values as practical, performative actions. The process of understanding people's values remains important and useful for advancing knowledge management (Langley et al. 2013) in companies and organizations.

In this approach, by a management of knowledge, advocated by the cultural leadership, the book does not aim at material scientific knowledge reduced to the acquisition of information. The latter is not immutable, unproven, but appears uncertain, because "scientific knowledge is not a proven knowledge, but it represents a knowledge that is probably true" (Chalmer, 1987). The book targets rather in the approach by a management of knowledge «knowledge management» (Brown, 1999), the intelligence, the value of knowledge, of the person who is a universal, lasting and immutable value. The firm tends to become the place of work where the dignity of man, the value of the person are revealed in a capitalist economic model characterized by increased competition and dominated by the law of the market.

This is what made certain economic thinkers like Delors[9] (1925) say that "the European economic model must be based on three principles: competition which stimulates, cooperation which strengthens and solidarity which unites", or as Antoine Riboud[10] Rational economic reasoning alone cannot lead to a working-class population unprepared to accept the laws of the market. You have

[9] Jacques Delors, born on 20 July 1925 in Paris, is a French economist and politician.

[10] Antoine Riboud (1918-2002), born in Lyon on Christmas day, Antoine Riboud was a public man, but very discreet about his life. Proud to be self-taught, he left a book of memoirs with the revealing title of the last in the class. A tribute to this industrial captain who marked his time and the economic history of Lyon and France.

to be able to listen and talk to him. It's not easy. The misunderstanding of the economy by workers is matched only by the misunderstanding of their system of values by leaders."

In contrast to this criticism directed against rational economic reasoning, other economists both ethnographers and sociologists like Sauvy (1994), bring a nuanced reflection and value the model of rational capitalist reasoning dominant in the absence of an alternative substitute: «If capitalism persists despite its imperfections and injustices, it is because there is no presentable replacement». Between these two trends, let's say one capitalist and the other sociological, the company is faced with the contradictory consequences of globalization, and the social responsibility of the company. This contradictory issue obliges the company to call on creativity, the intelligence of employees to move from skills management to knowledge management, especially under the effect of technological change.

Knowledge and knowledge have quickly become the key resource needed in all sectors of the economy. If knowledge is the power of "Knowledge is Power" as Bacon (1561–1626) put it, the finality of "knowledge management" This need is first and foremost to optimize decision support by promoting the availability of intelligence and facilitating strategic analyses. The new management of knowledge, understanding and respect for the values of others would indeed be the moderating counterweight of the New World, globalization, individualism, exclusion and the veneration of profit.

Our contribution producing knowledge, the knowledge that Girin (1989) calls «ordinary scientists», emanates from academic achievements and especially from field experiences, observations and management of men. The book is therefore part of a practical research dimension that requires us to stick to facts and causal relationships between facts. Then, the work of the book gives science a possibility, among others, to know the truth of the world and bring benefits to humanity through knowledge acquired.

Existing facts or acquired knowledge? What are we talking about?

A key paradox arises between self-evident facts and scientific knowledge: can science claim to see reason beyond mere facts? If facts, in themselves, are neutral and objective, do they possess autonomous authority? Or can scientific interpretation, which is mediated by theories and frameworks, challenge the notion of objective facts? This book discusses the arguments supporting the primacy of facts and the overarching role of science in understanding reality.

The view that one cannot be right against the facts is that the facts are what they are and that it would then be absurd to be right against the facts, since the facts are the index of truth. The facts have a force of their own, objective, a force in itself that could not be questioned. However, this thesis forgets that the facts can be misleading as Descartes pointed out in his metaphysical meditations: a stick plunged into water appears as broken, a square tower appears round. Science has precisely the objective of overcoming appearances, illusions and establishing truths from reasoning, produced by reason, against facts that come essentially from the senses. The idea that one cannot be right against the facts is challenged when the facts are misleading.

The proponents of this concept of misleading facts believe that facts do not exist and are only constructions of our mind. Thomas Khun, shows that the facts are never crude, neutral, but come from an interpretation, and a mental construction. Even the scientific data are in reality, not neutral, and come from the measuring instrument that issued them and the scientific theory that serves as their framework (KUHN will speak of a scientific paradigm). Facts are thus, and above all, interpretations constructed by conceptions that preexist to them.

This is already what Kant said in the criticism of pure reason in the following terms: our perceptions are not raw data of the world transmitted by the senses, but they are constructions structured by the categories of our understanding and conditioned by our reason: the tree I see is not the tree itself, but the tree as it appears to me, product of the combination of my sensitivity and my understanding." Schopenhauer said that the world was above all «my representation», it is not a given objective as neutral, that is to say a presentation, but a representation, that is to say a presentation again, which is partly produced by myself.

In the wake of this doctrine that favors the priority of facts and science, our observations and experiments remain at the heart of practical research which does not advocate a deductive mode (theory validated or refuted by facts), but inductive (theory based on observations). The book does not claim to have produced a theory, but it fuels the hope that enlightened researchers would be able to build it later on from our observations and the facts that exist.

The aim of the book is to provide the reader with an insight into the type of leadership deemed appropriate to save the managerial world in time and space. We consider that the contribution of researchers to the development of management sciences, to society and to the people who live in it, is not exclusively the result of conventional quantitative or qualitative surveys, but also emanates from reflections, thoughts, and observations that are the result of several years of field experience and management of men. The ideas of researchers, their vision of the world, and management of men, have produced in the past and can continue to produce added value to management sciences and humanity. Science itself progresses through ideas, observations, trial and error. "Scientific knowledge is not proven knowledge, but it represents knowledge that is probably true" (Chalmer 1987).

Managerial effectiveness is derived from experimentation and the right to error (MacMillan, 1982). In order to succeed in the future of management and leadership, Sample (2005) and Cost (2006) propose to show reflection, imagination and genius. It is in this evolutionary context of progress, and to advance the management of men and organizations towards a better future that the book presents in this essay of reflection, imagination and vision for a new type of cultural leadership. This type of leadership would be a new alternative paradigm supplanting the other existing types of leadership that have failed to think humanity, humanize management and allow people to live together in a village called planet Earth.

Our contribution to managerial thinking is not planning lunar plans (Hamel, 2009), but to think of a leadership that would be able to put into practice lunar plans and pilot strategic management for the benefit of all human beings on planet Earth.

The book believes that the human behavior that characterizes the types of leadership developed above is passive, controlled and determined by the external environment. Based on these observations, and the fact that the planet has not yet known a leader able to save it and ensure a survival worthy of living together, the work of the book aims to reflect on the conception of a type of supranational independent leadership, by touching somewhat on the field of philosophy and practical research.

The alternative leadership suggested to the reader aims at supplanting the different types of leadership reported in the literature. Indeed, the types of charismatic leadership, controlling (Blake and Mouton, 1964), distributed (Mintzberg [2008], shared [Luc, 2010], destructive Einarsen [2010], serving [Belet, 2013], democratic and spiritual [Vernazobres, 2016], or global [Donnet, 2020]; have shown their shortcomings, because they were all limited to a given population and geographical area [Figure 4].

Chart 4. Evolution of the type of leadership

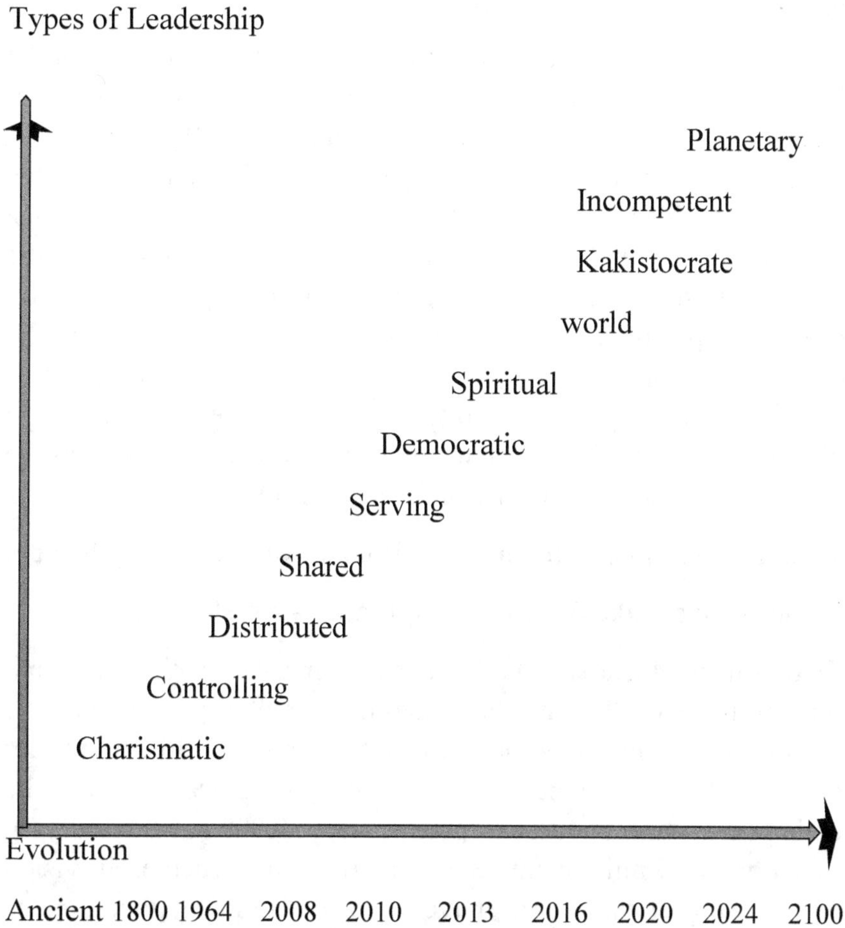

These types of leadership have failed to unite all human beings to live together on planet Earth. Certainly, living in an ideal city of Plato may not be within the reach of the human species because of the complex of power and domination of the human species (Freud, 1913 ; Adler 1966 ; and Enriquez, 1991). But aspiring to a better city than the present world seems possible with an alternative third type of leadership characterized by a form of "realistic idealism, based on knowledge rather than desires, dreams, big ideas and good intentions" (Bourdieu., 1970).

The book offers the reader who aspires to a better future, a global leadership that would transcend his national, regional or cultural affiliation. A type of leadership that Stogdill (1990) calls towards the end of the previous century, a good leader distinguished by his traits of intelligence, responsibility, independence, or what Enriquez (1991) calls the myth of good power in his work "the figures of the master". History through the ages has been marked indeed by different types of leaders whose behaviour was influenced by the external environment of their time. From this historical point of view, the book recounts the profiles of some ancient leaders, some nineteenth, twentieth and twenty-first century leaders, as well as the supranational futuristic leader of the next century.

7.5.2. Discussion of types of historical and contemporary leaders

Ancient leaders like Alexander and Mark — Aurèle

Two influential leaders who left a lasting mark on both ancient and modern history—through their visions, exemplarity, and symbolic legacies—are Alexander the Great and Marcus Aurelius. Alexander (356–323 B.C.) was reputed to have been only 12 years old when he embarked on his conquests, traveling over 30,000 km and unifying a territory of 57 million km². Seventy cities bear his name. His vision was to 'subject the whole universe to one form of government,' reflecting his desire to be the reconciler of the entire world and to organize a global community. Marcus Aurelius (121–180), Roman emperor, Stoic philosopher, and writer, also practiced philosophy while exercising power. His goal was to bring about societal change grounded in ethical principles.

Perceived as a great legislator, Marc-Aurèle promoted the reform of civil law in order to integrate more equity and humanity (protection of orphans and minors, respect for the rights of slaves and freedmen...). According to him, all glory is ephemeral and does not allow escape from death.

The leaders of the twentieth and twenty-first century

Theories based on the character traits of leaders like Alexander, however, have their limits in some nineteenth-century leaders like Napoleon, or twentieth-century as Joan of Arc, Abraham Lincoln, Mahatma Gandhi, mao TSE Toung, Winston Churchill, Charles of Gaul, Kamal Atatürk, Nelson Mandela. They were all respected leaders and yet it seems that there is no common characteristic among them and have only acted as leaders for a specific population category and geographical area. Just like the current leaders of the twenty-first century who act as leaders, only for a geographical space, and one category of population (first the greatness of America, first the health of the Europeans, first vaccinating the Russians, first the vaccine for the Chinese). This type of leader does not care about the major and global concerns of the planet.

The good intentions suggested by some continental leaders, to remove patent copyright of vaccine invention for the benefit of other poor populations, remain ephemeral without results, and reflect the enduring divide between rich and poor, north and south, east and west on Earth. Far from being transformational leaders of the world, current leaders, driven by a nationalist sentiment, only serve the expectations of a part of humanity and a geographical part of the planet. The current leadership is stripped of an ideal that aims to serve the human being, regardless of their social and geographical position. Today, management of men appears indeed, a selfish management generating wealth for some and poverty for others.

Could a supranational, humanistic cultural leadership be capable of saving Earth's management? Is an extraterrestrial crisis or threat necessary to inspire such a global leadership and move beyond the parochial limitations of national or continental leadership?

7.5.3. The new supra-national cultural leadership as savior of the planet

In answering the question of whether saving the planet is part of a logic of supranational cultural leadership, our theoretical contribution is to defend the idea that the twenty-second century futuristic alternative leadership, would be the one who would hold both the attributes of authority power and transformational leadership, to humanize world management, save humanity and safeguard planet Earth from any health crisis or hypothetical extraterrestrial threat.

The book does not aim at a cultural leadership of the spiritual type (Fourboul, 2016) or hypermodern (Tronc, 2016), or a global leadership itself questioned (Donnet, 2020), to the extent that the notion of global management or world leadership is closely linked to the models of French-speaking or Anglo-Saxon advanced countries. Rather, the book aims at an alternative type of independent and supranational cultural leadership. Stimulated by a hypothetical extraterrestrial crisis or threat, the alternative, strong and enlightened cultural leadership would be able to create around it a total mobilization of planet Earth.

This supra-national cultural leadership is about a need to return to the old values of justice and equity, and to live together on this planet Earth around a law for all following an enlightened and responsible leadership. Hans Jonas (1991) was the first German philosopher to introduce the concept of responsibility of present generations towards future generations, which became the basis for sustainable development principles at the United Nations. Hans Jonas (1991) has indeed looked at this question of global leadership, considering the hypothesis of an enlightened dictator able to achieve the sustainable development of the planet and avoid the risk of destruction of the conditions for a common life on earth.

Contemporary Anglo-Saxon scholars (Aguilera et al., 2022) advocate a return to core moral values and justice, aiming to foster global coexistence free from rejection and discrimination—under the framework of a universal law and independent supranational leadership. They cite examples of diverse, independent leaders and academics who propose that integrating moral and social considerations into management can help evolve capitalism toward a more balanced relationship between market, society, humanity, and nature—guided by a truly global leadership.

In the face of various challenges related to the exercise of abuse of power that favours profit, at the expense of moral values and sustainable development, certain philosophical approaches can come to the aid of decision-makers to humanize management and save the planet. The book cites researchers Risse and Wollner (2019), who advocate for example a philosophical plea for a new global contract (New Global Deal) between employers and employees, while Elizabeth Anderson (2017) examines the power of leaders and analyses how employers regulate the lives of employees and why no one talks about it. Other authors (Kitcher and Keller 2017) contemporary to Risse and Wollner denounce the power of certain leaders over future generations, especially regarding climate change. In their book (The Seasons Alter: How to Save Our Planet in Six Acts), the authors suggest to leaders six ways or six tracks to save our planet Earth.

The merit of researchers Risse and Wollner (2019) is to have conceptualized corporate power abuse in terms of injustice, offering a useful roadmap for understanding multinational power abuse. These, driven by an abusive selfishness based on profit and not moral values, indeed generate in the researchers' sense, an abusive discrimination and reflect an arbitrary and irresponsible use of their power of leadership. The works consulted thus offer a critical view of certain types of decision-making leaders who have failed to control abuses of power due to their incompetence and limited capabilities. It follows that recourse to philosophical precepts and moral values is ultimately the semantic foundation of a society governed by a law for all and by a supranational leadership planetary savior of humanity (Aguilera et al, 20 212 022).

Moving away from the archaic typology of incapable leaders, concerned with their prerogatives and domination, researcher Isabelle Barth (2023) adopts a corrosive critique of these dysfunctional figures. In her recent book, she proposes "management is dead, management lives". , to discover a new emerging figure of the leadership that she calls the swarm harmonizer leader, perceived as a true conductor. Barth (2024), in his latest book " The Kakistocracy or the Power of the Worst: A Journey to the Heart of Incompetence", goes even further when she believes that world business is characterized by the reign of incompetent mediocres. Isabelle Barth (2024) raises the question of how a leader, a boss, came to a position of responsibility by being incompetent.

The second question is how he can remain in office when everyone knows that he is incompetent. Based on studies and research, the author provides an original critical reading of the power link within organizations. She deciphers the world of incompetence, that is to say that of kakistocracies! For Barth (2019), the corporate world is too neglectful of its human capital. The world of management that is invested in the search for the daily and concrete life of the company seemed to move away from the field of philosophy that deals more with the thoughts of ideas than with the real concrete life of companies. However, the multifaceted economic, social, ecological, managerial and even cultural crisis has called into question the best-assured certainties that are shaking up the boundaries of different scientific disciplines. The world of management is beginning to perceive the need to think differently from managers (Barth, 2023).

As a result, the world of philosophers seeks to deal more with the concrete affairs of life in the company. The contribution of philosophy to management thus allows to prevent management crises and save the lives of humans on planet Earth. The ecologist Michel Tarrier had imagined in 2010 a certain green dictatorship (Presses du Midi, 2010) , an «ecocracy», not arbitrary, but coercive insofar as freedom stops where the planet begins. In the same sense, to save planet Earth, Michel Santo, believes in 2019 (in Accueil, Analyse, Débat, Culture, Économie et politique) that we must reduce individual freedoms by a tyranny «benevolent and enlightened».

If ecologists advocate for a 'benevolent and enlightened tyranny,' one of the primary arguments presented by researcher Mathilde Szuda in 2019 is the implementation of individual and collective rationing—ensuring everyone has access to essential goods and services in equitable amounts. This would involve regulating all consumption and overconsumption through a firm intervention by political authorities. Given that state intervention in the economy often tends toward authoritarianism, the key questions become: how can individual freedoms be curtailed, and how can citizens be persuaded to accept such measures?

At the first question of how to make citizens give up a part of their individual freedom, some philosophers advocate coercion. The idea was born in the 70s with the American political scientist William Ophuls who advocates for example a takeover by «ecologistesrois». Hans Jonas, philosopher and father of the precautionary principle, evoked in 1979 the hypothesis of a "benevolent tyranny, well informed and animated by the right understanding of things" if men could not impose on themselves the moderation necessary for their survival.

It remains to be seen who would lead this green dictatorship, this enlightened benevolent tyranny. Intellectuals? Scientists? These, despite their good intentions, would they be commendable? Are these benevolent tyrants incorruptible? According to the historian of science and environment Valérie Chansigaud, questioned in 1979 by Libération : « Attacking freedoms in the name of a superior interest is the model for all authoritarian regimes, which always end up favouring one class ». Hans Jonas, questioned by Der Spiegel on the possibility of a «kind of enlightened economic dictatorship in which philosophers would be kings», he replied that the renunciation of individual freedom was inevitable . He felt that the "green dictatorship" was not therefore a desirable horizon, but rather a warning intended to convince the individual to give up some of his freedom on his own.

On the second question of how to get citizens to consent, some people think about the solution of democracy. Questioned by Libération, the philosopher Dominique Bourg explains that the «green dictatorship» would thus pass through a referendum. But in order to have the consent of citizens, they still need to be informed and aware citizens. Others, like Agnès Sinaïqui in 2019, say that we should not " settle for a referendum and people would be able to give up certain things if they were trained, and if they had a sense of justice".

For Sinaï, a society can choose sobriety if there is a form of equitable sharing of efforts. It is not so much the regime that should be changed, but the capitalist ideology that animates it, because authoritarian governments of this world are rarely a model in terms of ecology, as pointed out in 2018, historian Jean-Baptiste Fressoz, researcher at the CNRS, who does not hesitate to speak of «carbofascism». The environmental activist Michel Sourrouille considers that in 2019, when a country is going through difficulties, "there is a tendency to entrust its destiny to a strong man or woman."

At that time, he believes, the green dictatorship would appear as a lesser evil...

CONCLUSION

This chapter aims to explore the relationship between power and leadership within management. Drawing on a broad but not exhaustive body of literature, the book seeks to answer whether safeguarding global management depends more on power or leadership—particularly, which should be emphasized in management education to humanize practices. Its contribution lies in highlighting the differences and overlaps between these concepts and demonstrating how humanistic power and leadership can help organizations attain a more sustainable society.

Based on both classical and contemporary theories, the discussion points toward the emergence of a new form of independent, humanistic, and supranational cultural leadership—one capable of saving the planet and fostering coexistence free from discrimination and domination.

CONCLUSION OF PART THREE

In the question of whether culture can influence human behaviour, the book has shown that culture exerts both a negative and positive influence on human behaviour (chapter five). In the negative approach to cultural influence, the book explains to what extent this negative approach is a brake on sustainable development based on work and studies in cross-literature. The book then sought to shed light on the positive approach to cultural influence, while showing that culture is a vector of sustainable development capable of saving the world according to research and work mentioned above.

If culture can save the world, the relevant question is how? The answer given in chapter six, explaining that culture can save the world through cultural intelligence, artificial intelligence and unavoidable cultural change. The book has demonstrated how cultural intelligence can save the world through performance indicators and a cultural intelligence quotient that is perceived differently depending on whether the reader is positioned in the American or French approach.

In the context of the power and leadership relationship with management, we asked ourselves the question in chapter 7, whether saving management is a matter of power or leadership that should be promoted in management schools to humanize management. Our contribution is to have revealed the differences in perception between the two concepts and shown how power and leadership can help management and companies achieve their goals.

The discussion based on old and contemporary theories of power and leadership suggests the emergence of a new type of independent, humanistic and supranational cultural leadership, who would be able to cure management and save the planet from discrimination and conflicting domination.

GENERAL CONCLUSION

The book concludes with a general conclusion which is structured around three unifying axes. The essay approach on culture as a nerve of peace in the world, suggests a reminder of the introductory thought, a synthesis of the theoretical contribution and the limits of the work carried out.

Reminder of the introductory approach

The book provides, in its preliminaries, clarifications on the human politics that characterizes a mosaic of culture in the universalist sense of the term. It is a new sense of culture that wants to be universal and dominant. The mosaic of culture underlaid by human politics can also be explained by the human species. From this point of view, the book shows that the culture that belongs to the human species, contains several meanings: anthropological, sociological, evolutionary and change. The anthropological meaning means a scientific anthropology based on cultural relativism. The sociological meaning of peoples' customs is linked to social representations based on values and norms. The evolutionary meaning of culture is reflected in a confrontation between the notion of culture and that of civilization. In the sense of cultural change, the book highlights the complexity of the phenomenon of cultural change and the difficulties of reducing resistance to change.

The issues of cultural change in its relationship with its socio-political environment appear indeed complex and disparate. In relation to the sciences, the book notes that the gap between the natural sciences and the spiritual sciences of culture still exists. Thus, a bridge between the philosophy of the exact sciences and the philosophy of the humanities and social sciences deserves to be established to constitute critical passages. Also, in relation to the world, culture cannot be seen as synonymous with the Americanization of the world, but as the triumph of inclusive cultural hypercapitalism aimed at a world culture through the globalization of local reinterpretations. From now on, man is only culture and in the end everything is cultural.

Since everything is cultural, concepts such as cultural management and sustainable development can be better understood through academic theories and debates. This book seeks to establish a connection between sustainable development and cultural management, emphasizing how management practices contribute to sustainability. In addition, it highlights the role of culture itself in advancing sustainable development, drawing on the perspectives of UNESCO, the United Nations, African nations, and other countries. However, some critical reflections question whether the emphasis on culture's contribution to development might be a distraction or a decoy.

This debate leads to the emergence of cultural diversity in its form of national and corporate culture, or in its form of cultural conflict. Indeed, the cultural dimension in private companies is part of a national culture within which the company establishes its own corporate culture. The book provides an insight into examples of cultural diversity and cultural management in countries such as Morocco, France, and UNESCO's 2030 Cultural Agenda.

To the question of whether culture can influence behaviour in the world, it is shown that culture can exert both a negative and a positive influence according to cross-approaches in French, English and Arabic literature. Proponents of the negative influence of culture view the reactive profile of business leaders, and their passivity to take initiatives as barriers to economic growth and sustainable development. In contrast to this belief, the proponents of culture's positive influence on human behaviour argue that culture is dynamic and constantly evolving towards human progress, and a vector for adaptability and sustainable development.

From the perspective of saving the world, the book demonstrates how cultural intelligence can succeed in saving the world through performance indicators and a cultural intelligence quotient, according to the American and French approach. To do this, the book explains the different aspects of cultural intelligence that may be present in the perception of different researchers and decision-makers. Culture cannot succeed in saving the world without the contribution of artificial intelligence that is developing more and more in this century. The idea of saving the world means, in the end, a cultural change that can only be realized through the contribution of a decision-maker with a leadership logic and a supranational vision.

In response to the question of whether saving global management is a matter of leadership or power, the elements of the answer revealed differences in stakes and perception between the two concepts, and showed how humanistic power and leadership can help management and companies to achieve the goals of a more sustainable society. The discussion based on ancient and contemporary theories of power and leadership suggests the emergence of a new type of leadership, cultural, independent, humanistic and supranational. This new type of leadership would be able to save the planet and allow us to live together without discrimination and conflicting domination.

In this vein, the book aims to deepen the understanding of cultural leadership and contribute to the development of future theories—integrating management learning with practical leadership development.

Theoretical contribution

In its theoretical contribution, the book tries to explain by the added value of knowledge, that leaders who are convinced of the competitive advantage of a management of knowledge try to use a management mode no longer centered on power, but on the values of ethics and meaning and on a coherence between their speech and their actions (Porcedda, Lapierre, 2008). The process of understanding people's values remains crucial to advancing knowledge management (Langley et al. 2013) in companies and organizations.

This approach, by a management of knowledge, does not aim at the material scientific knowledge reduced to the acquisition of information, because the latter is not proven, but uncertain (Chalmer, 1987). The chosen approach, targets rather the management of knowledge, intelligence, the value of knowledge which is a universal, sustainable and immutable value. The theoretical contribution of the work of the book producing knowledge that Girin (1989) calls «ordinary scholars», emanates from academic achievements and especially field experiences, observations and management of men.

It is a need to return to the ancient values of justice and equity and to live together in this planet Earth around a law for all, following a leadership not selfish nationalist, but supranational enlightened and responsible. While Hans Jonas (1991) was the first German philosopher to address this issue of global leadership, other contemporary Anglo-Saxon authors (Aguilera et al., 2021, 2022) are moving in the same direction to return to societal moral values and justice, to escape the technical grip that mechanizes human values.

In his essay "Reading the technological society to understand the mechanization of values and its ontological consequences ", Lindebaum (2021) questions how to understand in practice this technique that mechanizes values while materiality is "subordinated" values (Hinings & Greenwood, 2015). The author analyses the different degrees of value mechanization which can influence in practice the different consequences, either for a better dimension or for a worse dimension. Lindebaum (2015) recognizes that the technique or technology can be used for pro-social purposes or cause massive individual and societal harm if not controlled.

The first implication of the author's analysis is the trend towards the mechanisation of values shifting attention to means rather than ends Selznick (1957). Second, an excessive focus on the effectiveness of the technique tends to emphasize "techniques" that are normally neutral and available for any purpose. On the other hand, Selznick offers a similar warning when he draws attention to the drift that constitutes the tendency to detach oneself from the ends of institutional and community life. However, to remove the "ends", because of empirical and practical work, leads to create conditions of "tyranny of means and powerlessness of ends" (Krygier, 2015). The means can indeed exercise this tyranny, when we confuse cause and effect. The cause of hypertension, for example, is defined in the biological field using technology, when in reality hypertension is a social effect. As a result, socio-economic conditions should be addressed as the causes of hypertension. For Lindebaum (2015), confusing causes and effects is not just a matter of non-information. , but requires the need for social scientists to know empirical data.

Managerial contribution

Cultural leadership plays a vital role in addressing crises in strategic management (Beaumont, 1993) and knowledge management (Brown, 1999). In a society plagued by management dysfunction, much of management knowledge tends to focus on developing tools rather than fostering a genuine understanding of organizational experience (Gaulejac, 2005). The disconnect between theory and practice, between prescribed strategies and achievable outcomes, is a significant shortcoming in many managerial endeavors.

The contribution of the book to managerial planning is not to plan lunar plans (Hamel, 2009), but to think of a leadership that would be able to put into practice lunar plans and pilot strategic management for the benefit of all human beings on planet Earth. The work of the book emphasizes that the contribution of researchers to the development of management sciences, strategic management and humanity is not exclusively the result of conventional quantitative or qualitative surveys, but also emanates from reflections, thoughts, and observations that are the result of several years of field experience and management of men. The ideas of researchers, their vision of the world, and management of men, have produced in the past and can continue to produce added value to management sciences and humanity.

Science advances through ideas, observations, experimentation, and the willingness to learn from errors (MacMillan, 1982). Similarly, managerial effectiveness depends on experimentation and the acceptance of failure as part of the learning process. To thrive in the future of management and leadership, researchers like Sample (2005) and Cost (2006) emphasize the importance of reflection, imagination, and innovative thinking.

It is in this evolutionary context of progress, and to advance management that the book presents in its conclusions a managerial contribution aimed at a new type of cultural leadership. This type of supranational leadership, would be the alternative supplanting the other types of existing leadership, nationalist and selfish, who did not manage to manage humanity, and allowed to live together in a village called planet Earth. In doing so, the book aims to shed light on how power and leadership can humanize management and save the planet.

From this analysis, it becomes evident that power and leadership can serve as foundational paradigms for developing a supranational, cultural leadership capable of preserving management and safeguarding Earth. The ultimate aim is to foster a world built on coexistence free from rejection and discrimination, governed by universally applicable principles under the guidance of an independent, global leadership.

This enlightened foresight, based on knowledge management, would be realistic and possible, not based on the abuse of power, incompetence, and selfish desires for domination, because "there are no underdeveloped countries, but only under-governed countries". (Drucker, 2005).

Limits of the contribution of the work

The contribution of the book, however, contains certain limitations related to errors inherent in any theory, thought or vision confronted with other subsequent realities. The right to error of the researcher makes it possible to advance science, knowledge, human management and the organization of planet Earth. If the error is human, it differs however from the fault which does not mean failure (Berthet, 2018; Lourei, 2021).

Given that there is no way to avoid mistakes in business, claiming the right to error does not mean accepting decision errors but rather trying to reduce or stop them (Autistiser, Berthet, 2021). Engaging in a right to error approach means choosing to make it a learning task in management schools and field experience contexts. Human error remains ultimately a lever of innovation that frees confidence and creativity.

BIBLIOGRAPHICAL REFERENCES

A

Adler N. (1994), Organizational Behaviour: A Multicultural Approach. French translation of 2° édition, 324 pages.

Adler, A. (1966), knowledge of man: study of individual character, Paris: Payot,

Aguilera, R. V., Aragón-Correa, J. A., Marano, V (2022), « Rethinking corporate power to tackle rand societal challenges: lessons 002), "Understanding Cultures and Implicit Leadership Theoriesacross the Globe: an Introduction to Project GLOBE", Journal of World Business, Vol. 37, 2002, pp. 3-10

Aguilera, R. V., Aragón-Correa, J. A., Marano, V. & Tashman, P. A. (2021): "The corporate governance of environmental sustainability: A review and proposal for more integrated research, in Journal of Management, 47 (6), 1468–1497.

Ahmadi, A., Vogel, B. (2022), "Knowing but Not Enacting Leadership: Navigation the Leadership Knowing-Doing Gap in Leveraging Leadership Développent, in the Academy of Management Learning & Education, Manuscript, I'd AMLE-2020-0534-RES.R2

All-Arkoubi. K & McCourt. W (2004). "The politics of HRM: waiting for Godot in the Moroccan civil Amy Chua 'World on Fire: How Exporting Free Market Democracy Breeds Ethnic Hatred and Global Instability

André Malraux (1901 — 1976), Ang Soon and Linn Van Dyne (2008), Handbook of Cultural Intelligence

Arcand, G. (2006), The Role of National Culture in the Relationship between HRM Practices and Organizational Performance: The Case of Banks in 22 Countries in North America, Europe and Asia. Doctoral thesis, Université Paul-Verlaine UFR « Études supérieures de management ». Management et management. — Metz, 2006

Argyris C. (1995), know to act. Paris, Interéditions, 330 pages.

Ashton, J. (2021), The Nine Types of Leader: How the Leaders of Tomorrow Can learn from the leaders of today, Publisher : Kogan Page; 1 st édition (3 Janv. 2021), 288 pages.

Aubert, N. (1998), « relations of power and leadership », in Traité de sociologie du travail, 600 PP, Dir by Michel De Coster et al., Edition of Boeck Supérieur, Collection : « Ouvertures sociologiques » pages 443 To 474

Autissier, D, Berthet, V. (2021), stop To decision errors ; know and manage cognitive biases with the cognitive Bias Inventory, EMS edition, 112 pages.

Avenier MJ (2009), « Bridging a reputed impassable gap: building scientific knowledge relevant to practice », in Revue management et avenir, n° 30, p. 188 -206.

Aycan, Z., Kanungo, R., Mendonca, M., Yu, K., Deller, J., Stahl, G. & Kurshid, A. (2000), 'Impact of culture on human resource management practices: a 10-country comparison', Applied Psychology, Vol. 49, No 1, pp. 192-221.

Aycan, Z., Kanungo, R., Mendonca, M., Yu, K., Deller, J., Stahl, G. & Kurshid, A. (2000), 'Impact of culture on human resource management practices: a 10-country comparison', Applied Psychology, Vol. 49, No 1, pp. 192-221.

Aycan, Z., and all (2001), Impact of Culture on Human Resource Management Practices: a 10 — Country Comparison » First Published in Psychologie appliquée 49 (1):192-221.

B

BaileyJ. R. (Ed.) (2002), 'Refracting reflection: Views from the inside', in the Academy of Management Executive, vol. 1, no. 1, p. 77.

Barabel. M. Meier. O. (2008). International Human Resource Management, Dunod Edition, 139

Barakat H. (1993), The Arab world: society, culture, and state. University of California Press (Berkeley), 368 pages.

Barbe Philippe, 2006, l'antichoc des civilisations. Médiations méditerranéennes, France, L'Aube, Monde en cours, 172 p.

Bardes M., Piccolo R.F. (2010), « Goal Setting as an Antecedent of Destructive Leader Behaviour, » When Leadership Goes Wrong, IAP 2010 édition, pp. 3–22.

Barney, J. & Rangan, S. (2019). Editors" comment : Why we need a special issue on New. Theoretical perspectives on market-based economic systems? Academy of Management Review, 44 (1), 1–5

Barnouw, V. (1963). Culture and Personality. Homewood, IL : Dorsey Press.

Barth, I. (2019) Le Manager et le Philosophe. Edition the passer 384 p

Barth, I. (2023) management is dead, long live management! : Change your beliefs and certainties. In Edition EMS 114 p

Barth, I. (2024) the kakistocracy or the power of the worst: Journey to the heart of incompetence. Edition EMS 176 p

Bass S. (2002), sustainable development strategies : a resource book. Edition OECD Publishing, 358 p.

Bateson. G, and Watzlawik. P. (1972). The new communication. Paris, Le Seuil, 372 pages.

Bean D. F. (2001), « Equivocal Reporting: Ethical Communication issue, » Journal of Business Ethics, no. 29, 2001, pp.65-76.

Beaumont, P.B. (1993). Human resource management: key concepts and skills, London: Sages Publications ltd

Belet, D. (2013). The servant leadership: a powerful and humanistic paradigm to address the management crisis, Gestion 2000, pp.15-33.

Belet, D. (2016), « Le servant leadeurship » : paradigme alternatif et efficace de management des hommes » in le leadeurship, research and practices (Dir) Noguera et Plane, edition Magnard — Vuibert, April 2016, 214 pages ;

Benabdeljalil, N. (2007), "The management of enterprises in Morocco: between cultural and economic contingencies." International SME Review 202 (2007): 89–122. DOI: 10.7202/1008518ar

Benabdeljlil, N. (2007), "The management of enterprises in Morocco: between cultural and economic contingencies." International SME Review 202 (2007): 89–122. DOI: 10.7202/1008518ar

Benhida, Zakia; BRANCU, Laura. (2019), "Evaluation of the cultural intelligence profile of Moroccan and Romanian students". Journal of the International Journal of Management Sciences [S.l.], n. 2, j'une 2019. ISSN 2605-7158. Available at: >https://revues.imist.ma/index.php/RMPSG/article/view/16617/9134>. Date accessed: 12 June 2021

BENSA, A. (2006), The End of Exoticism. Essays in Critical Anthropology (2006), writing history [online], 8 | 2011, posted on 11 October 2014, accessed 7 June 2022. URL : http://journals.openedition.org/elh/551 ; DOI: https://doi.org/10.4000/elh.55

BENSA, A. (2006), The End of Exoticism. Essays on Critical Anthropology, Toulouse, Anacharsis (Essays), 2006, 364 p

Ben-Shahar, D.; Carmeli, A.; Sulganik. E. ; Weiss, D.(2022), power and dominant coalitions in family business, Academy of Management Review in Press, Published Online:25 Mar 2022 https://doi.org/10.5465/amr.2021.0007.

Bergeron, P.G. (2001). Dynamic Management: Concepts, Methods and Applications. Boucherville, QC : Gaëtan Morin editor.

Berthet, V. (2028), the error is human. At the frontiers of rationality, edition CNRS 20/09/2018

Bidi, G. and Bane, M.F. « Relations between socio-cultural practices, performance and ethics in the public service: a case of an African public administration », journal Question(s) de management ? ; NN31 February 2021, EMS Edition pp. 119-130

Bing S. (1992), crazy boss. NY : Pocket Books, 271 pages

Blake, R., and Mouton, J.S. (1964), the managerial grid: key orientations for achieving production through people, Houston, Texas. Gulf Pub, 1964, 340 pages

Bloom, A. (2018). The Disarmed Soul: Essay on the Decline of General Culture, ed. 1. Paris, France : Les Belles Lettres. 205 p

Boubacar. D (2004). Sociocultural factors and business start-ups in Guinea, exploratory study of the ethnic groups Peule and Soussou. Thesis presented at the Faculty of Graduate Studies, Université Laval.

Bourdieu, and Passeron, J. C. (1970), reproduction : elements of a theory of the educational system, Paris, les éditions de Minuit, col » le sens commun », 1970

Bouversse, J. (2004), « Bourdieu, savant et politique » in Presses universitaires de France Cités 2004/1 (n° 17), page 133 – 141

Boyer L, and Scouarnec. A (2009). La prospective des Métiers. Editions EMS, 352 pages

Boyer L. (2006), the management of men. Eyrolles-éditions d'Organisation, Paris, 232 p

Brannen J. (1999), "Reconsidering children and childhood: Sociological and policy perspectives", in the new family? Edited by Silva, E.B. and smart, C., editors. Sage, pp. 1-12.

Braudel, Fernand, 1969, written on history, Paris, Flammarion, Champs, 314 p.

Bremner, R. P. & Eisenhardt, K. M. 2022. Organizing form, experimentation, and performance: Innovation in the nascent civilian drone industry. Science Organization, forthcoming.

Brewster C., Sparrow P.R., Vernon G. (2007), international human resources management.2nd Edition, London, UK, Chartered Institute of Personal Development, 323 pages.

Bruckner, Pascal, 2002, le sanglot de l'homme blanc. Tiers-monde, culpabilité, haine d'soi, Paris, Seuil, Points, 1 st ed. 1983, 309 p.

Carlzon J (1986). The Pyramid Falls! Paris, InterEditions, 221 pages.

C

Chalmers aF (1987), what is science ? Paris : The paperback book, 286 pages.

Choueir, R (2008), "Cultural Shock and Clash of Cultures. Geography and Cultures », Electronic Edition URL : http://journals.openedition.org/gc/801

Choueiri, R. (2008). "Cultural Shock" and "Clash of Cultures". 5-20. 10.4000/GC 801

Chua. a (2007), The Burning World. Social Violence and Globalization, Seuil édition, New World books collection, 352 pages

Claude Allègre (2003), un peu de science pour tout le monde, Fayard, 2003. Galilée, Plon, 2002.

Claval, Paul, 2003, Géographie culturelle. Une nouvelle approche des sociétés et des milieux, Paris, A. Colin, Coll. U, 287 p.

Combalbert. L (2005), the Management of Crisis Situations, First edition at ESF Éditeur, «Entreprise» series, in Paris. 3rd edition in 2012 —206 pages

Conger, J. 2013. Mind the gaps: What limits the impact of leadership education. Journal of Leadership Studies, 6 (4): 77–83.

Cost S. (2006), the leader of the 3rd millennium, Organization Edition, 300 pages.

Crozier., Friedberg, E. (1977), "The actor and the system: Constraints of collective action", First published in 1977, in the collection "Sociologie politique".

D

D'Iribarne ; Henry ; Segal ; chevrier ; Globokar (1998), Cultures and globalization, Seuil, Paris 1998

D'Iribarne P. (1990), « Face l'impossible décentralisation des entreprises africaines », in Revue française de gestion n° 80, p. 28.

D'Iribarne P. (2004), « Business management and cultural diversity. Between tradition and modernity: a subtle equation in developing countries", in Futuribles, n° 295, pp. 57-70

D'Iribarne (1989), the logic of honour, Seuil, Paris 1989

Daniels and Radebaugh (2001),

Daniels, J.D., and Radebaugh, L.H. (2001). International Business. Environments and Operations. Reading : Addison-Wesley.

David S. Landes, The Wealth and Poverty of Nations: Why Are Some So Rich and Others So Poor. New York : W.W. Norton, 1998. 544 pp.

Day, D. V. 2000. Leadership development: A review in context. The Leadership Quarterly,11 (4): 581–613

Deffayet, S., Livian, Y. F., Petit, V. (2010). The art of command. Permanences and modes in leadership styles, Management, 2000, vol. 10, n° 5, pp. 85-99.

Defrenne J., Delvaux C. (1992), the management of uncertainty. Boeck & Larcier édition, 281 pages.

Demorgon J (2000), Complexity of Cultures and Interculturality. Saved 352 pages.

Denning S. (2000), The Springboard : How storytelling ignites action in knowledge-era organizations. Butterworth Heinemann, Boston, 248 pages.

DeRue, D. S. & Ashford, S. J., 2010. Who will lead and who will follow? A social process of leadership identity construction in organizations. Academy of Management Review, 35 (4): 627–647

Diamond J. (2005), Collapse: How Societies Decide to Disappear or Survive (collapse : How societies choose to Fail or Survive), published by Gallimaard, 2,006,664 pages

Dilts R., Bonissone G. (1995), tools for the future? Paris : La Méridienne, 464 pages.

Donnet, P. A. (2020), the global leadership in question: the confrontation between China and the United States, edition of l'Aube (28 May 2020), collection Monde en cours 224 pages

Drucker. P (2005). The future of management. Global village, 185 pages.

E

Earley, C. (2002) Research in Organisational Behaviour, volume 24, 358 pages

Earley, C., and Mosakowski, E. (2004), 'Cultural Intelligence', in Harvard Business Review magazine

Eddakir A. (2003), « Étude de la relation culture nationale-pratiques de management : cas du Maroc », Actes de colloque AIREPME, Agadir, October, 14 pages.

Eikeland O. (2006), 'Condescending ethics and action research', in Action Research, vol. 4, no. 1, p. 37-47Bartunek J.M. (2007), 'Academic-practitioner collaboration need not require joint or relevant research: toward a relational scholarship of integration', in the Academy of Management Journal, no. 50, pp. 1323-1333.

Einarsen S., Skogstad A., and Aasland M. S. (2010), "The Nature, Prevalence, and Outcomes of Destructive Leadership: A Behavioural and Conglomerate Approach," pp. 145-174, in When Leadership Goes Wrong, IAP edition 2010.

El Amrani, J. and M.A. Chebihi (2003), Culture et management au Maroc, Repères et perspectives, Rabat, no 4, hiver, p. 87-107.

El Aoufi (2000), "The social imperative in Morocco: from adjustment to regulation", economic critique no. 03 • autumn 2000 PP 53-79

El Aoufi, N. ; Hollard, M. (2004), « Les relations professionnelles au Maroc : violence et justification », Critique économique n° 12 • Hiver-printemps 2004 PP 5-36

El — Meligi, M. (2007), lead. A humanist vision of leadership, in the science and administration collection publication: 6 September 2007, 228 pages

Enriquez, E. (1991). Les figures du maître, Paris : Arcantère

F

Falipo, F. (2011), sustainable development, collection "Thèmes et Débats société" by Éric Klass ... pages

Ferdinand Tönnies 1855-1936) and Alfred Weber (1868-1958).

Ferro, Marc (ed.), 2003, le livre noir du colonialisme XVIe-XXIe siècle : de l'extermination à la repentance, Paris, Hachette Littératures (Pluriel-Histoire), 1119 p.

Fletcher, R. (1957), instinct in the light of recent Works in comparative psychology, international, universities press, inc. New York 336-337 PP,

Florida. R (2012), The Rise of the Creative Class, Revisited, New York, Basic Books, 2012,484 pp. » , the new review of work posted on October 29, 2016, accessed May 10, 2020. URL : http://journals.openedition.org/nrt/297

Fortin. A, and Warren J. P. (2015), Pratiques et discours de la contreculture au Québec, Septentrion, 270 pages.

Foucault. M (1976). La volonté de savoir. Volume 1, Gallimard, Paris, 248 pages.

Fourboul, C.V. (2016), « les valeurs du leadeurship spirituel », in le leadeurship, recherche et pratique (Dir) Noguera et Plane, édition Magnard — Vuibert, April 2016, 214 pages.

Fournier, LS (2009), « De l'utilité de la notion de culture », Journal des anthropologues, 118-119 | 2009, pp. 215-220. Posted July 1, 2014, accessed May 22, 2022. URL : http://journals.openedition.org/jda/4079 ; DOI: https://doi.org/10.4000/jda.4079

Freud, S. (1913), Complete Works — Psychoanalysis — Vol. XI : 1911-1913, Edition 3, Volume 11, 436 pages

Freund, J. (1965), what is politics? Ed. Sirey, 1965.

Friedman T.L (2005), a geometric world: the world is flat: A brief history of the twenty-first century, New York: Farrar. Strauss and Giroux, 496 pages.

Frimousse S., Peretti J.M. (2007), « La diversité ou la dialectique du semblable et de l'indifférent : Implication managériale », in Revue Management et Avenir, n° 14, p 109-116.

G

Gaby José Ababa Ekula (2007), Leadership and Power in the Organization, in ISM Dakar — Higher Diploma of Management 2007

Garaudy, Roger, 1977, for a dialogue of civilizations, Paris, Denoël, Les Coudées franches, 233 p.

Gaulejac, V. (2005), La Société malade de la gestion. Management ideology, managerial power and social harassment, Essays, publication of 07/01/2005, 288 pages,

Gauthier, C. (1989). "From a Soulless World to a Soulless World". Journal of Educational Sciences, Volume 15, Number 3, 1989, pp. 463-478. Digital release : November 26, 2009

Gauthier, V (2014), le savoir relié : vers un leadeurship intuitif et relationnel. Paperback — 28 August 2014

Gelfand M. J., Nishii LH., Raver, J. L. (2006), "On the nature and importance of cultural tightness-looseness," in Journal of Applied Psychology. 91, No 6, pp. 1225-1244

Girin J. (1989), «Methodical opportunism in research on the management of organizations», in communication to the study day «Action-research in action and in question», AFCET, Collège de systèmises, Ecole Centrale de Paris, 10 March 1989, 11 pages

Godelier, E. (2006), corporate culture. Publisher: La Découverte. Collection : Repères, 128 pages

Godelier, E. (2009), "La culture d'entreprise. Source de pérennité ou source d'inertie ? », Revue française de gestion (n° 192), pages 95 To 111.

Godet M (2007), le courage du bon sens, pour construire l'avenir autrement. Odile Jacob, 414 pages.

Godet M. (2001), Creating Futures : Scenario-planning as a strategic management tool. Economica, 280 pages.

Goodenough, W. (1971). Culture, langue et société. M.A. : Addison-Wesley.

Goudineau, Y. (2018), science et culture. Débat », anthropologue, directeur de l'École française d'Extrême-Orient de 2014 à 2018, est directeur d'études (« Ethnologie comparative de l'Asie du Sud-Est ») et actuel responsable du Centre EFEO de Chiang mai. P 239 — 246

Greffes (2004). « La Valorisation économique du patrimoine ». Bulletin des bibliothèques de France (BBF), 2004, n° 2, p. 141-142. Disponible en ligne : <http://bbf.enssib.fr/consulter/bbf-2004-02-0141-006>. ISSN 1292-8399.

Gregg, J., Earley. C, et ANG, S. (2003), Cultural Intelligence : Individual Interactions Across Cultures (15 juillet 2003), 400 pages.

Griffin, R.W., et Pustay, M.W. (2005)., International Business : A Managerial

Habermas, J. (1987), théorie de l'agir communicationnel, tome 1 : Rationalité de l'agir et rationalisation de la société. Paris : Fayard, 1987 à 1929),

H

Hamel G. (2009), 'Moon Shots for Management', in Harvard Business Review Press, février 2009, vol. 87, n° 2, p. 91-98.

Hans Jonas (1991), le principe responsabilité broché en français 1991 versions originales en allemand 1979 éditions cerf 336 pages

Harold D. (1950-12-01), éditeur : Yale University Press (1er janvier 1734), 333 pages

Hermann, C. F. (1963.), « Quelques conséquences de la crise qui limitent la viabilité des organisations », Science administrative Quarterly, vol. 8, n° 1, juin 1963

Herskovits (Melville J.) (1952), l'homme et ses œuvres, New York, Alfred Knopf, 1952

Herskovits, M. J. (1950), les bases de l'anthropologie culturelle. Édition électronique réalisée par Jean-Marie Tremblay, Paris : François Maspero Éditeur, 1967, 331 pages. Collection : petite collection Maspero, no 106.

Hinings, C. R. & Greenwood, R. (2015.), absent dans l'action : la contribution de Philip Selznick à la théorie institutionnelle contemporaine. Dans M. S. Kraatz et R. Flores (dir.), Institutions and Ideals : Philip Selznic's Legacy for Organizational Studies, vol. 44 : 121-148. Bingley, UKL : Emerald Group Publishing Limited.

Hirst, G., Mann, L., Bain, P., Pirola-Merlo, A. et Richver, A. 2004. Learning to lead : The development and testing of a model of leadership learning. The Leadership Quarterly, 15 (3) : 311-327

Hofstede (1980), « Culture and Organizations », International Studies of Management & Organization, vol. 10, 1 janvier 1980, p. 15–41 (lire in line [archive],

Hofstede, G. (1980). Motivation, leadership et organisation : les théories américaines s'appliquent-elles à l'étranger ? In D.W. Organ (Ed.), the applied psychology of work behaviour, 126-154. Boston : Irwin.

Hofstede, G. (1984). Culture's conséquences : International differences in work-related values. London : Sage.

Hofstede, G. (1993). Cultural constraints in management theories. Academy of Management Executive. 7 (1) : 81-93.

Hofstede, G. (1994). Vivre dans un monde multiculturel : comprendre nos programmations mentales. Paris : Les éditions d'organisation.

Hofstede, G. et Bond, M.H. (1988). The Confucius connection : From cultural roots to economic growth. Organizational Dynamics. 15 (1) : 4-21 (2001), Cultur's conséquences : Comparing values, behaviours, institutions and organisations across nations, London, Sage, 2001, 596 p.

Hofstede, G., et Bond, M.H. (1988). The Confucius connection : From cultural roots to economic growth. Organizational Dynamics. 15 (1) : 4-21.

HouranI, Albert, 1991, la pensée arabe et l'Occident, Paris, Naufal, 1er éd., 1983, 415 p.

House, R.J. (2001), « Cultural Acumen for the Global Manager : Lessons from Project GLOBE », Organizational Dynamics, Vol. 29, n° 4, 2001, pp. 289 – 305

House and all (2004), culture, leadership et organisations : l'étude GLOBE de 62 sociétés, Sage, Londres, 2004 12P. W. Dorfman & M. JavidanP. J. Hanges &

Huntington, Samuel, 2000, le choc des civilisations, Paris, Odile Jacob, poches, 1er éd.1996, 545 p. DOI : 10.3917/comm.066.0238

Husserl, E. (1976), la crise des sciences européennes et la phénoménologie transcendantale, Paris, Gallimard, 1976. F et préface de G. Granel (abrégé Krisis dans la suite du texte et des notes).

Husserl, E. (2012), la crise de l'humanité européenne et la philosophie. Introduction, commentaire et traduction par Nathalie

Depraz. Collection dirigée par Laurence Hansen-Løve Édition numérique : Pierre Hidalgo, La Gaya Scienza, © mars 2012

Huxley, J., Transhumanism (Transhumanisme), 1957. Industrial Environmental Crisis Quarterly, vol. 7, n° 2, 1993.

J

John Stuart Mill a System of Logic, Principes d'économie politique, Sur la liberté, l'utilitarisme, La soumission des femmes, Trois essais sur la religion,

K

Kabasakal H., Bodur M (2002), 'Arabic cluster : a bridge between East and West', in Journal of world business, n° 37, pp. 40-54

Kabasakal H., Bodur M. (1998), « Leadership, values and institutions : the cas of Turkey. Paper presented at the western academy of management,' Conferences, Istanbul Turkey Juin.

Kenneth R. Gray, Amine S. (2002), « Doing Business in Morocco. Thunderbird International Business Review, » dans Wiley Periodicals, vol. 44, n° 3, p. 379-398.

Kieser A., Leiner L. (2009), « Why the rigour-relevance gap in management research is unbridgeable », dans le Journal of Management Studies, vol. 46, n° 3, p. 516–533

Kitcher, P. et Keller, E. F. (2017). The Seasons Alter : How to Save Our Planet in Six Acts. Liveright publishing : Éditeur : Liveright Publishing Corporation (21 avril 2017) 288 p

Kotter, J. P. (1990) A Force for Change : How Leadership Differs from Management, New York : Free Press, 1990.

Kouzes J. M., Posner B. Z. (1991), the leadership challenge : How to get extraordinary things done. Jossey-Bass, 362 pages.

Kragh, S. U. (2016), « Tribe and villages in African organizations and business », Personnel Review, vol. 45, no 1, pp. 51 à 66.

Krober (tous) (1952), La nature de la culture, The University of Chicago,1952, 437 p

Kroeber, A.L., et Kluckhohn, C. (1952). Culture : a critical review of concepts and definition. Papiers du musée d'archéologie et d'ethnologie de Peabody. 47 (1) : 1 – 223

Krygier, M. 2015. Selznic's Hobbesian Idealism : its nature and its origins. Dans M. S. Kraatz & R. Flores (éd.), Institutions and Ideals : Philip Selznic's Legacy for Organisational Studies, vol. 44 : 21 52.

Bingley, UKL : Emerald Group Publishing Limited

Kuchinke, K.P. (1999), 'Leadership and culture : Work-Related Values and Leadership Styles among One Company's U.S. and German Telecommunications Employees', Human Resource Development Quarterly, 10 (2) (1999), 135,154. https://doi.org/10.1002/hrdq.3920100205

L

Lash S. et Urry J. (1993), Economies of Signs and Space, édition Sage Publications ltd, 368 pages.

Lasswell, H.D., at all (1950), Power and Society : A Framework for Political Inquiry,

Lazzarini, S. (2021) : Le capitalisme et la recherche en gestion : les pires moments, les meilleurs moments, Académie de la revue de gestion, sous presse.

Lecomte, J. (2016), les entreprises humanistes, édition les Arènes, 526 pages

Lee, L. C. (1963), une enquête sur la théorie de l'autoritarisme d'Erich Fromm, Claremont

–Levi-Strauss, C. (1958), Anthropologie structurale, Paris, Plon, 1958 Collections : Évolution. éditeur : Pocket (26 septembre 2003) poche : 480 pages.

– Levi —, Strauss, C. (1967), les structures élémentaires de la parenté, Paris et La Haye, Mouton, 1967. Éditeur École des Hautes Études en Sciences sociales, Parution 2017, Collection : En temps et lieu, 648 pages

Lewis. (1996), When Cultures Collide : Managing Successfully Across Cultures, éditeur N. Brealey Pub, 1996

Liauzu, Claude, 2005, empire du Mal contre grand Satan. Treize siècles de cultures de guerre entre l'islam et l'Occident, Paris, A. Colin, 356 p.

Likert. R, Graw. h (1961). News Patterns of Management. Traduction française : Le gouvernement participatif de l'entreprise, Paris, Gauthier-Villars, 1974, 279 pages.

Lindebaum, D (2021), « Reading the technological society to understand the mechanization of values and its ontological consequences », Académie de la revue de gestion 35 P, AMR-2021-0159-RE.R3

Lipiansky ; mm (1973), le structuralisme de Lévi-Strauss. Collection Bibliothèque scientifique, éditrice : Paris, Payot, 1973. 347 pages.

Lipman-Blumen J. (2005), « Toxic leadership : When grand illusions masquerade as noble visions », dans Leader To Leader vol.

Lipovetsky, G., et Serrou, J. (2008) La Culture-monde. Réponse à une société désorientée, collection : penser la société, édition Odile Jacob 224 p

Lipovetsy G. et Serroy J (2013), l'esthétisation du monde : vivre à l'âge du capitalisme artiste, édition Gallimard 496 pages

Livermore, D. (2009), Leading with cultural intelligence : the New secret To succès (2009), Éditeur : AMACOM ; 9.1.2009 Édition (octobre 1, 2009), 240 pages

Lourei, S. (2021), le droit à l'erreur : les bons collaborateurs font des erreurs, les bonnes entreprises le permettent, édition Dunod.

Luc, E. (2010), le leadeurship partagé, Presse universitaire de Montréal, collection parameter,

Lukes, S. M. (1974), « Relativism : cognitive and moral, » in the Aristotelian Society, supplementary, vol. 48 (19,974) https://www.jstor.org/stable/i380673?refreqid=excelsior%3A905c00ce955ecdc4b8a1ae266c9772a0, pp. 165–189+191–208 Publié par : Oxford University Press

Lukes, S. M. (2005). « Power : A Radical View, » (2e éd.) London : Palgrave Macmillan.

Lukes, S.M. (2021). « Power : A Radical View » (3e éd.) London : Palgrave Macmillan

Luthans, F., Welsh, DB et Rosenkrantz, S.A. (1993). What do Russian managers really do? An observational study with comparisons to U.S. managers. Journal of International Business Studies. 24 (4) : 741-761

M

Maalouf, Amine, 1998, les identités meurtrières, Paris, Grasset et Fasquelle, Le Livre de Poche, 189 p.

MacMillan I. C. (1982), « Seizing compétitive initiative », dans Journal of Business Strategy, vol. 2, ne° 4, p. 43–57.

Maltbia, D., Terrence E. (2009), A Leader's Guide to Leveraging Diversity – Strategic Learning Capabilities for Break-through Performance.

Marius Barbeau, A Le Kroeber (1946), Journal of American Folklore, V59, no 231, janvier-mars, éditeur : Literary Licensing, LLC (20 avril 2013), 102 pages

Martinez-Alier, J. (1992), « valeur économique valeur écologique », Revue Écologie politique No 1 —janvier 1992

Mattéi, Jean-François. (2011), « La crise de la culture européenne », le procès de l'Europe. Grandeur et misère de la culture européenne, sous la direction de Mattéi Jean-François. Presses universitaires de France, 2011, pp. 175-219. Chapitre III la culture et les cultures Jean-François Mattéi dans le procès de l'Europe (2011), pages 95 à 134. Chapitre V la crise de la culture européenne Jean-François Mattéi dans le procès de l'Europe (2011), pages 175 à 219

Mauss, M. (1971), Essais de sociologie, Paris, Le Seuil, 1971 (Collection « points essais, sciences humaines ») Poche : 252 pages.

Max Weber « L'éthique protestante et l'esprit du capitalisme,

Mayer, Arno, 2002, Les Furies.1789.1917. Violence, vengeance, terreur, Paris, Fayard, 1 ère, éd., 2000, 680 p.

McCall, M. W. 2010. Peler l'oignon : Se familiariser avec le développement du leadership fondé sur l'expérience. Psychologie industrielle et organisationnelle, 3 (1) : 61-68.

McClelland, D. (1970), "The two faces of power," Journal of International Affairs, vol. 24, no 1, 1970, pp. 29–47 ISSN : 0022 – 197X, 0022–197 X

McMahon, G.C., Virick, M. et Wright, P.M. (1999). Perspectives théoriques alternatives pour la gestion stratégique des ressources humaines revisitées : progrès, problèmes et perspectives. Dans P.M. Wright, L. Dyer, J.W. Boudreau et G.T. Milkovich (éd.), Research in Personnel and Human Resources Management : Strategic Human Resources Management in the Twenty-First Century, Vol. 4, 99-122. Stamford, CT : Jai Press Inc.

Mehenou Amouzou (2015), « Culture et développement en Afrique ». Publié par Guinee7.Com le 11 mai 2015

Meier, O. (2019), Management interculturel, collection management sup 6e Édition Dunod 336 pages

Merci J., Jardat R. (2007), "Induction as an institutionalized and institutionalizing practice – retail banking and consultancy in France," dans : AIM Gnosis Conference, 6-7 septembre, Londres, UK, pp. 66-87

Merkens H. (1990), "le management interculturel", dans le site www. ofaj.org (office Franco-allemand pour la jeunesse), n° 16, 11 pages.

Meyer. E. (2014), The Culture Map : Breaking Through the Invisible Boundaries of Global business Relié, Affaires publiques ; Édition illustrée (27 mai 2014), 288 pages

Mieszala J. C., Sibony O. (2009), "La prospective est-elle utile aux entreprises ?", in Societal Numéro 63 - 1er trimestre 2009, p. 34-40.

Millot M., Roulleau JP. (2005), les relations sociales en Europe, édition liaisons, 362 pages.

Millot M., Roulleau JP. (2011), "Les leadeurs ignorés", in tous les leaders, dirigés par Peretti J M., éditions d'organisation, p. 169-173.

Mintzberg, H. (2008), "Leadeurship at Community hips", Gestion. Revue internationale de gestion, vol. 33, n° 3, p. 16-17.

Morgan, L.H. (1877), Ancient society, or Researches on the Lines of Human Progress from Savagery through Barbarism to Civilization. First published, 1877, London : MacMillan and Company. Traduction française par H. Jaouiche, 1971. Paris : Éditions Anthropos, 1971, 653 pages.

N

Nouiga M. (2003), la conduite du changement par la qualité dans un contexte socioculturel. Essai de modélisation systémique et application à l'entreprise marocaine. Thèse de doctorat, École Nationale Supérieure d'Art et Métiers, Centres d'Enseignement et de Recherche de Paris, 245 pages.

O

Olivier Toutain, O ; Ballereau, V. (2017), "Vers un leadership humaniste fondé sur la valeur des relations", dans entreprendre & innover 2017/2 (n° 33), page 86 à 92

Oruh, E.S, Dibia. C (2020), "Employee Stress and the Implication of High-Power Distance Culture : Empirical Évidence from Nigeria's Employment Terrain" (accepte/in press) in Employee Relations, 12.05.2020. Contribution à la revue » Article. Édit EUR « Emerald Group Publishing Ltd. ».

P

Pentland B.T., Feldman M.S. (2005), « Organizational routines as a unit of analysis », in Industrial and Corporate change, vol. 14, n° 5, pp. 793-815.

Perrineau. P (1975) « sur la notion de culture en anthropologie », Revue française de science politique,/année 1975/25-5/pp. 946—968

Pesqueux Y. (2007), gouvernance et privatisation. Édition PUM, 258 pages.

Pesqueux, I. (2016), « la culture nationale en sciences de gestion ». Master. France. 2016. sel — 01400477 Hal archive ouvertes,

Petriglieri, G. et Petriglieri, J. L. (2015). Can Business Schools Humanise Leadership? Academy of Management Learning & Education, 14 (4), 625–647.

Petriglieri, G., Wood, J. D. et Petriglieri, J. L. (2011). De près et en personne : bâtir les fondements du développement des leaders par la personnalisation de l'apprentissage en gestion. Academy of Management Learning & Education, 10 (3), p. 430-450.

Pettigrew A. (1993), Managing Change for Competitive Success Editor? Blackwell Publishers, 336 pages.

Pillé, I. (2011), Intercultural Communication a Critical Introduction. Edition Edinburgh University Press, 208 pages. 2de édition : Edinburgh University Press, 2017. 227 p.

Piller, I. (2017), intercultural communication : A Critical introduction. Edinburgh University Press. PP 456

Pras B. (2007). Management et islam vers une convergence de valeurs. Revue française de gestion 2007/2, n° 171, p. 91-95.

Probst. GJB, Ulrich H (1989). Pensée globale et management, résoudre les problèmes complexes, les Éditions d'organisation, 314 pages.

Q

Quinn, R. W., Spreitzer, G. M. et Lam, C. F. 2012. Construire un modèle durable de l'énergie humaine dans les organisations : explorer le rôle critique des ressources. The Academy of Management Annals, 6 (1) : 337-396

R

Regourd, S. (2004) : « L'exception culturelle revient sur le devant de la scène », La Croix, 18 juin 2013 (ISSN 0242-6056, lire en ligne [archive], consultée le 27 juillet 2017)

Reinecke, J. ; Ansari, S. (2021). Microfoundations of framing : The international production of collective action frames in the Occupy Movement. Academy of Management Journal, 64 (2), 378–408

Renier (Romain), la culture contribue sept fois plus au PIB que l'industrie automobile dans La Tribune Web du 3 janvier 2014

Risse, M., & Wollner, G. (2019). On Trade Justice : A Philosophical Plea for a New Global Deal. Oxford University Press : Oxford.

Rivers, W. H. R (1914), The History of Melanesian Society, Cambridge, University Press, 1914, en deux volumes, p. 474

Roche, G (1992), « la notion de culture » extraits du chapitre IV : « Culture, civilisation et idéologie », de Guy Rocher, Introduction à la sociologie générale. Première partie : l'action sociale, chapitre IV, p. 101-127. Montréal : Éditions Hurtubise HMH ltée, 1992, troisième édition.

Rogovsky, N. (1996). IHRM practises in multinational corporations : Developing IHRM integrative Framework : University of Pennsylvania.

Rosen L. (2003), 'The Culture of Islam : Changing Aspects of Contemporary Muslim Life', in Virginia Quarterly Review, Summer2003, vol. 79, numéro 3, p. 97.

Rotary, N. (2019), le Nouveau Monde cherche ses nouveaux dirigeants. Leadership humaniste, les éditions Trédaniel (8 octobre 2019), 183 pages

S

Said, Edward, 1980, L'Orientalisme. L'Orient créé par l'Occident, Paris, Seuil, 1er éd., 1978, 392 p.

Sample S. (2005), devenez des grands leaders. Éditions d'Organisation, 239 pages.

Samson, Steven Alan, « David S. Landes : The Wealth and Poverty of Nations : Study Guide » (2006). Publications et présentations de la faculté. 141.

Schein. E.H (1985), Organizational culture and leadership, San Francisco : Jossey-Bass Publishers, 1985, 358 pages.

Schneider, S. C., et Demeyer, A. (1991). Interpreting and responding to strategic issues : The impact of national culture. Journal de gestion stratégique. 12 : 307-320.

Schuler, R.S., et Rogovsky, N. (1998). Understanding Compensation Practice Variations across Firms : The Impact of National Culture. Journal of International Business Studies. 29 (1) : 159-177.

Schwartz S. H. (1994), 'Beyond individualism/collectivism : New cultural dimensions of values', in Individualism and collectivism : theory, method and applications, Dirigé par Kim U., Triandis H.C, Kagitçibasi C, Choi S-C, Yoon G., Thousand Oaks : Sage Publications, p. 85-122.

Schwartz, S. H. (1997), 'Values and Culture', in M. D. Carr & J. F. Schumaker (Eds.), Motivation and Culture, Routledge, New York, 1997, pp. 69-84

Selznick, P. (1957) Leadership in Administration : A Sociological Interpretation. Harper & Row, New York, 62, 67-68.

Sergeeva, A., Bhardwaj, A. & Dimov, D. 2022. Une réalité changeante et un avenir inconnaissable : Reveal the wider potential of pragmatism. Academy of Management Review, this issue services' Int. J. of Human Resource Management 15:6 September 2004 978–995

Shrivastava, P., Midriff, I. I., Miller, D. & Miglani, A. (1988), « Understanding industrial crisis », Journal of Management Studies, juillet 1988.

Sow (2009), « Droit et responsabilités culturelles. L'importance des responsabilités et droits culturels dans le développement », intervention en session plénière. Campus euro africain, Maputo, 25 juin 2009, Mozambique.

Sparrow, P., Schuler, R. S., et Jackson, S.E. (1994). Convergence ou divergence : Pratiques et politiques en matière de ressources humaines pour un avantage concurrentiel à l'échelle mondiale. International Journal of Human Resource Management. 5 (2) : 267-299

Spector B. (2007), Implementing Organisational Change, theory and practice. Pearson Prentice Hall, 205 pages.

Spencer, H. (1895), le principe de l'évolution, réponse à lord Salisbury, décembre 1895, évolution, Darwin, histoire des sciences, sélection naturelle

Spencer, H. (1857), « Progress, Its Law and Causes » in Westminster review (London, England : 1852 numéros OCLC : 26 747 836

Stefan Lagrosen (2003) « Exploring the impact of culture on quality management, » the International Journal of Quality & Reliability Management, Vol. 20 Issues : 4, pp. 473-487, https://doi.org/10.1108/02656710310468632

Stogdill — 1990 —, Handbook of Leadership : Theory, Research, and Managerial Applications — relié —

T

Tahiri, F. [2021] « Le leadership au Maroc », in Dir Fadoua Tahiri [2021], les pratiques du leadership dans les entreprises privées marocaines. Edition EMS, 126 pages

Taylor S., Beechler S., Napier N. – 1996 – , « Towards an Integrated Theory of International Human Resource Management », in the Academy of Management Review, vol. 21, n° 4, pp. 959-985.

Teggart, F. – 1916 – , Prolegomena to history. The relation of history to literature; philosophy and science, Berkeley, University of California Press, 1916. Brochure de 140 pages.

Thévenet M. [2010], « Le déclin provisoire de la culture d'entreprise », humanisme et Entreprise 2010/5 [n° 300], pages 77 à 84

Thévenet M., Vachette J. [1992], Culture et comportements. Vuibert, 241 pages.

Thomas Werquin — 2008 — intervenant a juin 2008 dans international-conférence on cultural Economics à Boston — Impact of major cultural events and equipment on urban development a critical analysis of case studies

Fortin. à [2000], produire la culture, produire l'identité, Sainte-Foy [Québec] : Presses de l'Université Laval. 264 pages

Toynbee, Arnold, 1951, la civilisation à l'épreuve, Paris, Gallimard, NRF, 282 p.

Toynbee, Arnold, 1964, Le monde et l'Occident, Paris, Gonthier, Médiations, 189 p.

Tribou G. [1995], l'entrepreneur musulman : l'islam et la rationalité d'entreprise. Ed l'harmattan. 235 pages.

Trompenaars, F. [1993]. Riding the waves of culture. Chicago : Irwin Laurent, A. — 1983 —. La diversité culturelle des conceptions occidentales de la gestion. International Studies of Management and Organizations. 13 : 75-96

Trompenaars. F [1994]. L'entreprise multiculturelle. Maxima, 308 pages.

Tronc, B. [2016], « Ambiguïté dans le management et leadership hypermoderne, » in le leadership, recherche et pratique [Dir] Noguera at Plane, édition Magnard—Vuibert, avril 2016, 214 pages ;

Tylor, E.B. [1924]. Primitive Culture. Gloucester, MA : Smith.

U

Ulrich D. – 1989 – , « Tie the corporate knot : Gaining complete customer commitment », in Sloan Management Review, Summer, pp. 19-28.

Usunier, J.-C. — 1992 —. Commerce entre cultures : Une approche culturelle du marketing international. Paris : PUF.

V

Van de Ven A.H., Johnson P. – 2006 – , "Knowledge of theory and practice", in the Academy of Management Review, vol. 31, n° 4, pp. 802-821.

Vernazobres, F. [2016], « tous les leaders ? Quels leaders ? Évolution des théories du leadership et pratiques des grandes entreprises », dans le leadership. Recherches et pratiques [Dir], Noguera et Plane, édition Magnard — Vuibert, avril 2016,214 pages ;

Vogel, B., Reichard, R., Batistič, S. et Černe, M. 2021. Un examen bibliométrique du domaine du développement du leadership : comment nous en sommes arrivés là, où nous en sommes et où nous allons ? The Leadership Quarterly. 32 – 5 –. 101 381.

W

Warnier, J.P. – 2004 – lost in translation? Globalisation des flux et courtage culture

Wéber, M. [1959), Le Savant et le politique, Plon, 1959.

Weick, K. [1988]. » Enacted sense making in crisis situations. » Journal of management studies, 1988.

Wolton, D. [2004], « Information et communication : dix chantiers scientifiques, culturels et politiques ». Dans Hermès, La Revue 2004/1 [n° 38], pages 175 à 18

Wood P. [2002], Diversity : The invention of a concept. Encounter, permanent, papé, V336 pages.

Worms [2013]. Article « pouvoir », « Notions communes », édition., les 100 mots de la philosophie. Presses universitaires de France, 2013, pp. 9-44,

Z

Zellweger, T. M., & Zenger, T. R. 2022. Entrepreneurs as scientiste : Une approche pragmatique pour produire de la valeur à partir de l'incertitude. Académie de révision de la gestion,

STATISTICS

SIZE
- Words: 92 488
- Lines: 11438
- Paragraphs: 2408
- Reading time: 5:33

PERFORMANCE
- 00 errors per 100 words

COMMON WORDS
- Culture: 1299
- Lead: 377
- Power: 370
- Management: 331
- Development: 316
- Durable: 271
- Change: 243
- Human: 207

BIBLIOGRAPHICAL REFERENCES: 270

TABLE OF CONTENTS

PART TWO

PART THREE.

www.ingramcontent.com/pod-product-compliance
Lightning Source LLC
LaVergne TN
LVHW052245200926
848481LV00002B/281